Vincenzo Buonassisi is a lawyer by education, but his professional life has been devoted to cuisine rather than the courtroom. He is a member of the prestigious *Accademia Italiana della Cucina* and ranks with Luigi Carnacina at the top of the list of Italian food authorities. He is a well known author on food, but *The Classic Book of Pasta* is his masterwork, the result of nearly 30 years of collecting and compiling recipes.

Elisabeth Evans, the translator of *The Classic Book of Pasta*, spent some time in Italy while studying for her languages degree from Oxford University. She has worked as a recipe translator for the famed La Varenne cooking school in Paris, where she also studied, and is the author of *Great Cooks* for which she conducted research into early Italian chefs. She is now a freelance translator specializing in Italian cooking and art and lives in the Channel Islands with her family.

Vincenzo Buonassisi
THE CLASSIC BOOK OF PASTA

Translated by Elisabeth Evans

Futura

A Futura Book

First published as *Il Codice della Pasta* in 1973
by Rizzoli Editore, Milano.

First published in Great Britain in 1977 by
Macdonald and Jane's Publishers Limited

This edition published in 1985 by Futura Publications,
a Division of Macdonald & Co (Publishers) Ltd, London & Sydney
Italian edition © 1973, Rizzoli Editore, Milano.
Translation © 1976 Macdonald and Jane's Publishers Limited.
U.S./Canadian edition © 1976, Lyceum Books, Inc., Wilton,
Connecticut, U.S.A.

The typographical design for this edition was adapted from
that created for the original Italian edition by John Alcorn.

ISBN 0 7088 2784 5

Printed in Great Britain by
The Guernsey Press Company Ltd,
Guernsey, Channel Islands.

Futura Publications
A Division of
Macdonald & Co (Publishers) Ltd
Maxwell House
74 Worship Street
London EC2A 2EN
A BPCC plc Company

Contents

INTRODUCTION

A BRIEF HISTORY

Pasta is such a brilliant invention that it would be nice to set up a monument to the man responsible, but the origins of all flour and water compounds are as remote as prehistoric man himself. Let it be enough to recognize his genius in discovering the infinite possibilities of grain as a versatile and nourishing food. First he left grain to soften in water and made the happy discovery of fermentation. Then, when cooking pots had been developed he began grinding grain between two stones to make a finer dish. The most ancient Romans had a sort of floury soup called *pultes* (from which, centuries later, came *polenta*), occasionally improved by the addition of vegetables. *Pultes* and beans, both being essential to survival, were at one point a sacred food eaten at religious gatherings.

At some stage this floury soup may have overcooked into a solid mass, or fallen onto the hearth and baked like a pizza. Nomadic or pastoral areas have dishes that descend from this first baked pasta, like the Mexican *tortilla*, or the *piddene* from Romagna. Before long the baked pasta was being cut up into strips, and these also ended up in the pot with the vegetable soup. In Salento there was a dish of Arabic origin called *circeri e trii*, chick peas and strips of pasta, while the Greeks introduced their own *laganono* or *lasanon* to southern Italy when it became Magna Grecia. Tagliatelle are to this day called *laganelle* and a pasta rolling pin is a *laganaturo* in those regions.

The Romans took over the food and the word. Horace tells of a dish of leeks, chick peas and *lagano* in his Satires. Pasta was also eaten by the Etruscans, who decorated their tombs with many scenes of domestic life, including a rolling pin and indented wheel for pasta. Actual recipes from Roman times have come down to us from a later period in the famous *De Re Coquinaria* by the still-obscure Apicius, probably written in the 3rd century.

There is a chapter dedicated to pasta dough, including recipes for fried strips served with pepper and honey, or cooked in hot oil and served with *garum*, the ubiquitous Roman sauce made of fish innards.

A radical change came over pasta when someone thought of cooking it directly in soup without baking the dough first, then of eating it without so much liquid. Sometime in the Middle Ages the dough was just rolled out and cut into strips, or pieces of varying shapes and sizes were made into the first gnocchi. These were sometimes given a twist or wrapped round little iron pins (like knitting needles) or millet stalks, since the hole or cavity helped them to cook better. Thus, the first macaroni were born. However, there was much confusion between the two, a fact still reflected by the habit in the Veneto to this day of calling gnocchi macaroni.

By 1041 they were common enough words and food for a fool to be known as a *gnoccone* or *maccherone*, but the pasta itself was made and served rather differently from present-day macaroni. Honey and sugar were the usual accompaniments—a tradition which lives on in the Calabrian *sucamele*. The hole was a delicious and convenient way of sucking up the honey. Cristoforo da Messisbugo, famous carver at the Court of Ferrara in the 16th century, gives recipes for fried macaroni with honey, butter, cream cheese and cinnamon in his best-selling handbook of etiquette and court cuisine, *Banchetti*. This combination of flavours was popular until the 18th century.

Meanwhile, pasta was developing into many different shapes and sizes across the regions of Italy, from fettuccine to pappardelle. Stuffed pastas such as *tortellini* probably appeared in Emilia in the Middle Ages, and by the 13th century ravioli were well-known. As for *pasta secca*, and more especially dried pasta with a hole, it had its own rather special history. It may have been invented by the Arabs as a way of preserving flour during the long caravanserai across the desert, and they certainly introduced it into Sicily and southern Italy. It spread to other Mediterranean regions, including Spain, where the words *sfidelli* and *fidellini* (the thinnest sort of pasta) probably originated. The Italian climate, and particularly the Tyrrenian coast, was ideal for drying pasta dough and the water was perfect to mix and cook it, so dried pasta found a natural home in Italy.

A belief still lingers that Marco Polo brought dried pasta to Italy, but there is plenty of evidence to disprove it. For example, in 1279 a Genoese notary made an inventory of effects belonging to his client Ponzio Bastone, including a chest full of *maccheroni*—obviously dried rather than fresh pasta. Marco Polo was still in the East at that date. This Genoese chest reveals that *maccheroni* meant any form of dried pasta, just as in southern Italy *trii* meant any sort of fresh pasta. Marco Polo did in fact bring some pasta back from Java, and mentioned that it was "similar to our own lasagne." It was made with flour ground from the breadfruit tree and must have been something of a curiosity to the Italians, who were already connoisseurs of pasta.

By the 14th and 15th centuries pasta was a fairly common dish, but still too expensive to be a staple in the Italian diet. It must have had a different consistency from modern pasta as Platina, the Humanist and cookery writer, gives a recipe in his famous work *De Honesta Voluptate ac Valitudine* for *vermiculos* (a Latin form of *vermicelli*) that needs cooking for one hour. One of the main differences between pasta then and now was the absence of tomato sauce. The tomato first came from Mexico and Peru in the 16th century, but it took time for people to trust such a poisonous-looking fruit, and to adapt it to the Italian climate and soil. Tomatoes found a real home in Naples eventually—the colour must have had something to do with it—and probably made their first encounter with pasta in that very city.

The tomato changed Italian cooking in many ways, and may have hastened the demise of that ancient preference for sweet and savoury mixtures with pasta. When pasta and tomatoes became a more popular combination between the 17th and 18th century, Naples was the undisputed home of the dish. A whole folklore grew up around the subject, illustrated by 18th-century prints showing *lazzaroni* or Neapolitan urchins eating pasta by lowering it into their mouths without the assistance of any fork or spoon. This was in fact the common method of eating it and Gennaro Spadaccini, a chamberlain at the Bourbon court in Naples, made pasta an acceptable food for royal banquets by inventing a modern four-pronged fork to spare visiting foreigners the embarassment of eating it with their hands. His master, King Ferdinand II, hated any meal without spaghetti, so the Chamberlain was richly rewarded.

Italian migrations spread the fame of pasta to other parts of the world, in particular to North America. President Thomas Jefferson (1743-1826) brought back a pasta press from his visit to Italy, and Yankee Doodle's feather called "macaroni" must have popularized the dish still further. Thereafter all American cookbooks mention pasta. One published in 1792 suggested cooking it for three hours in water and 10 minutes in broth. Later versions reduced the time to 90, then 45 minutes. A 1932 U.S. Navy cookbook suggests three minutes for cooking pasta, while the revised 1944 edition lengthens the time to 20 minutes. Another book suggests housewives use the tile-test for pasta:throw a forkful of cooked pasta at the kitchen wall, and if it adheres to the tiles the pasta is ready to serve.

Italians came to regard their national dish with affection, although Leopardi considered it a symbol of stupidity (and was reprimanded by Croce for such wayward thinking). Rossini complained of the poor quality of French pasta in Paris, and Verdi did the same from St. Petersburg. Byron knew enough about the subject to link pasta and aphrodisiacs, and made Cerere offer vermicelli, oysters and eggs as a powerful aid to passion. This is not so far-fetched in the light of recent American findings which prove that spaghetti and tomato sauce are a very complete food, rich in Vitamin E which is beneficial to the reproductive system.

The only doubt which lingers concerns the fattening qualities of pasta, although vegetarians have claimed it is harmful only when combined with meat and animal fats. All these things are, like food in general, a matter of habit and taste upon which no amount of evidence, scientific or otherwise, will have the least effect. However, there can be no argument about the enormous versatility of pasta. It has already been adapted by enough people around the world and over the centuries to prove its worth. As long as flour of any kind remains a valuable part of our diet, the number of pasta-eaters in general will increase naturally with the expanding population.

ABOUT THIS BOOK

Versatility is the keynote of pasta cookery. There must be several thousand ways to prepare pasta, many of which are in this book. For the modern cook the most appealing aspect is that rules and instructions are of secondary importance to imagination and availability in the Italian kitchen. Pasta can accommodate readily to what you have and what you have time to do.

There are recipes here for preparing and serving pasta with a wide variety of ingredients. The recipes are grouped into chapters according to the main ingredient—pasta with vegetables, dairy products, eggs, fish and shellfish, white meat, red meat, pork and game. Within the chapters the recipes progress from the simplest combinations, such as pasta with garlic and olive oil, to the more complicated, such as Neapolitan carnival pie. Look for recipes at the beginning of a chapter if you are in a hurry and towards the end if you have more time. All the recipes trace their origins to the finest tradition of Italian regional cooking and have been carefully adapted to modern use without losing any of their authenticity. Footnotes to certain recipes give some of the many regional variations. All recipes make from four to six servings.

Remember that pasta offers scope for endless experimentation and improvisation. If you haven't got the exact ingredients for a certain recipe, try substituting something else. Types of pasta are suggested for each recipe, but this depends on tradition and personal taste. You can always use any variety of commercial or home-made pasta that suits you. Some recipes require ingredients hard to find outside Italy, in which case an alternative is suggested where possible, although sometimes it may be disappointing compared with the original. There are many good Italian groceries that import all the ingredients used, if not fresh, at least in tins/cans or jars, so explore the market thoroughly and ask the grocer's advice if you have any problems. Some of the principal Italian ingredients used are explained in the sections that follow.

COOKING PASTA: THE BASIC RULES

Pasta is always cooked in boiling, salted water in a large pan so there is no danger of it sticking together. Use at least two pints of water for every four ounces of pasta, or four quarts for one pound. Let the water come to a rolling boil, then add about ½ teaspoon salt for each pint of water, or a bit less if the sauce is to be salty (e.g., with anchovies). Put in all the pasta at once, allowing about two or three ounces per serving, then turn the heat up to maximum immediately so that the water returns to the boil quickly. The cooking time will vary according to the type of pasta. Fresh egg pasta can cook in as little as five seconds from the time the water returns to the boil, and stuffed fresh pasta from 5–20 minutes depending on how long it has been kept, while dried commercial pasta takes anything up to 20 minutes according to sizes.

Obviously the indications on a package of pasta are not meant to be taken too literally. The only way to see if pasta is cooked is to test a little bit between your teeth. It should be tender, but firm—only experience can teach you the true meaning of *al dente*, the Italian expression for perfectly cooked pasta. When the pasta is *al dente*, drain it in a colander as quickly as possible. Shake the colander to remove the water, although in some recipes it is best to leave a little of the water on the pasta to help dissolve certain ingredients such as cheese in the accompanying sauce. Sometimes the pasta is forked directly out of the pan, shaken gently and dropped onto the plates piping hot, but this requires a good deal of skill or the plate may become as watery as the pan. When the pasta has been drained in a colander, return it to the pan and add a little oil to make it nice and slippery before adding the sauce itself. Some people prefer to serve the sauce directly on the individual helpings of pasta, but it is easier to mix it effectively if it is poured into the pan, then transferred immediately to a very hot, deep serving bowl and given one more stir. And it is always best to handle pasta with wooden implements to avoid breaking it.

MAKING PASTA

Pasta is made by mixing flour and water, or flour and eggs in varying proportions. The classic pasta dough is made with three to four ounces of flour (and never more than four ounces) per egg. The number of eggs can be reduced, however, or they can be eliminated if the taste does not blend well with the other ingredients or with the sauce. The best pasta is *always* made with pure semolina flour.

Temperature is an important factor when making pasta. Always try to work in a moderate temperature, away from draughts. Choose a firm, large work surface, preferably of unvarnished wood, although formica will do. Put the flour in a mound and make a well in the centre, then break in the eggs and gradually beat them lightly with a fork or your fingers, supporting the mound with one hand so the egg does not spill out. Gradually draw in the flour, working it into the eggs with your fingertips. Add a good pinch of salt and continue working in the flour, slowly at first, then more rapidly and energetically as it becomes firmer. A tablespoon of oil can be added to the eggs to make a smoother dough, and if it seems too stiff you can add a few tablespoons of warm water; only experience can tell you what is necessary.

If the eggs are very large or "absorbent" you may need to add more flour if the dough seems moist and sticky, but of course never exceed four ounces of flour per egg. Knead the dough, pressing it with the heel of your palm and fingertips until it is smooth and even. Form it into a ball, scraping all the crumbs off your hands. Wash and dry your hands, then knead again, folding and turning the dough often for about ten minutes. Wrap the dough inside a damp cloth and allow it to stand and rest for a half hour. Then divide it in two and work with one half while the other remains covered with the cloth to prevent it drying out.

The final rolling out must be done quickly and lightly, and once you have mastered the technique it is not difficult. Begin by rolling the ball away from you, then turning it one quarter and repeating the procedure so the dough keeps an even circular shape. Remember to roll away from you rather than down onto the board, and stop when the dough is about ⅛-inch thick. Give it a final thinning by wrapping it round the rolling pin and stretching it with a sideways pressure of your hands. Unroll the pasta, turning the pin slightly so you have a different part of the sheet, dust any sticky section very lightly with flour, and repeat the same process several times until the pasta is almost paper thin and transparent. This should not take more than ten minutes or the dough will dry out.

The pasta is then ready to cut and stuff according to the instructions in the individual recipes for stuffed pasta. For tagliatelle, fettuccine, etc. let the dough dry with about one third of the sheet hanging over the edge of a table or chair on a clean cloth. Turn it every ten minutes so a different part hangs over each time; the whole process should take about 30 minutes. The pasta is ready when the surface has a rather leathery appearance. When the dough is ready, roll it up on the rolling pin and unroll on the work surface. Fold over gently into a flat roll about three inches wide and cut crosswise into the desired thickness of noodle with a very sharp knife until the entire roll is cut. Open out the noodles very carefully onto a cloth and let them dry five minutes longer. Gather up the cloth and drop the noodles directly into the boiling water.

If you have a pasta machine—and it can be a great boon to making home-made pasta—by all means use it to do the work for you. Simply follow the instructions given with the machine. Uncooked flat noodles can be kept uncovered in a cool place for as long as a month, but not when the pasta is stuffed for the filling deteriorates. An interesting variation of egg pasta is *pasta verde* or green pasta, made by adding spinach puree to the pasta dough as described in recipe 191, TAGLIATELLE VERDI WITH BUTTER AND PARMESAN. The spinach puree makes for a softer, creamier kind of pasta, but does not really alter the flavour very much.

One of the splendours of pasta cooking is the pasta pie, such as the PASTICCIO DI LASAGNE ALLA MESSISBUGO, recipe 370, in which the pasta and sauce are cooked in a very short pastry case. This *pasta frolla* is a soft crumbly pastry mixture made with flour, butter or lard and egg yolks (or sometimes water). The ingredients and method of preparation are given in the recipes for each *pasticcio* (or *timballo* as they are sometimes called), but do not be confused if some *pasticcio* recipes are just for a baked pasta dish— Italian names are never very definite due to variations from region to region. The best type of pie dish to use for a pasta pie is a 9½-inch spring-form pan which can be removed when the pie is cooked. This is easier if the pastry case is "baked blind" before adding the pasta and sauce. Cover the bottom of the pan with a circle of greaseproof or waxed paper, line the bottom with the pastry, weigh it down with dried peas or rice and bake until firm and golden in a hot oven. Bake the top crust on a separate baking sheet, weighed down also with peas or rice. You then need only heat the pie through for a few minutes with its pasta filling.

VARIETIES OF PASTA

Pasta is made in a wide range of shapes, each of which in turn is made in an even wider variety of sizes, thicknesses and textures. All have different names and many of the same types of pasta are known by different names in different regions of Italy. The types of pasta called for in the recipes in this book are the more common varieties available in many supermarkets and certainly in all well-stocked Italian markets. Following is a brief description of these pasta types:

angolotti—small, crescent-shaped dumplings usually stuffed with meat. These are most often home-made but can sometimes be bought commercially.

bucatini—a thicker and hollow version of **spaghetti**, also known as **perciatelli**.

capellini—"hair thin," translated literally, this is one of the very thin varieties of flat **spaghetti**; **capelli d'angelo**, "angel's hair," is the thinnest of all.

cappelletti—the word means "little hats" and this pasta variety is a dumpling cut in the shape of a small, peaked hat and stuffed with chopped chicken breast, pork, mortadella/bologna, cheese and nutmeg. Usually home-made, it can also be bought ready-made in certain shops.

conchiglie—small, rounded shells (the name means "seashells"), available in either ridged or smooth varieties. The cavity is excellent for trapping meat sauces and other thick sauces.

farfalle—a small pasta variety, shaped like a bow tie.

fettuccine—the Roman version of the egg noodle, a bit narrower and thicker than the variety from Bologna known as **tagliatelle.**

fusilli—a "slip-proof" **spaghetti**, spiral in shape; **tortiglioni** and **rotelle** are slightly different versions of the same pasta type.

lasagne—the broadest pasta noodle, about two inches wide, available either ridged or smooth.

lasagne verdi—a specialty of Emilia-Romagna, this is green lasagna with spinach added to the basic pasta dough.

linguine—a flat **spaghetti**; **tagliolini** is a thinner version of the same pasta type.

macaroni—the general term for all commercially made dried pasta. The **macaroni** called for in the recipes in this book is some version of the popular elbow **macaroni** or cut, slightly curved tubular pasta. **Maccheroncini** is a thinner, smaller variety.

orecchiette—the name means "little ears" which pretty well describes this small, shell-shaped pasta.

pansotti, panzerotti—a stuffed dumpling similar to **ravioli** but triangular in shape, usually home-made but sometimes available commercially.

pastina—the general term for a whole group of tiny pasta varieties including **anellini, ditalini** and **stellette,** used most often in soups.

penne—another of the varieties of pasta with a hole; a short, tubular pasta about ¼ inch in diameter and 1½ inches long.

quadrucci—the name translates "little squares" which is just what these are, little squares of **tagliatelle** noodles.

ravioli—the best-known pasta dumpling, square-shaped and stuffed generally with meat and spinach or cheese.

rigatoni—a ridged, tubular macaroni, about ½ inch in diameter and 2 inches long.

spaghetti—thin, solid pasta strings; the most commonly known and served pasta type, called **vermicelli** in southern Italy. **Spaghettini** (**vermicellini**) is a thinner variety.

tagliatelle—long, thin egg noodles, about ¼ inch wide; the pasta specialty of Italy's culinary capitol, Bologna.

tagliatelle verdi—green **tagliatelle** noodles, the result of spinach added to the basic noodle dough.

tortelli, tortellini—small, ring-shaped pasta dumplings (**tortellini** are about half the size of **tortelli**) with a stuffing similar to **cappelletti**. Like **cappelletti**, these are most often made at home but can sometimes be bought ready-made in certain shops.

trenette—from Genoa, a somewhat narrower and thicker version of the Bolognese **tagliatelle** or egg noodle.

tubetti, tubettini—tiny narrow tubes of pasta about ¼ inch in diameter; **tubetti** are about ½ inch long, **tubettini** about ¼ inch long.

vermicelli, vermicellini—other names for **spaghetti** and **spaghettini**, used particularly in Naples and the regions of southern Italy.

zite—a slightly smaller and smooth-surfaced version of **rigatoni**; **mezze zite** is half the size of regular **zite**.

HERBS AND FLAVOURINGS

Herbs love Italian sunshine and are widely used in cooking because they are so plentiful and delicious. Few precise quantities for herbs are given in these recipes because Italians just use imagination, availability and experience when adding them to the cooking. In more northern climates you may not be able to make such generous use of fresh herbs, but in most recipes that should be no reason to put you off, with the exception of Genoese *pesto*, which really does require fresh basil. Herbs freeze well and both frozen or dried they can serve well through the long winter months, although fresh herbs are always best. Try not to wash your herbs as it spoils the flavour; just brush or wipe them with a cloth unless they are very muddy.

Here are some of the herbs and flavourings most widely used in pasta cooking:

basil (*basilico*)—a very aromatic herb used to flavour tomato sauce, salads and soups. It is delicious combined with a piquant cheese or just with oil and pasta.

bay leaves (*alloro*, *lauro*)—used for soups and sauces, or in meat *ragu*. One small leaf is enough to flavour the average sauce or *ragu*.

borage (*boraggine*)—used like spinach for stuffed pasta. It is only good fresh —it loses its flavour when dried.

chervil (*cerfoglio*)—similar to parsley, but with a more delicate flavour. It is used in cheese mixtures for stuffed pasta.

celery (*sedano*)—Italians use the leaves as well as the chopped stem as flavouring for *ragu* and many sauces, to give a strong, salty taste.

cloves (*chiodi di garofano*)—used in strongly flavoured *ragu* and in dumpling mixtures, especially with liver.

capers (*capperi*)—often used in cold pasta dishes with tomatoes and olives.

cinnamon (*cannella*)—widely used in the past for pasta recipes that included sugar, it is now sometimes used for stuffed pastas with meat or cheese fillings.

fennel (*finocchio*)—the root stem of Florentine fennel and the stalks and leaves of wild fennel are both used for sauces, the most famous of which is Sicilian sardine and wild fennel sauce.

garlic (*aglio*)—used very widely to flavour oil for a sauce before adding other ingredients. Remove the skin by banging down sharply on the clove of garlic with the flat part of a knife. Add the crushed garlic to the oil, let it brown, then discard; or finely chop the garlic and leave in the oil when brown. In southern Italian cooking a lot of garlic is used, but you can always adjust the amount given in any recipe, especially since cloves of garlic vary greatly in size and flavour.

mint (*menta*)—used especially in Roman cooking with fish and vegetables, and mixed with cheese in pasta fillings.

nutmeg (*noce moscata*)—used to heighten the flavour of certain dishes. Grate whole nutmeg directly into many pasta sauces (such as bechamel) and fillings (with spinach and ricotta), or for gnocchi mixtures.

oregano—a sweet, highly flavoured herb—actually, **wild marjoram**—used a great deal with tomatoes and other vegetables. It is closely related to **sweet marjoram** (*maggiorana*) and they are both used to flavour butter and oil, and in fish sauces.

parsley (*prezzemolo*)—Italians use mainly the uncurled variety of parsley, but curled parsley has an excellent flavour too. It makes a simple accompaniment for pasta on its own with oil and butter, and is also much used in combination with other ingredients.

pepper (*pepe*)—freshly ground black pepper adds a delicious flavour to many pasta recipes and should be available on the table also. White peppercorns give a stronger flavour.

hot chili pepper (*peperoncino*)—the Italian version of chili pepper is small and pointed, and can be stored dried for use in cooking. Some peppers are more powerful than others, so begin with a small piece to flavour the cooking oil, and add more according to taste. The seeds are the hottest part of all. If no whole pepper is available substitute any variety of hot red powdered pepper, depending on the strength required. It is used particularly in combination with other piquant flavours like anchovies and garlic, and with tomatoes.

sweet pepper (*peperoni*)—also known as pimientos, they are all members of the capsicum family. Used in many sauces and *ragus* to give colour as well as flavour. Use fresh or tinned/canned—they are often called roasted pimientos. Roasting is the method of removing the outer skin. Roast fresh pepper by holding the pepper over a naked flame and gradually revolving it so it is browned on all sides. Moisten your fingertips and immediately peel off the skin. Grilling or baking is also possible but is less effective for regular browning all over.

rosemary (*rosmarino*)—a powerful herb which should be used with discretion. It gives a pleasant flavour to oil or butter and is used in lamb and pork *ragu*.

saffron (*zafferano*)—best bought in little packets of the crocus pistils themselves, rather than as powder. A pinch of saffron added directly to the sauce or dissolved in two tablespoons warm water is enough for most sauce recipes.

sage (*salvia*)—a few sage leaves are often added to butter when it is melted for the pasta sauce. It is good fresh or dried, but avoid powdered sage.

salt (*sale*)—Italians prefer to use sea or coarse salt in cooking.

thyme (*timo*)—used in a bouquet garni for *ragu*, as well as to flavour melted butter, and occasionally a bechamel sauce.

ITALIAN CHEESES

bel paese—a soft, bland cheese from Lombardy which, like **fontina**, has good melting qualities for *au gratin* dishes.

caciocavallo—similar to **provolone**, but probably more ancient (*cacio* is the old name for cheese). It has a strong sharp flavour and should be used with care.

fontina—a fat, firm, creamy cheese from Piedmont which has little holes rather like gruyere, and is used for grating over pasta dishes.

gorgonzola—a blue-veined cow's milk cheese from Lombardy. Less piquant varieties are usually used with pasta.

grana—a hard cheese made from skimmed milk, of which there are various regional varieties. The best known is **parmesan** (*parmeggiano*), from the region of Parma, and is widely used in Italian cooking. Good parmesan is expensive but it does make all the difference in a dish where it is a main feature of the ingredients. Freshly grated parmesan is best in cooking; keep a piece wrapped in foil in the bottom of the refrigerator. If you buy grated parmesan, keep it in small quantities in an airtight container in a cool place other than the refrigerator.

groviera—an Italian imitation of Swiss gruyere from Lombardy. Use any sort of gruyere or emmenthal for recipes that call for **groviera** if the cheese is not available.

mascarpone—a cream cheese from Lombardy, it can also be replaced by other varieties of cream cheese.

mozzarella—the same type of cheese as **scamorza**. Traditionally, the latter is made with cow's milk in areas north of Monte Cassino; in the south, the cheese is made with buffalo milk and called **mozzarella**. A Neapolitan specialty, it melts forming delicious strings and is very good for pasta dishes *au gratin*.

pecorino—there are many regional varieties of this hard sheep's milk cheese; the best are considered to be **pecorino romano** and **pecorino sardo**. In Italy, it tends to be cheaper than parmesan so is more widely used in cooking, but the flavour is less versatile. You can use a mixture of grated parmesan and **pecorino** (or **romano**, as it is known in North America) for a change.

provolone—a bland, yellow cheese made from buffalo or cow's milk which comes in many shapes and sizes (often looking like a yellow pear). It gets very hard when kept and is grated for many pasta dishes.

ricotta—soft ewe's milk cheese. When it is unavailable substitute a soft cream cheese, but *not* cottage cheese.

scamorza—see the description under **mozzarella**.

BROTHS AND SOUPS

Pasta asciutta is cooked in water (or sometimes stock) and drained, while *pasta in brodo* is cooked in stock and served as a soup. Some people prefer to cook the pasta in water before adding it to the soup, since the starch can cloud the pristine clarity of a true consomme, but this obviously depends on the type of soup in question. It is worth having well-flavoured and interesting stock or *pasta in brodo* is in danger of being insipid. Of course, when the pasta itself is highly flavoured you need worry less about the stock. Stuffed pasta like ravioli can be served in a weaker stock than plain pasta like quadrucci, or the many commercial varieties of small pasta. The best stock of all is made with meat as well as bones, but a perfectly delicious "household stock" can be kept permanently replenished from remains and leftovers so long as you boil it for at least ten minutes every day and use some very well-flavoured ingredients (this is not for clear soup, however). The best thing is to keep different types of stock in the freezer so you can use them at will. Following are some of the basic broths and soups used in pasta cooking:

chicken stock (*brodo di pollo*)

1 chicken	1 bay leaf
1 onion stuck with 2 cloves	peppercorns
1 carrot	salt
1 stick celery	

Put the chicken in a large pan, cover with cold water, bring to a boil and add the other ingredients. Simmer for about two hours, until the chicken is tender, then remove for another use. Add the giblets to the stock, simmer for a half hour, then boil until the stock has reduced and the flavour seems well concentrated. Strain very well, cool and remove the fat. Cooked chicken is used in many pasta recipes so it is worth using a whole chicken—a capon is even better—to obtain the stock. You can also chop some of the chicken flesh very finely and heat it in the stock with the pasta to make a real chicken soup.

meat stock (*brodo di carne*)

3 lb. beef and/or veal bones, including veal knuckle and beef marrow bone	1 carrot
	1 onion
	1 stick celery
2 lb. beef such as shin, chuck or silverside	bay leaf
	peppercorns
salt	

Cover the bones and meat with about three pints cold water, bring slowly to a boil, skim and add the other ingredients. Simmer very slowly for at least three hours, then strain, leave to cool, and remove the fat from the surface. This stock can obviously be made with different bones or simply with the lean meat. Meat and bones make a strong stock so you will be able to use more water and have a larger quantity. Remember, you can use any meat cooked in stock for other dishes.

For a really delicious *brodo ristretto* or concentrated meat stock, omit the bones if desired, and cook the lean beef with a whole chicken. Remove the chicken and beef when tender and boil the stock until it reduces by half. This can be made into excellent clear soup or consomme.

consomme

1 quart stock	1 small onion
8 oz. raw minced shin of beef	1 small stick celery
whites and shells of 2 eggs	

Bring the cold stock to a boil with the beaten egg whites and the washed and lightly crushed shells, the chopped onion and celery, whisking all the time. Let the liquid rise in the pan, remove from the heat and allow to settle. Return to the heat and simmer for 30 minutes. Strain through a scalded cloth.

Stock cubes or tinned/canned beef or chicken bouillon or consomme make a useful alternative when no stock is available. Taste carefully before and during cooking, however, since they can be quite salty and may need less extra seasoning.

vegetable soup (*minestra di verdura*)

When you are making a thick soup with vegetables and pasta it is best to remove about half the vegetables after they are soft, put them through a food mill and return them to the pot to thicken the soup before adding the pasta. Have a separate pan of water or stock boiling while the soup is cooking. If it seems too dry you can add a few extra ladles of boiling water, otherwise the pasta may stick together.

ragu

From the French *ragout*, this usually refers to a meat sauce with pieces of meat cut up and served in it. It is obviously related to stew, but the meat is more finely chopped or minced. Use good, lean meat to make a **ragu** and mince it yourself, if possible. This makes a juicier sauce to serve with any sort of pasta.

meat gravy (*sugo di carne*)

The juice from braised or roast meat, together with the fat or liquid used in the cooking (such as oil or wine), makes a delicious *sugo* or gravy to mix with pasta. It is usually boiled after the piece of meat has been removed (to be served as another course) to reduce and thicken it, but sometimes a little flour is added to the vegetables fried in the oil before adding the meat, and then stirred into the liquid. The time-honoured tradition of cooking the *stracotto*—"extra-long cooked" meat—very gently in a well-covered pan is considered the best way to get a really rich and delectable gravy, especially in Naples where it is something of a specialty. Modern ovens tend to dry out meat cooked for as much as six hours, but over an open fire you could calculate the distance from the heat to make the *stracotto* simmer with tiny, almost imperceptible bubbles. Quite small pieces of meat (1½ to 2 lb.) are used, but now for long cooking it is more economical to buy a larger piece or joint, and reduce the time to about three hours so that the meat is still edible, as well as having a delicious gravy. After long, slow braising, the juices that harden on the sides of the pan have a lovely flavour in themselves, and the ever-inventive Italian housewife will use the same unwashed pan to cook a bean soup like the famous Paduan specialty *pasta e fagioli* to take advantage of that extra meaty taste.

ITALIAN PORK SPECIALTIES

Over the centuries, the Italians have developed some really delicious ways of cooking and preserving the pig and every region has its own jealously guarded secrets of salting, curing and sausage making. Many of these pork specialty products are exported and it is worth trying to use them in preparing recipes in this book because they have a very special flavour which can never be quite the same as any substitute. This is due to a stronger blend of salt and spices used in the preserving process, and often to the diet and growing environment of the pigs themselves. Here are some pork specialty products commonly used in traditional pasta cooking:

cotiche, cotenne—fresh pork rind cooked with meat or vegetables to give richness and flavour to a sauce, as well as a slightly gelatinous consistency.

guanciale—similar to **pancetta**, but more delicate in flavour since it is cut from the pork cheek not the belly. It is more difficult to obtain and you can substitute **pancetta** or bacon if necessary.

lardo—the top layer of fat from the back which has been salted and has, like all fat, absorbed the very best of the flavour in the preserving process. It is used to flavour sauces and ragu, or diced and fried on its own. Fat salt pork can be used in the same way when necessary.

pancetta—a similar cut of pork belly or breast as bacon, but the preserving process gives it a more piquant, spicy flavour that blends especially well with pasta. It is usually sold sliced from a roll and can be kept in the refrigerator for a few days.

prosciutto—ham, which can be raw (*crudo*) or cooked (*cotto*). Parma ham is the most famous variety of raw **prosciutto**. The pigs come from defined areas in the Parma region and the hams are as lightly salted as possible and then air-cured in the very special breezes that blow around the Parma hills. Other regional raw **prosciutto** is exported from Italy, but any form of salted uncooked ham can be used when necessary.

salami—there are hundreds of varieties of these highly seasoned salted sausages, the best of which are made from pure pork although some regional varieties use other meats as well. *Mortadella* is one well-known variety, known also as Bologna sausage. It is milder than most other salamis and has a lovely smooth, firm texture. For pasta recipes with salami you can use any variety; the spicier ones, with peppercorns or fennel seeds, for example, go particularly well.

salsiccia—fresh pork sausage, usually made from shoulder of pork with added spices but without all the additives of ordinary sausages. They can be obtained at good Italian groceries, especially the variety known as *luganega* from northern Italy, and are well worth buying for recipes calling for fresh pork sausage.

strutto—now made industrially by a centrifugal process that draws all the fat out of the unwanted parts of the pig and clarifies it to make lard. Other lard can be used as a substitute, but it should preferably be made from pork fat.

sugna—prepared at home, especially in country areas, by rendering down the best parts of pork fat, particularly from the back nearest the skin. The ancient method of preserving this form of home-made lard with herbs and seasonings in earthenware pots or bladders gives it a very special flavour which is hard to imitate, although pork dripping makes a good substitute since it has a good flavour of its own.

MISCELLANEOUS INGREDIENTS

anchovies (*acciughe, alici*)—tinned/canned anchovies in oil can be used in any of these recipes, but they are not as tasty or economical as the salt-cured whole anchovies available in most Italian groceries. These are sold loose by weight and it takes no time to fillet them: wash off the salt, hold the tail and scrape off the skin, dorsal fin and bones attached to it. Split the anchovy in two with a sharp knife, remove the spine and the flour fillets. Use immediately, or keep them up to two weeks in a dish arranged in layers and completely covered with oil. Anchovies have a very pungent flavour, so adapt the amounts suggested according to taste.

breadcrumbs (*pangrattato*)—where breadcrumbs are required in these recipes use crisp breadcrumbs made by slowly baking slices of stale bread in a slow oven, then pounded in a mortar, grated or put in a blender. They can also be bought from Italian groceries.

large breadcrumbs (*mollica di pane*)—used to thicken sauces and dumplings. Use thickish slices of stale white bread without the crust, soften as directed in milk, stock or water, squeeze dry and crumble.

mushrooms (*funghi*)—the boletus variety of mushrooms (*funghi porcini*) are commonly used in Italian cooking. They have a lovely strong flavour which blends especially well with pasta and any tomato sauce or ragu. These mushrooms can be bought dried from Italian groceries; a little goes a long way—one ounce of dried mushrooms should be enough for the average sauce for six helpings of pasta. Soak them for 10–20 minutes in lukewarm water, then reserve the water to add to the sauce or ragu (but strain it first), and rinse the mushrooms under running water.

olive oil (*olio di oliva*)—recommended for cooking in all Italian recipes. In certain sauces the oil is one of the dominant flavours (e.g., uncooked marinated sauces) so it is worth using a good fruity olive oil. The best come from Sicily, Tuscany, Sardinia, Liguria, Lucca and Spoleto. There are also some good blends of olive oil and other vegetable oils available which are well flavoured and good for cooking. In country areas, in southern Italy in particular, various pork fats are used for cooking, some of which are described in the preceding section. They do, of course, add a special flavour but are often hard to find.

pine nuts (*pignoli*)—these little nuts have a special flavour and consistency that cannot really be replaced by any other sort of nut. They are usually available at Italian groceries.

seafood—most fish used in Italian cooking are native to the Adriatic and Mediterranean seas, so you will have to experiment with your own local fish in some recipes (suggestions are given) or else use the excellent imported tinned/canned varieties of seafood such as *vongole*, *cozze*, *polipi*, etc. Make sure they are preserved in their natural juices. If you add this to the sauce, check for saltiness as you may want to add less than usual.

tomatoes (*pomodori*)—Italian tomatoes benefit from a lot of sunshine and are well flavoured and succulent. The small *pomodori da sugo*, sauce tomatoes or plum tomatoes, are normally used for cooking because of their flavour, but you can experiment with any tomatoes available, using more or less according to size and ripeness. It is quickest simply to cut fresh tomatoes across and put them through a sieve or food mill before adding them to a sauce when the recipe specifies pureed tomatoes, and recipe 15 suggests different ways of preparing tomatoes for a sauce. Italian peeled tomatoes in tins/cans make a good alternative and can be sieved for a fine puree or just crushed on the bottom of the pan with a fork. Concentrated tomato puree is made with six pounds of tomatoes for every one pound of tomato puree, so it is very strong. Use with discretion, tasting the sauce before and after adding it. If it has a bitter flavour add one teaspoon sugar to counteract the acidity. It is best to dilute the concentrated tomato puree with a little water before adding. If you feel any tomato sauce lacks something, you can always add one or two teaspoons of concentrated tomato puree for extra flavour.

I
PASTA WITH VEGETABLES

SPAGHETTI OR VERMICELLI WITH GARLIC AND OIL   1

1 lb. vermicelli or spaghetti   olive oil
garlic

This is a very old and inexpensive way to serve pasta, still common in parts of
Apulia. Cook the pasta until tender and drain thoroughly. Place it in a very
hot serving dish with as much olive oil (use a green, fruity variety—the best is
from southern Italy) and crushed or chopped garlic as you like. Mix gently so
the pasta absorbs all the flavour of the garlic and oil, and in turn warms them
pleasantly. Then sit down and enjoy the simple pleasure of this humble dish.

CONCHIGLIETTE OR LUMACHINE WITH OIL AND LEMON JUICE   2

12 oz. conchigliette or lumachine   2 oz. spring onions/scallions
olive oil   salt and pepper
juice of 1 lemon   (chopped parsley, tomatoes)

Use a small concave pasta like conchigliette or lumachine. Cook the pasta and
drain thoroughly, then allow it to cool. Serve cold, preferably as an hors
d'oeuvre, dressed with a really fruity olive oil, salt and pepper and the finely
chopped or sliced spring onions/scallions.

Variations 1. Top with a handful of chopped parsley.
        2. Add a good, ripe tomato which has been seeded and chopped
            in pieces or diced.

SPAGHETTI WITH FRESH HERBS   3

1 lb. spaghetti   plenty of savory, marjoram, basil,
10 tablespoons olive oil   parsley, a little tarragon, chives, and
salt   a little thyme

The only difficulty with this recipe is finding the variety of the fresh herbs,
which is what gives the dish its perfectly balanced flavour. If you succeed, simply chop the herbs, or better still pound them in a mortar, in sufficient quantities to provide a generous tablespoon of the mixture for each serving. Cook
the pasta, drain well and serve with the olive oil and herbs.

SPAGHETTI OR VERMICELLI
WITH TOMATOES, OIL AND LEMON JUICE 4

1 lb. spaghetti or vermicelli	olive oil
1¾ lb. tomatoes	basil
juice of 1½ lemons	salt and pepper

Choose medium ripe tomatoes and skin them. (Dip them for a minute in boiling water to loosen the skins, but not long enough for the flesh to soften or cook.) Chop and remove the seeds without losing too much juice. Cook the pasta and drain well, then add the tomatoes and their juice, the lemon juice, salt and pepper and one or two tablespoons of good, fruity olive oil. Mix well; the hot pasta will thicken the sauce slightly. Sprinkle with a little basil to taste and serve immediately.

SPAGHETTI OR VERMICELLI
WITH UNCOOKED SAUCE—I 5

1 lb. spaghetti or vermicelli	salt and pepper
1½ lb. tomatoes	basil
8 tablespoons olive oil	(parsley and oregano)
2 cloves garlic	

Uncooked sauces that contain lemon juice are made at the last minute, before adding to the pasta, as in the preceding recipes. The more usual uncooked sauce is marinated for two hours or more and contains no lemon juice or vinegar, as the acid flavour would be overpowering. Here is one method of making this type of uncooked sauce: put the olive oil (a fruity oil from southern Italy is the best) in a deep serving dish with the skinned, seeded and chopped or diced tomatoes (retain as much of their juice as possible), the finely chopped garlic and a little basil, and marinate for at least two hours. Then season with salt and pepper and stir the sauce gently. Mix with the hot pasta and serve immediately.

Variations 1. Use whole crushed cloves of garlic and remove before adding the pasta.
2. Use parsley or oregano instead of basil; they are sometimes combined, but this is less interesting than having one dominant flavour.

SPAGHETTI OR VERMICELLI WITH UNCOOKED SAUCE—II   **6**

1 lb. spaghetti or vermicelli	4 oz. black or green olives
1½ lb. tomatoes	salt and pepper
8 tablespoons olive oil	basil
2 cloves garlic	(parsley and oregano)
1 hot chili pepper	

Put the oil, the skinned, seeded and diced tomatoes (remember to retain as much of the juice as possible), the chopped garlic, the pepper broken into two or three pieces, the seedless olives and some basil in a deep serving dish. Leave to marinate at least two hours, then add salt and pepper and remove the pieces of red pepper. Cook the pasta, drain well and mix with the uncooked sauce.

Variations 1. Add the crushed cloves of garlic and remove before adding the pasta.
2. Use parsley or oregano instead of basil.
3. If you use green rather than black olives the sauce should marinate a minimum of four hours, and as long as 24 hours.

SPAGHETTI WITH UNCOOKED BLENDER TOMATO SAUCE   **7**

1 lb. spaghetti	salt and pepper
1 lb. tomatoes	basil, parsley
olive oil	(parmesan)
1 or 2 cloves garlic	

The blender gives you a really thick tomato sauce which is perhaps less fragrant than marinated uncooked sauce, but has a special fragrance of its own. Use good, ripe Italian plum tomatoes and puree them in the blender with a handful of basil and a handful of parsley, salt and pepper and a little garlic, according to taste. Cook the spaghetti and drain very thoroughly (extra water spoils the consistency of the sauce), and mix with the blender sauce, adding a little olive oil—preferably a green, fruity variety from southern Italy.

SPAGHETTINI WITH GARLIC AND TOMATO   **8**

1 lb. spaghettini
2½ lb. tomatoes
6 cloves garlic
8 tablespoons olive oil
2 hot chili peppers

basil, oregano
celery
parsley
capers

Use small, ripe tomatoes; skin, seed and leave to drain a little to remove excess water. Place in a deep serving dish and marinate for about four hours with as much oregano, chopped capers, parsley and basil as you want, the crushed cloves of garlic, chopped red pepper and olive oil to cover. Cook the spaghettini and drain well. Remove the garlic and peppers from the sauce and serve with the hot pasta.

SPAGHETTI OR VERMICELLI WITH GARLIC, OIL AND PARSLEY   **9**

1 lb. spaghetti or vermicelli
8 tablespoons olive oil
6 cloves garlic

parsley
salt and pepper
(rosemary)

Heat the olive oil in a pan until smoking hot and lightly brown the chopped garlic; do not let it overcook or it will have a strong burnt flavour. At the last minute add a handful of coarsely chopped parsley and a good sprinkling of freshly ground pepper. Cook the pasta, drain well, mix with the sauce and serve immediately. The success of this simple dish depends on having the pasta and the sauce ready at exactly the same time, or some of the flavour will be lost. There should be enough oil to make the spaghetti nice and slippery (the Neapolitans have a word for it: sciuliarielli), but not so much that they are swimming in it.

Variations　1.　Put whole crushed cloves of garlic in the oil and leave them to cook a bit longer, then discard before serving. This gives a stronger flavour of garlic, which may upset the perfect balance of garlic and olive oil that should distinguish this dish.

　　　　　　　2.　Grind some pepper directly over the pasta after mixing with the sauce.

　　　　　　　3.　Sprinkle with red pepper and omit the black pepper for a more fragrant taste.

　　　　　　　4.　Use rosemary instead of parsley.

SPAGHETTI, VERMICELLI OR TRENETTE WITH GARLIC, OIL AND HOT PEPPER

1 lb. spaghetti, vermicelli or trenette
8 tablespoons olive oil
4 or 5 cloves garlic

1 hot chili pepper
(parsley, pecorino/romano)

As in the previous recipe you must have the sauce ready at the same time as the pasta. Heat the oil until it smokes, then add the chopped pepper (the hottest variety you can find) and the chopped garlic. Brown lightly and add the chopped parsley. Discard the pieces of pepper and the sauce is ready to serve with the hot pasta. It is a simple sauce with a good powerful flavour.

Variations
1. Neapolitan housewives have a method of adding one or two tablespoons of the water in which the pasta is cooking to the sauce to prevent the parsley from overcooking and losing its lovely green colour. The sauce is ready when all the water has been absorbed.
2. Add the hot pasta to the sauce in the pan, and stir so the pasta absorbs all the flavour.
3. Use whole crushed cloves of garlic and remove them before serving, although this gives a less interesting flavour.
4. Grind some pepper into the sauce when you add the parsley.
5. Add a little grated pecorino/romano or parmesan to the pasta after mixing it with the sauce.

SPAGHETTI OR VERMICELLI WITH BREADCRUMBS

1 lb. spaghetti or vermicelli
8 tablespoons olive oil
4 oz. stale white breadcrumbs

salt and pepper
(garlic, parsley)

This ancient and frugal dish comes from the southern part of Italy once known as Magna Grecia. Heat the oil, add the bread torn into crumbs, and fry lightly without burning. Season with salt and pepper and serve it with the hot pasta. This makes a very humble but also very appetizing sauce, and requires no other ingredients, although various unauthentic additions are sometimes made such as tomato or anchovy.

Variations
1. Cook a clove of crushed garlic in the oil and remove before adding the breadcrumbs.
2. Add a little chopped parsley to the sauce at the last minute, or better still sprinkle directly over the pasta.

1 lb. any variety of pasta	pepper
8 tablespoons olive oil	(parmesan)
1 lb. onions	

Another very ancient way of making simple food taste really appetizing. Heat the oil in a pan, add the coarsely chopped or sliced onions and cook until transparent and soft. Add a generous sprinkling of pepper and serve with any sort of hot pasta, such as spaghetti, bucatini, or penne.

Variation   For a richer flavour, sprinkle with grated parmesan after adding the sauce.

VERMICELLI OR BUCATINI WITH TOMATOES AND LEMON JUICE **13**

1 lb. vermicelli or bucatini	juice of 1 lemon
½ lb. tomatoes	pepper
olive oil	basil or parsley

Cook the pasta in plenty of boiling, salted water. Choose firm ripe tomatoes; skin, seed and chop them in strips. When the pasta is half cooked strain well, return to the pan and add just enough olive oil to moisten the pasta without drowning it, the lemon juice, tomatoes, a little basil or parsley and some freshly ground pepper. Mix together and continue cooking until the sauce has finished cooking the pasta. Test frequently to see it does not become too soft.

VERMICELLI OR SPAGHETTI WITH TOMATOES, NEAPOLITAN STYLE **14**

1 lb. vermicelli or spaghetti	salt
12 tomatoes	(parmesan or pecorino/romano,
basil	oil, pepper)

This Neapolitan recipe dates back to the early days of the tomato in Italy. Between the seventeenth and eighteenth centuries, tomato and pasta were married together for the first time when Neapolitan street vendors or succarenari sold portions of pasta for two cents. Their portable kitchens, equipped with enormous cauldrons for boiling the pasta, were set up all along the little streets or squares of Naples. The cooked pasta hung in long lines on poles placed over the cauldron to keep the pasta hot. Two cents worth of macaroni—al due—gave you a large forkful sprinkled with grated cheese. There are numerous illustrations of lazzaroni or urchins lowering such a fork-ful into their mouths on some high day or holiday. The cheese is piled up on a big dish beside the cauldron with a couple of carnations stuck in it and a garland of peppercorns as part of the instinctive Neapolitan love of colour and display. The tomatoes are less in evidence, but they are there all the time, cooking in a pan over the heat. They were good ripe tomatoes, cooked by slitting down the side so they could simmer in their own liquid and nothing else. When this evaporated they were left to finish cooking in their own heat. Anyone lucky enough to have another cent was entitled to a portion of the tomatoes—al tre—so the tomatoes were originally an accompaniment rather than a proper sauce. Heat the tomatoes in a pan until the skins burst and let them cook in their own liquid, just adding pepper and a little basil, for about ten minutes—until the liquid evaporates and the basil flavours the tomatoes. Beware of cooking them much longer or the tomatoes may burn. This deliciously simple accompaniment is then ready to serve with the spaghetti or vermicelli. It has an added advantage for weight-watchers: the sauce contains no fat at all.

Variations 1. Serve grated parmesan or pecorino/romano separately, as in the original version al due.
          2. Add a little fresh olive oil and some pepper to the pasta and tomatoes.

SPAGHETTI, VERMICELLI, BUCATINI OR LINGUINE WITH TOMATO AND BASIL   15

1 lb. spaghetti, vermicelli, bucatini, or linguine	salt and pepper
2 lbs. tomatoes	6 tablespoons olive oil
basil	(parmesan, pecorino/romano, fat salt pork or prosciutto fat)

Fresh, ripe plum tomatoes make the best tomato sauce, not only for their colour and flavour, but also because they have a clearer juice than other varieties. There are various ways of preparing the tomatoes before you add them to the oil in the pan. If they are fresh you can cut them in half and leave to drain for at least 15 minutes, and then pass through a food mill to eliminate the seeds and skins. Or they can be dipped in boiling water for one minute to facilitate removing the skins. Peel, quarter, remove the seeds and chop the tomatoes. If you are using tinned/canned tomatoes, drain them well, place in a pan and mash with a fork. Heat the oil in a pan and add the tomatoes. Salt and pepper to taste, add a few chopped basil leaves and cook about 30 minutes, until slightly thickened. Serve over the hot pasta.

Variations 1. Just before serving, grate a little pecorino/romano or parmesan over the top of the pasta.
2. The pasta seasoned with this sauce can also be served cold.
3. Use fat salt pork or prosciutto fat instead of oil to prepare the sauce.

SPAGHETTI, VERMICELLI, BUCATINI OR LINGUINE WITH TOMATOES AND THYME **16**

1 lb. spaghetti, bucatini, linguine or vermicelli	salt and pepper (parmesan, pecorino/romano, pork dripping, sugna or prosciutto fat)
2 lb. tomatoes	
6 tablespoons olive oil	
thyme	

Make the sauce with oil and tomatoes, as in the previous recipe, then add a little thyme and cook until thick and well blended. Serve with the hot pasta and freshly ground black pepper. The thyme gives a completely different flavour to the tomato sauce.

Variations 1. Serve grated parmesan or pecorino/romano separately.
2. Use pork dripping, sugna or prosciutto fat instead of olive oil.

SPAGHETTI WITH BAY LEAVES—I **17**

1 lb. spaghetti	10 bay leaves
4 tablespoons olive oil	salt and pepper
1 onion	cinnamon
1 lb. tomatoes	

This is another ancient recipe from southern Italy which has a surprisingly modern and appetizing flavour. Heat the oil, lightly brown the sliced onion and add the pureed tomatoes. Add the bay leaves, season with salt and pepper and a pinch of cinnamon. Mix well, remove the bay leaves and serve with the hot pasta.

Variation Omit the cinnamon. However, its flavour does blend well with the bay leaves.

34

SPAGHETTI, VERMICELLI, BUCATINI OR LINGUINE WITH GARLIC AND TOMATO   **18**

1 lb. spaghetti, vermicelli,
bucatini or linguine
2 lb. tomatoes
6 tablespoons olive oil

1 hot chili pepper
salt and pepper
(fat salt pork, pork dripping,
prosciutto fat or sugna)

Prepare the sauce in the usual way (see recipe 15) with the oil and tomatoes, then add the pepper broken into small pieces. When the sauce is cooked you can remove the pepper or not according to taste. Serve with the hot pasta.

Variation   Use fat salt pork, pork dripping, prosciutto fat or sugna instead of olive oil.

SPAGHETTI WITH TOMATOES AND GARLIC   **19**

1 lb. spaghetti
1½ lb. tomatoes
4 tablespoons olive oil
2 cloves garlic

oregano
capers
(pecorino/romano)

This is a classic Neapolitan dish. Heat the oil and add the finely sliced garlic. Before it browns add the skinned, seeded and chopped tomatoes. Cook for a few minutes, add a handful of capers and a pinch of oregano, then serve with the hot pasta.

Variation   Serve grated pecorino/romano separately.

SPAGHETTI, VERMICELLI, BUCATINI OR LINGUINE WITH PEPPER AND TOMATO   **20**

1 lb. spaghetti, vermicelli,
bucatini or linguine
6 tablespoons olive oil
3 cloves garlic
salt and pepper

2 lb. tomatoes
(parsley, basil, oregano,
tomato puree, white wine,
fat salt pork, pork dripping,
prosciutto fat or sugna)

Heat the oil and add the finely sliced garlic. Before it starts to brown add the tomatoes prepared in the usual way (see recipe 4). Season with salt and pepper. Cook for about 15 minutes and serve with the hot pasta.

Variations   1. Add a handful of chopped parsley to the sauce before serving.
2. Add some small basil leaves, or chopped large leaves to the

sauce five minutes before serving.
3. Add a pinch of oregano.
4. Add whole crushed cloves of garlic and discard before serving.
5. Use tomato puree instead of whole tomatoes, but dilute to taste with a little lukewarm water. Watch the sauce when it is cooking in case you need to add a few more tablespoons water.
6. Add a little white wine when the garlic is cooking in the hot oil, then add the tomatoes immediately.
7. If the tomatoes are really ripe, Neapolitans often add ½ teaspoon sugar to the sauce with the seasonings to counteract the acidity.

SPAGHETTI, VERMICELLI, BUCATINI OR LINGUINE WITH TOMATOES, GARLIC AND BREADCRUMBS

21

1 lb. spaghetti, vermicelli, bucatini or linguine	1 lb. tomatoes
3 cloves garlic, crushed	olive oil
salt and pepper	2 tablespoons dry breadcrumbs

Heat the oil and lightly cook the crushed garlic. Add the skinned, chopped tomatoes, salt and pepper. Cook for a few minutes and add the breadcrumbs to give a nice consistency to the sauce. Serve over the hot pasta.

SPAGHETTI, VERMICELLI, BUCATINI OR LINGUINE WITH TOMATOES, GARLIC AND PARSLEY

22

1 lb. spaghetti, vermicelli, bucatini or linguine	2 lb. tomatoes
2 cloves garlic	6 tablespoons olive oil
1 stick celery	1 carrot
1 small bunch parsley	1 onion

Cook the celery, carrot and onion in a little water until soft. Take two tablespoons of this water with a little finely chopped parsley and add to a tomato and garlic sauce prepared in the usual way (see recipe 20). Cook until the sauce thickens and serve with the hot pasta.

1 lb. spaghetti, vermicelli,	basil
bucatini or linguine	salt and pepper
2 lb. tomatoes	(carrot, parmesan or
6 tablespoons olive oil	pecorino/romano,
1 onion	fat salt pork,
1 stick celery	prosciutto fat or sugna)

Heat the oil in the pan and add the sliced onion and chopped celery. When the onion starts to brown add the tomatoes prepared in the usual way (see recipe 4). Cook over moderate heat until the sauce thickens, season with salt and pepper. Add the basil towards the end and serve with the hot pasta.

Variations 1. Add some chopped carrot with the celery.
2. Serve the pasta with grated parmesan or pecorino/romano.
3. Use fat salt pork, prosciutto fat or sugna instead of olive oil.

SPAGHETTI OR VERMICELLI WITH TOMATOES AND BRANDY **24**

1 lb. spaghetti or vermicelli	4 tablespoons brandy
5 tablespoons olive oil	2 lb. tomatoes
½ onion	salt and pepper

Heat the oil in a pan and add the finely sliced or chopped onion and cook until transparent without letting it colour. Remove from the heat and add the brandy, stirring until the sauce thickens. Return to the heat and add the tomatoes prepared in the usual way (see recipe 4). Season with salt and pepper and continue cooking without letting it boil for a few minutes, then serve with the hot pasta.

SPAGHETTI OR VERMICELLI WITH TOMATO, GARLIC AND ONION

1 lb. spaghetti or vermicelli	salt and pepper
5 tablespoons olive oil	parsley
2 lb. tomatoes	(oregano, basil,
1 clove garlic	pecorino/romano, salt pork,
½ onion	prosciutto fat, sugna)

Heat the oil in a pan and add the finely sliced onion and garlic and a little chopped parsley. When the onion starts to colour add the tomatoes, prepared in the usual way (see recipe 4). Season with salt and pepper and cook until thick. Serve with the hot pasta.

Variations 1. Add a little oregano to the tomatoes.
2. Add basil instead of parsley, and oregano to taste.
3. Serve grated pecorino/romano separately.
4. Use fat salt pork, prosciutto fat or sugna instead of oil.

SPAGHETTI OR VERMICELLI WITH TOMATOES AND HERBS

1 lb. spaghetti or vermicelli	parsley
2 lb. tomatoes	mint
5 tablespoons olive oil	1 small piece hot chili pepper
1 onion	salt
2 cloves garlic	(pecorino/romano or parmesan)
celery leaves	

This is another variation on the tomato, garlic and onion sauce, but it has a rich assortment of flavours which you can alter according to taste. Heat the oil in the pan with a small piece of pepper. Discard the pepper and add the finely sliced onion. Cook until transparent (do not let it brown) and then add the thinly sliced garlic (or use crushed cloves of garlic and remove them before serving). Add a few leaves of mint and celery and a little parsley, and the tomatoes prepared in the usual way (see recipe 4). Season with salt and pepper and cook with the lid on the pan, checking occasionally to see there is enough liquid (you may need to add a few tablespoons of hot water towards the end), but the sauce should be fairly thick and the ingredients well blended before it is ready to serve with the hot pasta.

Variation Serve grated parmesan or pecorino/romano separately.

1 lb. spaghetti or vermicelli	2 tablespoons tomato puree
5 tablespoons olive oil	6 oz. dry white wine
½ onion	salt and pepper
1 clove garlic	(fat salt pork,
1 stick celery	prosciutto fat or sugna)

Heat the oil and cook the chopped or finely sliced onion, the chopped celery and finely sliced garlic, then add the dry white wine. Cook until the wine starts to steam and evaporate and add the tomato puree. Continue cooking over low heat, and if the sauce seems to be thickening and drying out dilute with two or three tablespoons of hot water, preferably from the pan where you are cooking the pasta. Season with salt and pepper. When the sauce has thickened nicely without becoming solid it is ready to serve with the hot pasta.

Variation Use fat salt pork, prosciutto fat or sugna instead of olive oil.

SPAGHETTI OR VERMICELLI
WITH GARLIC AND OLIVES 28

1 lb. spaghetti or vermicelli	½ lb. black olives
5 tablespoons olive oil	parsley
2 cloves garlic	(capers, pepper, breadcrumbs)

Heat the oil and add the finely chopped garlic. Before it starts to brown add the coarsely chopped olives and a good handful of chopped parsley. Cook for a few more minutes and then serve with the hot pasta.

Variations 1. Add a tablespoon of capers with the olives.
2. Serve freshly ground black pepper with the sauce.
3. Add some breadcrumbs browned in a little olive oil to the finished sauce.

1 lb. spaghetti or vermicelli	2 cloves garlic
5 tablespoons olive oil	basil
2 lb. tomatoes	salt
½ lb. black olives	(hot chili peppers)
1 tablespoon capers	

Coarsely chop the seeded olives. Peel, seed and chop the tomatoes keeping as much of the juice as possible. Finely slice the garlic and put in a pan with the oil, all the other ingredients and a little basil. Leave to marinate for about an hour. Cook over moderate heat until the liquid has reduced and the sauce has a good strong colour and flavour. Serve with the hot pasta.

Variation Add a few pieces of hot chili pepper to the oil and remove before serving.

MACCHERONCINI WITH OLIVES AND WINE 30

1 lb. maccheroncini	parsley
1 lb. green olives	pepper
dry white wine	breadcrumbs
2 cloves garlic	(parmesan)
3 tomatoes	

The white wine in this recipe betrays French influence. Chop the seeded olives and cook them in just enough white wine to cover, together with the chopped cloves of garlic, or whole, crushed cloves which are discarded before serving. Season with pepper and add a handful of chopped parsley. As soon as the cooking liquid evaporates and the olives are well flavoured remove from the heat and mix with the hot pasta. Put in a greased ovenproof dish, cover the pasta with slices of tomato, sprinkle with breadcrumbs and brown for a few minutes in a hot oven.

Variation Sprinkle a little grated parmesan on the pasta together with the breadcrumbs.

PENNE OR CONCHIGLIE WITH GREEN OLIVES

1 lb. penne or conchiglie
5 oz. green olives
2 lb. tomatoes
2 tablespoons capers
1 onion

2 sticks celery
2 tablespoons vinegar
6 tablespoons olive oil
salt and pepper
(gherkins, mint)

Heat the oil and brown the finely sliced onion; add the tomatoes, which you have put through a food mill, the seeded and chopped olives, the chopped celery and the capers. Season with salt and pepper and cook until the sauce has thickened. Add the vinegar and cook until it starts to evaporate; if it dries out too much add a couple of tablespoons of lukewarm water. Mix with the hot pasta and serve cold.

Variation Serve topped with slices of gherkin and chopped mint.

FRIED PASTA (ANY VARIETY)

1¼ lb. pasta (any variety)
6 oz. olive oil

salt and black pepper
parsley

This is another old Neapolitan recipe. First cook the pasta in plenty of lightly salted boiling water. Drain well, then fry a little at a time in very hot oil. Drain the pasta and season with salt and freshly ground black pepper. Top with sprigs of parsley which you have blanched, drained well and fried for a minute in the hot oil.

BAKED ZITE, MANICHE OR RIGATONI WITH TOMATOES

1 lb. of the larger variety of pasta
(e.g. zite, maniche or rigatoni)
1 lb. tomatoes
salt and pepper
2 or 3 cloves garlic

olive oil
parsley
(basil, oregano,
hot chili pepper or
paprika)

Grease an ovenproof dish and put in the sliced tomatoes. Sprinkle with the chopped garlic and a little salt and pepper. Cover with plenty of olive oil and bake in a moderate oven for ½ hour. When cooked, put the tomatoes in a large serving dish, add the hot pasta and mix well.

Variations 1. Use basil or oregano instead of parsley.
2. Add a little finely chopped hot pepper or a pinch of paprika.

VERMICELLI OR BUCATINI AND TOMATO RING 35

1 lb. vermicelli or bucatini
3 lb. tomatoes
basil or oregano
olive oil

breadcrumbs
salt and pepper
(parmesan)

Use round medium-sized ripe tomatoes. Cut them in half and place in a baking dish with a little oil, cut side down. Make a second layer with the cut side face up. Sprinkle with salt and pepper and a little basil or a pinch of oregano. Arrange the uncooked pasta on top like the spokes of a wheel (the gaps in between the pasta will help it cook). Add two further layers of tomatoes arranged as for the first two layers, then another layer of pasta and two final layers of tomatoes. Moisten with plenty of oil, sprinkle with breadcrumbs and bake in a moderate oven for about 15 to 20 minutes, or until the pasta is cooked.

Variation Add two more layers of tomatoes and pasta to make an even higher mound.

MACARONI (MESSE ZITE, ZITE) RING WITH TOMATOES 34

1 lb. macaroni,
messe zite or zite
4 lb. tomatoes
olive oil
6 tablespoons breadcrumbs

basil
oregano
salt and pepper
2 cloves garlic
(olives, capers)

Fry the breadcrumbs in two tablespoons oil with one finely sliced clove of garlic and add a pinch of oregano. Season with salt and pepper. Cut the tomatoes in half across and put one layer in a greased baking dish, cut side up. Sprinkle with a little basil and some breadcrumbs. Make a second and third layer of tomatoes and breadcrumbs with layers of uncooked pasta in between. Moisten with olive oil and bake in a moderate oven for about 1½ hours, or until the pasta is cooked. A similar recipe to the previous one, but the larger variety of pasta needs a longer time to cook.

Variations 1. Use only four tablespoons of breadcrumbs between the layers of tomato and pasta. Mix the rest with the oil, chopped garlic, oregano and seasoning and pour over the final layer of macaroni. This prevents the top from overcooking.
2. Add a few seeded chopped olives and capers between the layers of tomatoes: too many may spoil the flavour of this richly aromatic dish.

MACARONI (PENNE, MEZZE ZITE, ZITE) WITH ONIONS

1 lb. macaroni, penne,
mezze zite or zite
3 large onions
salt and pepper

tomato sauce or
concentrated tomato puree
3 tablespoons olive oil

Here the onion is not just a flavouring in the sauce, but the main point of the dish. Use large, firm onions. Peel, finely slice them and cook in the oil over low heat until soft and transparent, but not brown. Then add enough tomato sauce (see recipe 15) to add colour and flavour to the onions without drowning them (the original version of this recipe contains no tomatoes). If you are using tomato concentrate, dilute well with lukewarm water before adding to the onions, and a couple more tablespoons when the puree is cooking with the onions to keep the sauce fairly liquid. Season with salt and pepper. Mix well with the hot pasta so the onions are evenly distributed.

Variation Cook the onions until they dissolve into a puree before adding the tomato.

SPAGHETTI OR VERMICELLI WITH TOMATOES AND CELERY

1 lb. spaghetti or vermicelli
5 tablespoons olive oil
1 lb. tomatoes
½ onion

3 sticks celery
salt and pepper
(carrot)

Celery is the dominant flavour in this sauce, so do not be afraid to use generous quantities. Fry the chopped onion in the oil and add the finely chopped celery. When they begin to brown add a pinch of salt and some pepper and the peeled, seeded and chopped tomatoes. Cook until the tomatoes are soft and serve with the hot pasta.

Variation Mix a little grated carrot with the celery.

1 lb. orecchiette
1 lb. broccoli spears
olive oil

garlic
salt and pepper
(hot chili pepper)

Boil the broccoli just enough to cook the stems while the tips remain firm and green. Drain and reserve the water to cook the pasta. Finely slice the garlic and soften in olive oil, then add the broccoli and fry gently. Season with salt and pepper and serve with the hot pasta.

Variation Fry a hot chili pepper broken in pieces in oil before adding the garlic and broccoli, then discard.

ORECCHIETTE WITH BROCCOLI SPEARS AND TOMATOES 39

1 lb. orecchiette
1¼ lb. tomatoes, pureed
1¼ lb. broccoli spears
4 tablespoons olive oil
1 clove garlic

parsley
salt and pepper
(cauliflower florets,
pecorino/romano)

Cook the broccoli without letting it get soggy. Drain and reserve the water. Cook the orecchiette in this water. Heat the oil in a pan and add a clove of crushed or finely sliced garlic (to be discarded before serving), the tomato puree together with a handful of chopped parsley, salt and pepper. Mix the hot pasta with the broccoli and tomato sauce and serve immediately.

Variations 1. Use cauliflower florets instead of broccoli.
2. Serve grated pecorino/romano separately.

BUCATINI OR MACCHERONCINI WITH BROCCOLI, PINE NUTS AND RAISINS 40

1 lb. bucatini or maccheroncini
1 lb. broccoli spears
4 tablespoons olive oil
1 onion

1½ tablespoons pine nuts
2 tablespoons raisins
salt and pepper
(cauliflower florets)

Cook the broccoli so they are firm but tender, drain and use the water to cook the pasta. Heat the oil, add the finely sliced onion, the pine nuts and raisins, previously softened in warm water. Cook until the onion is soft, add the broccoli spears and season with salt and pepper. Serve with the hot pasta.

Variations 1. Cook the pasta, drain well, then add to the broccoli spears in the pan. Mix for a minute over the heat, then serve.
2. Eliminate the pine nuts and raisins, although they are an original feature of this ancient recipe.
3. Use cauliflower florets instead of broccoli.

BUCATINI OR MACCHERONCINI WITH BROCCOLI SPEARS, PINE NUTS, RAISINS AND SAFFRON   41

1 lb. bucatini or maccheroncini	1½ tablespoons pine nuts
1 lb. broccoli spears	2 tablespoons raisins
4 tablespoons olive oil	saffron
1 onion	salt and pepper

Saffron completely alters the flavour in this variation on the previous recipe. Use one pinch to one tablespoon of lukewarm water, added to the other ingredients in the pan just before the broccoli spears (or cauliflower florets).

BUCATINI WITH ONION   42

1 lb. bucatini	salt and pepper
6 large onions	(pecorino/romano)
6 tablespoons olive oil	

Peel the onions, slice thinly, and cook them with just enough olive oil to cover until the onion softens without browning. Keep stirring gently with a wooden spatula so the onions cook uniformly in the middle of the pan. Cook the bucatini, drain well and add to the pan when the onions are soft. Mix in a little fresh oil, salt and pepper, cook for a couple of minutes and serve.

Variations 1. Bake the pasta and onions for a few minutes in the oven.
2. Serve grated pecorino/romano separately.

SPAGHETTI WITH COURGETTES/ZUCCHINI

1 lb. spaghetti	olive oil
5 courgettes/zucchini	salt and pepper

Serve the courgettes/zucchini and fry them in hot oil. Cook the spaghetti, drain well and add the vegetables and their oil. Season with salt and pepper.

Variation Add the cooked, drained pasta to the courgettes/zucchini in the pan, and let them cook together a little so the pasta absorbs their flavour.

SPAGHETTI WITH COURGETTES/ZUCCHINI AND TOMATOES—I

1 lb. spaghetti	olive oil
6 courgettes/zucchini	salt and pepper
3 tomatoes	basil
1 onion	(garlic)

Wash, dry and dice the courgettes/zucchini. Heat the oil in a pan with the chopped or finely sliced onion. Add the vegetable, a few basil leaves, the skinned, seeded tomatoes cut in strips and cook until the courgettes/zucchini are soft. Add the hot pasta, stir a little to give added flavour, then serve.

Variation Add a crushed clove of garlic to the pan and discard it before serving.

SPAGHETTI WITH COURGETTES/ZUCCHINI AND TOMATOES—II

1 lb. spaghetti	basil
5 courgettes/zucchini	olive oil
3 tomatoes	salt and pepper
1 onion	(garlic)

Wash, dry and dice the courgettes/zucchini. Heat the oil in the pan, add the onion, the vegetable, basil, the skinned, seeded and sliced tomatoes. When the courgettes/zucchini are beginning to soften, dilute the contents of the pan with boiling water or a light stock. Add the uncooked spaghetti broken in short pieces and cook until al dente.

Variation Cook a whole crushed clove of garlic in the oil and remove before serving.

CONCHIGLIE AND COURGETTES/ZUCCHINI SALAD
46

1 lb. conchiglie
4 courgettes/zucchini
olive oil

lemon juice
salt and pepper

Clean, slice the courgettes/zucchini and fry them in the oil. Cook the conchiglie, drain well and leave to cool. Mix the pasta and cold vegetable in a serving dish with olive oil, lemon juice, and salt and pepper to taste.

SPAGHETTI OR VERMICELLI WITH PUMPKIN FLOWERS
47

1 lb. spaghetti or vermicelli
1 onion
1 clove garlic
olive oil
1 pinch saffron

½ lb. (about 5 dozen)
pumpkin flowers
parsley
salt and pepper
tomato sauce

Fry the finely sliced onion in the oil together with the chopped garlic and the pumpkin flowers, a little chopped parsley and the saffron (dissolved in a little warm water). When almost cooked add a few tablespoons of oil and tomato sauce (see recipe 15). Serve with the hot pasta.

VERMICELLI OR SPAGHETTI WITH AUBERGINES/EGGPLANT— I
48

1 lb. spaghetti or vermicelli
3 large aubergines/eggplant
olive oil
coarse salt

1 clove garlic
parsley
(½ hot chili pepper)

The success of this dish depends on a traditional Sicilian way of preparing the aubergines/eggplant. Peel the vegetables or not, according to taste, and cut them into quite thick, broad slices. Sprinkle with coarse salt and leave for a few hours—or better still overnight—to remove the bitter flavour. This is best done by laying the slices on the back of a curved plate and then covering them with another lightly weighted plate so the pressure forces the water to run down the curved surface. Fry the slices in plenty of hot oil in which you have lightly browned a thinly sliced clove of garlic (or it may be crushed and then discarded when brown), together with a little chopped parsley. Transfer the vegetable slices from the pan onto absorbent paper to remove any excess oil. Boil the pasta and drain well, then combine with the vegetables in a large dish, reserving a few slices to crown this delicious-looking mound. Add a little fresh olive oil and serve immediately.

Variation   You can also fry a little hot chili pepper in the oil together with the garlic, and then discard it. N.B. Always choose 'male' aubergine/ eggplant which have a slight protuberance on the opposite end to the stalk: they have fewer seeds and are less watery so they cook much better than 'female' ones.

VERMICELLI OR SPAGHETTI WITH AUBERGINE/EGGPLANT— II   49

1 lb. spaghetti or vermicelli	garlic
3 large aubergines/eggplant	parsley
olive oil	pepper
coarse salt	hot chili pepper

A variation on the previous recipe. Dice or slice the aubergine/eggplant and leave to stand sprinkled with coarse salt and covered with a lightly weighted plate for a few hours. Heat the oil in a pan, add the garlic and the chili pepper, then the parsley and vegetable slices. Cook for 15 minutes over moderate heat and then more gently over lower heat so the slices lose some of the oil absorbed in frying and are crisper and more tasty. This works best with small slices. Mix with the hot pasta, adding a little fresh olive oil and some freshly ground black pepper.

BAVETTE WITH AUBERGINES/EGGPLANT AND GARLIC   50

1 lb. bavette	3 aubergines/eggplant
6 tablespoons olive oil	2 cloves garlic
grated parmesan	pepper

Peel the aubergines/eggplant, cut in fairly thick slices and parboil in plenty of water. Discard the water and add fresh boiling water, together with two tablespoons olive oil. Cook the slices until just tender, drain and keep warm. Cook the pasta in the vegetable water. Meanwhile, heat the rest of the oil and the chopped garlic (or whole crushed cloves of garlic to be discarded before serving). Mix the pasta and the vegetable slices in a serving dish, adding the hot oil from the pan and the grated parmesan. Serve hot.

Variation Heat the oil in a really large pan and add the vegetable slices and the pasta so they cook together for a couple of minutes.

VERMICELLI OR SPAGHETTI WITH AUBERGINES/EGGPLANT AND TOMATOES 51

1 lb. vermicelli or spaghetti
3 large aubergines/eggplant
olive oil
coarse salt

garlic
parsley
pepper
6 tablespoons tomato sauce

Slice or dice the aubergines/eggplant, sprinkle with coarse salt and leave to stand for one hour under a weighted plate. Fry with the garlic and parsley, as in the preceding recipes. Make the tomato sauce as in recipe 15 with just oil and tomatoes. Add to the hot pasta with the vegetable slices and season with plenty of freshly ground pepper.

VERMICELLI OR SPAGHETTI WITH AUBERGINES/EGGPLANT AND PEPPERS 52

1 lb. vermicelli or spaghetti
2 aubergines/eggplant
2 sweet peppers
olive oil
coarse salt

hot chili pepper, ground
parsley
garlic
6 tablespoons tomato sauce

Dice the aubergines/eggplant, sprinkle with coarse salt and leave to stand one hour covered with a weighted plate. Fry the garlic and parsley in olive oil and add the diced vegetables with a pinch of ground chili pepper. Use good fat sweet peppers; clean them and cut in strips and cook with the vegetables. Make a tomato sauce with olive oil and tomatoes (see recipe 15). Cook the pasta, drain well and mix with the tomato sauce, aubergines/eggplant and peppers.

BUCATINI OR LINGUINE WITH SWEET PEPPERS

1 lb. bucatini or linguine	parsley
1 lb. sweet peppers	salt and pepper
1 lb. tomatoes	capers
4 tablespoons olive oil	(pecorino/romano)
garlic	

The best way of making this Calabrian recipe is to roast the peppers under a hot grill, and then wet your fingertips and peel them carefully. Remove the seeds and cut the peppers in strips. Heat the oil in a pan with a chopped clove of garlic (or crushed clove which you will discard before serving). Choose small, ripe tomatoes, skin, seed and chop them (or put them through a food mill) and add to the garlic in the pan. Cook for a few minutes, then add the sliced pepper; cook a little longer until the sauce is well blended. Add a few capers and a handful of chopped parsley, season with salt and pepper and serve with the hot pasta.

Variations 1. Add the pasta to the sauce in the pan and stir a little so it is well mixed.
2. Serve grated pecorino/romano separately.

SPAGHETTI, VERMICELLI OR LINGUINE WITH SWEET PEPPERS

1 lb. spaghetti, vermicelli, or linguine	parsley
1 lb. sweet peppers	1 teaspoon sugar
3 tablespoons olive oil	1 tablespoon vinegar
garlic	salt

This recipe is from Emilia. Finely chop the peppers, a little parsley and a clove of garlic and put in a pan with a pinch of salt, enough oil to moisten and a few tablespoons of water. Bring to a boil and cook covered for ½ hour over moderate heat. Check to see if more water is needed as the sauce cooks. When the peppers are almost soft add one teaspoon of sugar and one tablespoon of vinegar. Cook for another few minutes, but the sauce should not be allowed to thicken too much. It is an excellent accompaniment for any sort of boiled pasta.

SPAGHETTI, VERMICELLI OR LINGUINE WITH SWEET PEPPERS AND TOMATOES **55**

1 lb. spaghetti, vermicelli or linguine
¾ lb. tomatoes
3 tablespoons olive oil
1 teaspoon sugar
salt

¾ lb. sweet peppers
garlic
parsley
1 tablespoon vinegar

Make the sauce as in the previous recipe; finely chop the peppers, parsley and garlic and cook with the olive oil, some water and salt. Bring to a boil uncovered, add the pureed tomatoes, sugar and vinegar. Serve with the hot pasta.

SWEET PEPPERS STUFFED WITH SPAGHETTI **56**

6 sweet peppers
olive oil
black olives
salt and pepper

¾ lb. spaghetti
capers
tomato sauce

Wash 6 big peppers, roast them under a hot grill or broiler and remove the outer skin with moistened fingers. Cut a lid from the top and carefully remove the stem and seeds. Fill with the spaghetti cooked in the usual way and mixed with some tomato sauce (see recipe 15), capers and seeded black olives (or other ingredients, according to taste; Neapolitan housewives use any available leftovers, but the tomato, olive and caper flavours blend best with the peppers). Cover the stuffed peppers with their lids and place them in a greased baking dish; moisten with oil and bake until soft. In Naples the peppers are then left to stand a little, reheated and served.

SHORT PASTA AND PEAS **57**

1 lb. short pasta
(cannolicchi or tubettini)
salt

1 lb. shelled peas
3 onions

This is the most rustic and frugal version of a soup made for centuries in Apulia. Cook the peas with very little water and the chopped onion until tender and well flavoured. Cook the pasta and add to the peas, onion and whatever liquid is left in the pan. It should be served as a fairly thick soup, so alter the quantities of liquid in the pan according to taste.

CANNOLICCHI AND PEA SALAD 58

12 oz. cannolicchi
1 lb. shelled peas
olive oil

lemon juice
parsley
salt and pepper

Cook the pasta and drain well. Cook the peas until just tender. Mix the pasta and peas in a serving dish with oil, lemon juice, salt and pepper and chopped parsley. Serve cold.

BUCATINI WITH ASPARAGUS 59

1 lb. bucatini
1 lb. asparagus tips
(only the most tender part)

6 tablespoons olive oil
salt and pepper
(tomatoes, parmesan)

Heat the oil in a pan, but do not add garlic or onion as it would spoil the delicate flavour of the asparagus. Cook the asparagus in the oil with salt and pepper over low heat so it is tender wittout disintegrating. Serve the asparagus and the oil from the pan with the hot pasta, or add the hot pasta to the pan, mix very gently and serve.

Variation Add pureed tomato to the asparagus when you start to cook it in the pan. This combination of flavours may not appeal to everyone; if you do include tomato, serve grated parmesan separately.

BUCATINI, SPAGHETTI OR PENNE WITH ARTICHOKES 60

1 lb. bucatini, spaghetti or penne
4 tablespoons olive oil
2 cloves garlic
salt and pepper

8 globe artichokes
1 tablespoon vinegar
parsley
(parmesan)

Use very small, young artichokes. Remove the outer leaves, trim the tips and cut them into quarters. Remove chokes. Soak the artichoke quarters in vinegar and water until you are ready to cook them. Heat the oil, add the chopped garlic, or whole crushed cloves of garlic which you discard before serving. Add the artichokes and cook over low heat so they soften without frying. When almost done, season with salt and freshly ground black pepper and a good handful of chopped parsley. Serve with the hot pasta, or add the hot pasta to the pan for a minute or two to cook with the artichokes.

Variation Serve grated parmesan separately.

BUCATINI, SPAGHETTI OR PENNE
WITH ARTICHOKES AND OLIVES
61

1 lb. bucatini, spaghetti or penne
6 globe artichokes
12 black olives
1 tablespoon vinegar
parsley

4 tablespoons olive oil
2 cloves garlic
salt and pepper
(green olives, parmesan)

Clean, trim the artichokes, cut into quarters, remove chokes and leave to soak in vinegar and water. Drain and cook in the oil over low heat so they soften without frying (if necessary add a little warm water to the pan). When nearly cooked season with salt and pepper, add the seeded chopped olives and a handful of chopped parsley and serve with the hot pasta; or else add the hot pasta to the artichokes in the pan and cook for a minute or two together.

Variations 1. Use green instead of black olives.
2. Serve grated parmesan separately.

CONCHIGLIE AND ARTICHOKE SALAD
62

1 lb. conchiglie
olive oil
salt and pepper

6 globe artichokes
lemon juice

Clean, trim and chop the artichokes into quarters, remove chokes, then boil until tender. Cook the pasta; mix the artichokes and pasta in a serving dish, adding olive oil, lemon juice and salt and pepper. Serve cold.

PASTA AND POTATOES
63

1 lb. short pasta, such as
cannolicchi or tubetti
1¼ lb. potatoes
6 tablespoons olive oil
¾ lb. tomatoes
salt and pepper

1 onion
parsley
(pecorino/romano, parmesan,
carrot, celery, beef stock,
bacon, tomato puree)

This is one of the most delightfully rustic dishes in all Italian cooking; you can vary the ingredients according to taste and it always tastes delicious. The basic recipe is: heat the oil in a pan and cook the finely sliced onion. Add the pureed tomatoes, salt, pepper and a handful of chopped parsley. Cook for a few minutes, then add the potatoes, which you have peeled and cut in small pieces. Cover with warm water and continue cooking over a low heat so the water does not boil. When the potatoes are ready add the hot pasta, and the dish is ready to serve.

Variations 1. Add a mixture of chopped bacon, celery, carrot and parsley to the oil when you cook the onion.
2. Use beef stock, or a mixture of stock and water to cook the potatoes in the pan.
3. Use the equivalent amount of concentrated tomato puree diluted in water, instead of ordinary pureed tomatoes.
4. Serve grated pecorino/romano or parmesan separately.

FARFALLE OR CANNOLICCHI WITH POTATOES AND HERBS

64

1 lb. farfalle or cannolicchi	parsley
1 lb. potatoes	salt and pepper
1 stick celery	(parmesan)
chervil	

Peel the potatoes and cut into small pieces, then cook in a little salted water without boiling. When half cooked add the chopped celery and a little chopped parsley and chervil. Raise the heat, add the pasta and cook until both are done.

Variation Serve grated parmesan separately.

SPAGHETTI OR VERMICELLI WITH VEGETABLES AND HERBS

65

1 lb. spaghetti or vermicelli	2 carrots
2 potatoes	garlic
2 sticks celery	salt and pepper
4 tablespoons olive oil	(onion, tomatoes, parmesan)
basil	

Peel and chop the potatoes and carrots and chop the celery. Heat the oil in a pan with one or two sliced cloves of garlic, or crushed cloves of garlic, which you remove before serving. Add the other vegetables, a few basil leaves and season with a small pinch of salt and some freshly ground black pepper. When almost cooked add the pasta broken into short pieces, and enough water to cover. Cook the pasta and serve together.

Variations 1. Use a finely sliced onion instead of garlic, or both onion and garlic together.
2. Boil the pasta separately, and then mix with the sauce in the pan just before serving.
3. Include two large peeled, seeded and chopped tomatoes with the other vegetables.
4. Serve grated parmesan separately.

FARFALLE OR STELLINE WITH VEGETABLES 66

1 lb. farfalle or stelline	2 potatoes
2 carrots	2 onions
2 turnips	1 stick celery
a few cloves	¼ lb. fresh green beans
salt and pepper	(parmesan)

Clean and chop the vegetables, then cook in boiling water with the onion stuck with a few cloves. When tender put the vegetables through a food mill and return to the pan. Cook the pasta in this thick vegetable soup and serve together.

Variation Serve grated parmesan separately.

FARFALLE OR STELLINE AND VEGETABLE SALAD 67

1 lb. stelline or farfalle	2 carrots
2 potatoes	¼ lb. shelled peas
1 stick celery	olive oil
lemon juice	salt and pepper

Chop the vegetables and boil until tender. Mix with the hot pasta, a little olive oil, lemon juice and salt and pepper. Serve cold.

VERMICELLI OR SPAGHETTI WITH APPLE 68

1 lb. spaghetti or vermicelli
3 lb. apples
1 stick celery

1 lb. tomatoes
4 tablespoons olive oil
hot chili pepper, salt

Heat the oil in a pan, add the pureed tomatoes and cook for a few minutes until thick. Peel the apples and either core and put in an electric blender, or pass through a food mill. Add the apple puree to the pan, season with salt and chili pepper, and add the celery which you have chopped and boiled until tender. Serve with the hot pasta. The apple gives a pleasantly delicate flavour.

BUCATINI OR CANNOLICCHI WITH BROAD BEANS 69

1 lb. bucatini or cannolicchi
2 lb. broad beans
or lima beans
parsley

1 onion
4 tablespoons olive oil
salt and pepper

Shell the beans and discard the pods. Heat the oil in a pan and cook the finely sliced onion until it starts to brown, then add the beans. Cook over moderate heat until they soften, season with salt and pepper and add a handful of chopped parsley. If they seem too dry add a little hot water. When the beans are tender mix with the hot pasta and serve, or add the hot pasta to the pan and cook for a minute together before serving.

SPAGHETTI OR VERMICELLI WITH DRIED BEANS 70

1 lb. vermicelli or spaghetti
4 tablespoons olive oil
1 onion
salt and pepper

1 lb. dried broad beans
or lima beans
(sugar, tomatoes)

Soak the beans, preferably for 12 hours, in cold water. Remove the outer skin and cook in a pan with a little water and a finely sliced onion. Season with salt and pepper and leave to cook uncovered for two hours over moderate heat. When the beans are tender add the olive oil, and then the hot pasta. Mix together well and serve.

Variation   Add ½ teaspoon sugar to the water when cooking the beans and some chopped tomatoes.

1 lb. avemarie, cannellini or chifferi (or any of the smallest type of pasta with a hole) 2 sticks celery	¾ lb. shelled broad beans or lima beans olive oil 2 carrots salt and pepper

Boil the beans until tender and put through a food mill. The puree should be quite thick. Boil the other two vegetables in lightly salted water and cut them in julienne or thin strips. Cook the pasta and mix all the ingredients in a serving dish, adding fresh olive oil and freshly ground black pepper.

PASTA AND DRIED KIDNEY BEANS WITH TOMATOES

72

10 oz. munnezzaglia (assorted pasta leftovers) ¾ lb. dried kidney beans 1 clove garlic 6 tomatoes olive oil	1 stick celery parsley salt and pepper (hot chili peppers, bacon, concentrated tomato puree)

Soak the beans as long as possible, preferably overnight. Otherwise use this less well-known method of preparing them: boil for ten minutes in plenty of water, drain well and, keeping them in the colander, hold under cold water turned on full and shake vigorously. Then cook them in plenty of water with a clove of garlic, a handful of chopped parsley, a chopped stick of celery, the skinned chopped tomatoes and salt. Cook with the lid on the pan and when the beans are almost done add the munnezzaglia (pasta left over in the bottom of different packets). Break any long pasta in shorter pieces. When the pasta is cooked the soup should be thick enough for a spoon to stand up in it. Serve with a little fresh olive oil and freshly ground black pepper in each serving.

Variations 1. When the beans are cooking in the pan you can add a few tablespoons olive oil before adding the pasta. Also add more olive oil to the individual servings.

2. Cook the beans in just water and nothing else, then fry the garlic in the oil, add the tomatoes and pepper and salt, and mix together in the pan.

3. Put one teaspoon of concentrated tomato puree in the pan with the oil, onion, garlic and celery. Also add a small piece of hot

chili pepper and remove before adding the other ingredients.
4. Puree some of the beans when they are almost cooked and add to the rest of the ingredients to serve.
5. Fry chopped bacon in the oil to give added richness, then the garlic, tomato and parsley and mix with the beans.

PASTA AND DRIED KIDNEY BEANS 73

¾ lb. pasta   1 lb. dried kidney beans
1 onion   1 carrot
1 stick celery   salt and pepper
olive oil   (parmesan)

Soak the beans for at least 12 hours, unless using the method described in the previous recipe. Put them in a large pan with the chopped onion, carrot and celery, and cover with plenty of cold water. Cook with two tablespoons oil and season with salt. When almost ready add the pasta (long pasta of any thickness, broken into smaller pieces). When the pasta is cooked serve with freshly ground black pepper. Grated parmesan may be handed round separately.

PASTA AND LENTILS 74

1 lb. tubettini or other sorts of pasta   1 stick celery
¾ lb. lentils   salt and pepper
2 cloves garlic   (stock)
olive oil

Soak the lentils for at least 12 hours and cook with plenty of salted water, chopped garlic, or whole cloves of garlic which you discard before serving, and the chopped celery. Cook over a moderate heat, adding more liquid if necessary. When almost done add the pasta and cook until al dente. Put all the ingredients in a serving bowl and add fresh olive oil and freshly ground black pepper; you should have a good thick soup. Another way of cooking the lentils is to boil them without the vegetables and when they begin to soften remove from the heat and carefully drain off most of the water. Add fresh boiling water, return to the heat and after a few minutes add the rest of the ingredients.

Variation When the lentils soften remove some of the water and replace with a light stock before adding the pasta.

1 lb. laganelle
(Neapolitan for tagliatelline)
¾ lb. dried chick peas
or kidney beans
olive oil
salt and pepper

1 teaspoon bicarbonate of soda
2 cloves garlic
oregano
(onion, celery, bayleaf, parsley,
bacon, hot chili pepper)

This soup seems to be called 'Thunder and Lightning' because of the effect it can have on your stomach—a Neapolitan touch of humour. Laganelle is their word for the tagliatelline they cook with chick peas and its use is many centuries old. It comes from the Latin laganum and the Greek laganon, meaning a flour and water dough cut in strips. Of course other sorts of pasta can also be used for this recipe. Soak the chick peas at least 12 hours in warm water with one teaspoon bicarbonate of soda dissolved in it. Wash the chick peas and cook with plenty of unsalted water and when they begin to soften add the chopped garlic, salt and pepper and six tablespoons olive oil. Cook for at least four to five hours, adding boiling water as necessary. When almost cooked add a pinch of oregano and freshly made or commerical tagliatelline (they should be made without eggs and cut into short strips). When you use kidney beans the cooking time can be reduced.

Variations 1. When the chick peas start to soften, remove some from the pan and put through a food mill, then return to the pan to act as a thickener.
2. Use onion instead of garlic, or both. Also add chopped celery and a few bay leaves.
3. Add the fresh oil at the end instead of during the cooking, or put a little in the pan and a little in each individual serving.
4. Substitute chopped parsley for the oregano.
5. Add a pinch of hot chili pepper to the soup.
6. Add one teaspoon or more of fried chopped bacon.

¾ lb. laganelle (tagliatelline)	¾ lb. chick peas, dried
½ teaspoon bicarbonate of soda	1 onion
1 clove garlic	1 stick celery
1 bay leaf	2 or 3 ripe tomatoes
parsley	olive oil
salt and pepper	

This is a good resume of the origins of Italian cooking. The basic method of frying the tagliatelline and adding them to the chick peas so they finish cooking in their liquid is most unusual now, and is probably the same used at the time of Horace, who so lovingly describes a soup of chick peas, onion and laganum awaiting him at home. Originally the sheets of flour and water pasta dough were probably baked in a rustic fashion, spread out on large earthenware discs over hot stones, and were then cut into suitable strips and put into the soup. In the Middle Ages the laganum or laganelle became known as trii, which comes from the Arabic itryia, meaning dried pasta with a hole in it, but which was exactly the same pasta type as laganelle. The Greco-Latin name laganelle has remained in many other recipes. Clean and soak the chick peas for at least 12 hours in warm water with ½ teaspoon bicarbonate of soda and a little coarse salt dissolved in it. Drain, wash well again and cook in a large (preferably earthenware) casserole with plenty of water and one bay leaf. Halfway through the cooking drain the chick peas and return to the pan with more water already brought to the boil with onion, garlic, celery, chopped parsley and tomatoes which you have skinned, seeded and cut into strips. Continue cooking and add more boiling water is necessary so the chick peas never dry out. Heat plenty of oil in the pan and fry the laganelle or tagliatelline. When the chick peas are ready, add the pasta and the oil from the pan, mix so the soup is well thickened and serve.

Variation Fry only half the pasta and boil the rest in the normal way before adding to the chick peas.

BUCATINI WITH MUSHROOMS **77**

1 lb. bucatini	2 cloves garlic
¾ lb. fresh mushrooms	salt and pepper
olive oil	(lemon juice, onion, tomato)
parsley	

The best way to clean mushrooms is with a feather and without using any water. Clean and slice the mushrooms finely. Heat the oil with two cloves of chopped or sliced garlic and add the mushrooms. Cook over low heat without letting them fry, season with salt and pepper, and add extra water if the mushrooms seem too dry. Mix in a serving dish with the hot pasta, the oil from the pan, fresh oil to taste and a handful of chopped parsley.

Variations 1. Sprinkle the parsley on the mushrooms and when they are almost cooked, remove from the heat, add a little lemon juice and keep warm while the pasta is cooking. Mix together in a serving dish.
2. Fry the onion and garlic, then add the sliced mushrooms, salt, pepper, parsley and a few tablespoons tomato puree.

BUCATINI WITH MUSHROOMS AND TOMATOES—I 79

1 lb. bucatini	¾ lb. fresh mushrooms
olive oil	1 onion
parsley	¾ lb. tomatoes
dry white wine	salt and pepper

Ideally this recipe requires small, firm mushrooms found in the Gargano region, but of course any others can be used. Clean them well, chop or slice. Brown the onion in the oil, moisten with white wine and when it evaporates add the mushrooms and chopped tomatoes. Season with salt and pepper, add a handful of coarsely chopped parsley and when the mushrooms are cooked serve with the hot pasta.

BUCATINI WITH MUSHROOMS AND AUBERGINES/EGGPLANT 78

1 lb. bucatini	2 aubergines/eggplant
½ lb. fresh mushrooms	1 lb. tomatoes
2 cloves garlic	olive oil
sage	salt and pepper

Dice the aubergines/eggplant and leave sprinkled with coarse salt for one hour covered with a lightly weighted plate. Clean the mushrooms carefully and slice. Skin, seed and cut the tomatoes in strips, or put through a food mill. Heat the oil and add the finely sliced garlic and a few sage leaves. When the garlic starts to colour add the tomatoes, season with salt and pepper and cook until soft. Fry the diced aubergines/eggplant in another pan, at first over a high heat, then turn it down to moderate and add the sliced mushrooms. Add more oil if necessary as they cook. Cook the pasta, drain and add the tomato sauce. Arrange the vegetables on top and mix with the pasta only just before serving.

BUCATINI WITH WALNUTS—I 80

1 lb. bucatini
¼ lb. shelled walnuts
pepper

2 tablespoons olive oil
(pecorino/romano, parmesan)

A simple, piquant sauce: chop the walnuts and add to the hot oil, but be careful they absorb the flavour of the oil without burning. Mix with the pasta and add plenty of freshly ground pepper before serving.

Variation Serve grated pecorino/romano or parmesan separately.

BUCATINI WITH WALNUTS—II 81

1 lb. bucatini
1 oz. crumbs of soft bread,
coarsely crumbled
vinegar

¼ lb. chopped walnuts
1 clove garlic
olive oil
salt and pepper

This is a very old Sicilian or Neapolitan version of the previous recipe. Blanch the walnuts in boiling water to remove outer skin (this is not essential but gives a more perfect flavour). Pound the walnuts well in a mortar and add the bread, which you have soaked in water and squeezed out, one clove garlic and a little salt and pepper. As they blend to make a thick sauce add a little oil and a few drops of vinegar. Pass through a food mill, add a little more oil and vinegar to taste and serve with the hot pasta.

GNOCCHI OR CONCHIGLIE WITH
AUBERGINES/EGGPLANT AND WALNUTS 82

1 lb. gnocchi or conchiglie
a few slices of fried
aubergine/eggplant
24 shelled walnuts

a few tablespoons tomato sauce
olive oil
breadcrumbs

A Sicilian recipe: use a simple form of home-made gnocchi, or commercial gnocchi or conchiglie. Make a good thick tomato sauce (see recipe 15) and add the fried chopped aubergine/eggplant and the finely chopped walnuts. Combine with the hot conchiglie, reserving several tablespoons. Put the pasta in a greased ring mould, pour over the remaining tomato sauce, sprinkle with breadcrumbs and a little fresh oil and bake in a moderate oven about 30 minutes or until brown and crusty.

BUCATINI OR TAGLIATELLE
WITH WALNUTS AND SUGAR

1 lb. bucatini or tagliatelle	10 oz. shelled walnuts
¼ lb. breadcrumbs made	5 oz. sugar
from crumbled stale bread	1 pinch cinnamon
4 tablespoons olive oil	(nutmeg)

The combination of sweet and savoury flavours shows how old this recipe must be. Pound the walnuts in a mortar with the sugar and a pinch of cinnamon. Heat the oil and fry the breadcrumbs and add the walnut and sugar mixture: cook until the sauce thickens and serve with the hot pasta.

Variations 1. Blanch the walnuts in boiling water to remove the outer skins before pounding them with the sugar.
2. Add a pinch of nutmeg with the sugar and cinnamon.

TAGLIATELLE WITH WALNUTS
AND CANDIED FRUIT

1 lb. tagliatelle	½ lb. shelled walnuts
½ lb. candied	½ lb. sugar
citron and orange	2 tablespoons raisins
cinnamon	nutmeg
olive oil	

Pound the walnuts with the sugar and raisins and candied fruit, and add the cinnamon and nutmeg. Cook the tagliatelle, drain and add enough warm olive oil to make them nice and slippery. Add the walnut sauce and mix well.

MACARONI WITH ALMONDS
(14TH CENTURY RECIPE)

1 lb. macaroni	white wine
½ lb. almonds	apple or cherry jam
¼ lb. raisins	ginger
¼ lb. stale bread	cloves
vinegar	cinnamon

The ingredients are obviously a strange combination of flavours for modern taste, and even so some of the original ones have been excluded or adapted. Pasta was then always served with sweet things; for an interesting meal it is worth experimenting with this recipe. Fry the almonds and the bread and pound together in a mortar, adding the raisins. Moisten with the jam, a little white wine and vinegar (cooked must—residue from making wine—was used originally instead of jam; it is still available in certain parts of Emilia; agresto or bitter grape juice was used instead of vinegar, while the wine was actually wine, but not so dry as modern wine). Put through a food mill, add ginger, cloves and cinnamon (the original recipe says: in abundance) and serve with the hot macaroni.

PASTINA WITH PRUNES 86

1 lb. pastina
sugar

10 oz. cooked, seeded,
chopped prunes

Boil the pasta and add the prunes. Sprinkle with sugar and serve hot.

CONCHIGLIE WITH PINEAPPLE 87

1 lb. conchiglie
sugar and rum

1 lb. pineapple, diced

Cook the pasta, drain well and mix with the diced pineapple. Sprinkle with sugar, moisten with rum and serve cold.

II
PASTA WITH VEGETABLES AND DAIRY PRODUCTS

CAPELLINI WITH CREAM

1 lb. capellini
6 oz. thick cream

¼ lb. gruyere cheese
salt and pepper

Cook the pasta, drain well and mix with the cream, grated gruyere and a little pepper.

PASTA WITH BUTTER AND PARMESAN

1 lb. pasta such as
mezze zite, rigatoni or maniche
salt and pepper

¼ lb. butter
¼ lb. grated parmesan

Cook the pasta, drain well and add butter and parmesan. There is much argument about the organization of even this simple procedure: the two main alternatives are either to add the butter to the pasta in the hot serving dish, mix until the butter has melted and coats the pasta, then add the grated cheese and mix again; or, melt some butter with the pasta in the hot serving dish, then serve it out into individual dishes in which you have already put a piece of butter, and then let each person serve themselves with cheese and mix the whole lot together. The second method is better in that the pasta is stirred less and retains more heat, which helps to bring out the flavour. Freshly ground black pepper gives added perfection.

PASTA WITH MELTED BUTTER AND PARMESAN

1 lb. pasta
¼ lb. butter
¼ lb. grated parmesan

(parsley, pepper, sage,
stock/bouillon cube)

Boil the pasta and while it is cooking melt the butter by standing it in a small pan beside the heat, so it does not have to be cooked directly over the heat. Mix with the grated parmesan and pour over the hot pasta.

Variations 1. Add a handful of chopped parsley to the butter before adding the parmesan.
2. Grind some black pepper over the pasta before serving.
3. Add a few leaves of sage to the butter as it melts.
4. Dissolve ½ stock/bouillon cube in a little boiling water and add to the butter in the pan; heat a little longer so the mixture thickens slightly, then add some freshly ground black pepper.

SPAGHETTI WITH MELTED BUTTER   **91**

1 lb. spaghetti
¼ lb. grated parmesan
¼ lb. butter

salt
(pepper, nutmeg)

Heat three-quarters of the butter in a pan until it foams. Divide the remaining butter into each individual dish; mix the hot pasta with the melted butter and serve quickly. Serve grated parmesan separately.

Variations 1. Grind some black pepper over the pasta.
          2. Add a pinch of nutmeg to the pasta before serving.

GNOCCHETTI WITH BUTTER AND PARMESAN   **92**

1 lb. flour
¼ lb. grated parmesan
salt

5 oz. butter
sage
(mint)

Mix the flour with some water and a pinch of salt in a bowl to make a thick dough that will still run from a spoon. Drop spoonfuls of this dough into boiling water; it will rise to the surface like irregular-shaped gnocchi. Do not cook too many at a time, and allow five minutes for each spoonful of dough. Remove with a slotted spoon, drain well and serve with the butter melted in a little pan with a few sage leaves and the parmesan.

Variation Add a few leaves of finely chopped fresh mint to the dough.

CAPELLINI WITH BUTTER, CREAM AND PARMESAN   **93**

1 lb. capellini
3 oz. grated parmesan
6 oz. thick cream

¼ lb. butter
(pepper, cinnamon, nutmeg)

Cook the pasta in the usual way and mix with the butter and parmesan, then pour over the cream and serve immediately.

Variations 1. Add freshly ground pepper.
          2. Add a little cinnamon.
          3. Add cinnamon and nutmeg.

PASTA WITH CREAM

1 lb. linguine
1 tablespoon flour
6 oz. thick cream
parsley
grated parmesan

¼ lb. butter
1 onion
salt and pepper
nutmeg

Melt three-quarters of the butter in a pan and add the flour and chopped onion. When they begin to brown add the cream and stir well, then add salt and pepper, a pinch of nutmeg and a little parsley. Cook the linguine in plenty of salted water and mix with the remaining butter and then the sauce. Serve grated parmesan separately.

SPAGHETTI WITH SOUR CREAM

1 lb. spaghetti
6 oz. sour cream
salt
(nutmeg)

3 oz. butter
¼ lb. grated parmesan
paprika

Melt the butter in a large pan when the spaghetti is almost cooked. Add the drained spaghetti, stir quickly and add the sour cream, paprika (a good, relatively mild variety that blends well with the cream) and some of the grated parmesan. Mix well and serve the remaining parmesan separately.

Variation Add a pinch of nutmeg to the cream.

TAGLIOLINI WITH BUTTER, CREAM AND PARMESAN

1 lb. tagliolini
3 oz. grated parmesan
4 tablespoons cream

¼ lb. butter
(pepper)

Mix the hot tagliolini with butter and cheese, put in a greased baking dish, pour over the cream, sprinkle with more grated parmesan, then brown in a hot oven.

Variations 1. Serve with freshly ground black pepper.
2. Stand the baking dish in a bain-marie (a dish of hot water) and bake until browned in a hot oven.

1 lb. macaroni or	3 oz. butter
macaroni-type pasta, e.g. zite	3 oz. grated parmesan
3 tablespoons flour	24 oz. milk
breadcrumbs	salt (pepper)
nutmeg	

Make a bechamel by melting about half the butter, adding the flour and mixing well. Cook, stirring constantly, for two minutes without browning. Slowly add the boiling milk and a pinch of salt and nutmeg, stirring constantly to prevent lumps, so you have a smooth, velvety sauce. When it is almost ready cook the macaroni, drain well and toss with a good piece of butter, then add the bechamel—keeping a few tablespoons in reserve. Stir well, add three tablespoons grated parmesan and stir again. Have a greased baking dish sprinkled with breadcrumbs ready: put in the macaroni, cover with the remaining bechamel, dot with butter and sprinkle with a mixture of breadcrumbs and parmesan. Bake in a hot oven until brown.

Variation Add a little pepper to the macaroni at the end of the cooking time.

VERMICELLI WITH OIL, GARLIC AND BECHAMEL **98**

1 lb. vermicelli	2 oz. butter
3 tablespoons flour	16 oz. milk
1 entire head of garlic	olive oil
salt and pepper	

This combination of French and Italian cooking is a surprisingly delicious method of serving pasta. Make a fairly liquid bechamel by melting half the butter in the pan, stirring in two tablespoons flour and cooking over medium heat for two minutes without browning. Very gradually add the hot milk and a pinch of salt, but not nutmeg as the flavour would not blend well with the garlic. Boil the head of garlic in a little water and one tablespoon flour. When soft, put through a food mill, then add one tablespoon softened butter and blend well. Put in a pan with a little olive oil and some pepper; it should be liquid enough to make a good sauce. Cook the vermicelli and add first the garlic and oil puree, then the bechamel. Mix well and serve.

1 lb. macaroni-type pasta,
e.g. zite
3 tablespoons flour
2 tablespoons tomato puree
salt and pepper

3 oz. butter
3 oz. grated parmesan
16 oz. milk
breadcrumbs

Make a bechamel by mixing two ounces of butter, three tablespoons flour and proceeding as in the previous recipe. Add salt and the hot milk and stir until smooth. Add the tomato puree in sufficient quantities to make the sauce the colour and flavour you want. Cook the pasta, add the butter, the bechamel (reserve a few tablespoons) and the grated parmesan. Put in a greased baking dish and cover with the remaining sauce and a mixture of breadcrumbs and grated parmesan, then dot with butter. Bake in a hot oven just until brown.

SPAGHETTI WITH TOMATOES AND MILK **100**

1 lb. spaghetti
¾ lb. tomatoes
4 oz. milk
salt

4 tablespoons olive oil
1 onion
sugar
grated parmesan

This is a curious, but very pleasant combination of flavours. Heat the oil, add the chopped onion, the pureed tomatoes, and a pinch each of sugar and salt to counteract the acidity of the tomatoes (this is important for when the milk is added). Cook until all the ingredients are well blended, then add the milk and stir gently until the sauce thickens. Serve with the hot pasta and grated parmesan.

PASTA WITH BUTTER AND TOMATOES—I **101**

1 lb. pasta
2 oz. butter
basil
grated parmesan

2 lb. tomatoes
salt and pepper
(parsley, sage, peeled tomatoes)

Break the tomatoes with your hands—it is always better to use metal utensils as little as possible when preparing vegetables as they can alter the flavour. The same applies to fruit; peaches taste quite different if cut with a metal knife. Cook the tomatoes in the old Neapolitan way; put them in a pan without any water or oil, add a little basil and a pinch of salt, then cook over very low heat for about ¾ hour, then put through a food mill. Melt the butter in a pan, add the tomato puree, season with salt and pepper and a little more basil, then serve with the hot pasta. Serve grated parmesan separately.

Variations 1. Use parsley instead of basil, or both.
2. Add broken sage leaves to the melted butter instead of the parsley and basil.
3. Chop tomatoes roughly, then add directly to the butter and cook for a few minutes.

PASTA WITH BUTTER AND TOMATO—II **102**

1 lb. pasta e.g. linguine
3 oz. butter
basil

2 lb. tomatoes
salt and pepper
3 oz. grated parmesan

Melt the butter in a large pan, add the tomato puree prepared as in the previous recipe and a little basil. Heat until the butter and tomatoes are well blended and season with salt and pepper. Have the pasta ready at the same time as the sauce, then add the hot pasta to the pan, mix well, sprinkle with the parmesan and continue stirring until the cheese has blended with the other ingredients. Serve more grated parmesan separately.

BUCATINI WITH BRANDY **103**

1 lb. bucatini
2 tablespoons butter
1 onion
1 small carrot
salt and pepper
2 tablespoons brandy

2 tablespoons olive oil
1 lb. tomatoes
1 stick celery
parsley
sugar

Heat the oil and brown the chopped onion, celery and carrot. Skin the tomatoes, break them and remove the seeds. Add a pinch each of salt and sugar to counteract the acidity of the tomatoes, then the brandy. Cook until the sauce is thick and well blended, pour over the hot pasta and serve with plenty of freshly ground black pepper.

SPAGHETTI WITH BUTTER AND HERBS **104**

1 lb. spaghetti
2 cloves garlic
basil
grated pecorino/romano

¼ lb. butter
parsley
sage

Chop the garlic, a handful of parsley and of basil and some sage. Cook and drain the pasta, toss first in the butter then add the chopped herbs and grated pecorino/romano. This ancient recipe probably used to contain far more garlic: you can vary the quantities according to taste.

LINGUINE OR TAGLIOLINI WITH PARSLEY **105**

1 lb. pasta
½ onion
6 oz. milk

2 oz. butter
a good bunch of parsley

Melt the butter in a pan and cook the finely sliced onion until soft. Add the chopped parsley (the amount can be varied according to taste) and the milk. Mix well, add the hot pasta and continue stirring until the milk thickens and coats the pasta.

RIGATONI WITH RICOTTA **106**

1 lb. rigatoni
2 oz. butter
¾ lb. ricotta
salt and pepper

(parsley, fat salt pork,
prosciutto fat or sugna,
parmesan or pecorino/romano)

Another recipe from the ancient traditions of Latium, so also of Magna Grecia. Sieve the ricotta, add plenty of salt and pepper, then work it with a wooden spoon until it softens to a puree, if necessary adding a little hot water from the pan where the pasta is cooking. Add the melted butter and mix well. The rigatoni should be ready at the same time as the ricotta; mix well and serve with freshly ground black pepper.

Variations 1. Add melted prosciutto fat or sugna to the ricotta instead of butter.
2. Add one tablespoon chopped parsley.
3. Add a little grated parmesan or pecorino/romano.

1 lb. rigatoni	10 oz. ricotta
6 tablespoons olive oil	1½ lb. tomatoes
salt and pepper	onion
basil	(parmesan or pecorino/romano)

Heat the oil and add a little chopped onion. When it browns, add the skinned, seeded and chopped tomatoes, season with salt and pepper. Cook over low heat until soft, adding a few leaves of basil towards the end. Sieve the ricotta and work with a wooden spoon, adding some of the tomato sauce until the mixture is quite fluid. Cook and drain the pasta, add the remaining tomato sauce and then the ricotta mixture. Mix well and serve.

Variation Add a few tablespoons grated cheese to the pasta and also serve grated parmesan or pecorino/romano separately.

LASAGNE WITH RICOTTA **108**

1 lb. lasagne	¾ lb. ricotta
¼ lb. butter	salt and pepper
parsley	grated pecorino/romano

Sieve the ricotta, then work with a wooden spoon until it becomes a smooth paste, adding a few tablespoons hot water from the lasagne, salt, freshly ground black pepper and chopped parsley. When the pasta is cooked, drain, add some of the butter, reserving a little to grease the baking dish. Put a layer of lasagne on the bottom, cover with half the ricotta, sprinkle with pecorino/romano and dot with butter. Add a second layer of lasagne, ricotta and pecorino/romano, and then a final layer of lasagne. Dot with butter, sprinkle with more pecorino/romano and cook in a hot oven just until brown.

Variations 1. Mix the lasagne and ricotta together in a deep bowl, sprinkle over the pecorino/romano, then put in a baking dish to brown without arranging in layers.
2. Add one tablespoon of bechamel sauce (made with butter, flour and milk) to the sieved ricotta, although this rather alters the flavour. Do not use grated cheese as well.

SPAGHETTINI WITH RICOTTA AND MASCARPONE

1 lb. spaghettini
3 oz. mascarpone cheese
1 oz. butter
1 tablespoon soybean oil
salt and pepper

½ lb. ricotta
2 oz. radishes
1 tablespoon vinegar
(horseradish sauce)

Grate the radishes and leave to marinate for two hours with the vinegar and oil (do not use olive oil as this will alter the flavour). Mix the ricotta and the mascarpone with this marinade and work together to obtain a smooth sauce. Heat the butter and before it browns, add the sauce and stir well. Cook the pasta and drain it not too thoroughly as a little extra water will help dilute the sauce. Add the pasta to the sauce and mix together, then serve with freshly ground black pepper. This is a very delicate and attractive sauce.

Variation Instead of fresh horseradish, use three ounces of commercial horse-radish sauce, and then eliminate the marinade.

SPAGHETTI AND HERBS

1 lb. spaghetti
basil
chervil
1 tablespoon capers
2 oz. grated pecorino/romano

½ lb. ricotta
parsley
rosemary
6 tablespoons olive oil

Chop enough basil, parsley and chervil to have one heaped tablespoon of each. Also chop a few springs of rosemary and the washed capers. Heat the oil, add all these ingredients, then add the crumbled ricotta. Stir well and finally mix in the hot pasta. Sprinkle with grated pecorino/romano before serving.

MACARONI WITH SWEET RICOTTA

1 lb. macaroni (or zite,
penne, rigatoni, etc.)
1 good pinch cinnamon
salt

1 lb. ricotta
1 tablespoon sugar
(milk)

Sieve the ricotta, work in the sugar, cinnamon and several tablespoons of the water in which the pasta is cooking. You can also add salt if you feel the other flavours require it. Serve with the hot pasta.

Variation Work boiling milk into the ricotta instead of the pasta water.

1 lb. bucatini	½ lb. mozzarella
3 oz. butter	pepper
grated parmesan	(thick cream)

Cook the pasta, add the butter, parmesan and pepper and put in a greased baking dish. Cover the pasta with the sliced mozzarella, mixing it a little, but without letting the cheese touch the bottom of the dish. Sprinkle with more parmesan, dot with butter and brown in a hot oven.

Variations 1. Toss the pasta in melted butter before arranging in the baking dish; however the butter flavour may rather dominate the dish.
2. Pour a little cream over the pasta before putting it in the oven.

MACARONI WITH BECHAMEL AU GRATIN—II **113**

1 lb. macaroni (or zite,	3 oz. butter
mezze zite, maniche, penne, etc.)	3 tablespoons flour
34 oz. milk	½ lb. mozzarella
salt and pepper	grated parmesan
nutmeg	breadcrumbs

Make a bechamel sauce with butter, flour, milk and a pinch of nutmeg—the quantities given will make a fairly thin sauce. Cook the pasta and mix with half of the bechamel, some grated parmesan and freshly ground pepper. Put some of the remaining bechamel in the bottom of a baking dish, cover with a layer of the macaroni and bechamel mixture, sprinkle with more parmesan and top with slices of mozzarella and a few more tablespoons of bechamel. Make another layer of macaroni, parmesan and bechamel, sprinkle with breadcrumbs, dot with butter and brown in a hot oven.

Variation Make up in three layers: grease the bottom of the baking dish, divide the bechamel between the first and second layers of pasta and between the second and third layers.

SPAGHETTI WITH UNCOOKED MOZZARELLA AND TOMATO

1 lb. spaghetti
8 tablespoons olive oil
basil
salt and pepper
grated parmesan

1 lb. tomatoes
½ lb. mozzarella
oregano
(capers, small black olives)

This is one of the nicest of all the uncooked sauces. Peel the tomatoes, chop them and remove the seeds without losing too much juice. Leave to marinate in the oil, with plenty of basil (remember never to wash fresh basil; just clean it lightly with a cloth to retain all the flavour), a good pinch each of oregano, salt and pepper and a few tablespoons of parmesan, according to taste. You need no onion and garlic, and lemon juice would give too acid a flavour. Leave to stand at least two hours, then add the hot pasta and the finely sliced mozzarella, stir quickly so the cheese melts a little, then serve.

Variation Add small capers and seeded, chopped olives to the marinade.

FUSILLI WITH MOZZARELLA AND TOMATO

1 lb. fusilli
4 tablespoons olive oil
2 oz. grated pecorino/romano
oregano

1 lb. tomatoes
½ lb. mozzarella
salt and pepper

Heat the oil, add the puréed tomatoes, a pinch of oregano, the mozzarella cut in thin strips, the grated cheese and some salt and pepper. Mix well, then add the hot pasta, which should be commercial fusilli without egg, rather than a homemade variety.

Variation Prepare the sauce in a large pan and add the pasta to it over the heat so they cook together for a few minutes.

1 lb. macaroni	2 lb. tomatoes
6 tablespoons olive oil	¾ lb. mozzarella
basil	(fat salt pork,
salt and pepper	prosciutto fat or sugna,
grated parmesan	scamorza, ricotta)
breadcrumbs	

Make the tomato sauce with the oil, pureed tomatoes, basil and salt and pepper (see recipe 15). Cook the macaroni and mix with some of the sauce and grated parmesan. Pour half of this mixture into a well greased baking dish and sprinkle with breadcrumbs. Cover with the rest of the sauce, thin slices of mozzarella, more grated parmesan and finally the rest of the macaroni, more breadcrumbs, parmesan and a little oil, then brown in a hot oven.

Variations   1. Use fat salt pork, prosciutto fat or sugna instead of oil in the tomato sauce, and to grease the baking dish.
2. Use scamorza instead of mozzarella.
3. Add a little ricotta to the other ingredients; mix it with the tomato sauce and then pour over the pasta.

MACARONI WITH OLIVES AND MOZZARELLA **117**

1 lb. macaroni (or zite,	1 lb. tomatoes
mezze zite, rigatoni, etc.)	¼ lb. seeded olives
2 cloves garlic	½ lb. mozzarella
4 tablespoons olive oil	salt and pepper
grated pecorino/romano	oregano

Monte Faito, located on the Sorrentine peninsula where this recipe comes from, is covered with beautiful olive groves. Heat the oil in a large pan and cook the finely sliced or chopped garlic. Add the chopped tomatoes and the olives and season with salt. Mix with the hot pasta and the mozzarella cut in fine strips a pinch each or oregano and pepper and a few tablespoons of grated pecorino/romano. Cook for a few minutes so it thickens nicely and serve.

10 oz. macaroni (or zite, mezze zite, penne, etc.)	5 lb. tomatoes
	½ lb. mozzarella
olive oil	parsley
basil	breadcrumbs
grated pecorino/romano	garlic
grated parmesan	salt and pepper

Cook the pasta so it is less than al dente, or just over half cooked. The following sauce should be ready at the same time: heat four tablespoons olive oil with one clove of chopped garlic (or a crushed clove, to be discarded before serving), add the puree obtained from one pound of the tomatoes, and season with salt and pepper. Chop one clove garlic, some parsley and basil very finely and mix with a pinch of salt, some breadcrumbs and enough oil to bind. Thinly slice the mozzarella. Prepare three pounds of round, quite ripe tomatoes by cutting them in half, removing the seeds and draining to remove excess liquid. Spread a little of the chopped herb mixture on each tomato half, then pack them close together in an ovenproof dish (you may need two dishes), cut side up, and bake for ½ hour in a moderate oven so they cook without breaking up. Meanwhile, mix the half-cooked macaroni with the tomato sauce, add the mozzarella and equal quantities of grated parmesan and pecorino. Mix well. Finally, grease a large mould, arrange the baked tomato halves close together on the bottom so they are slightly overlapping at the edges and distribute the macaroni mixture on top. Make a final layer with the remaining one pound of tomatoes, cut in half. Sprinkle all with the bread-crumbs, moisten with a little fresh oil and bake in the oven for about ½ hour. The pasticcio will turn out better if you line the bottom with a circle and the sides with strips of buttered greaseproof or waxed paper.

ZITE WITH TOMATOES STUFFED WITH MOZZARELLA **119**

1 lb. zite	12 tomatoes
½ lb. mozzarella	3 oz. butter
3 oz. grated parmesan	basil
olive oil	salt and pepper

Skin round, fairly ripe tomatoes by plunging for a moment in boiling water, then cut a lid in the top and carefully remove the seeds and any excess liquid. Fill the tomatoes with diced mozzarella and arrange in a greased ovenproof dish, moisten with oil, sprinkle with a little crushed basil and salt and bake in a moderate oven until the tomatoes are soft on the inside and the mozzarella has melted and mixed with the tomato juice. Break the pasta and cook it so it is ready at the same time as the tomatoes, then drain it well, toss with butter and parmesan and a little pepper. Put the pasta in a greased ovenproof dish and arrange the stuffed tomatoes on top. This really sumptuous dish then only needs baking for a few minutes in a hot oven, and it is ready to serve.

SPAGHETTI WITH MUSTARD SAUCE **120**

1 lb. spaghetti
4 tablespoons olive oil
grated parmesan

1 lb. tomatoes
mustard, dry

Heat the oil, add a tomato puree made from the fresh tomatoes. Cook for a minute, then add one teaspoon or more (according to taste) of mustard. Cook the pasta in plenty of salted water, drain well and toss with the sauce. Serve grated parmesan separately.

Variation Make a larger quantity of sauce and use some of it to mix with the hot spaghetti. Spread half the mixture on the bottom of a greased ovenproof dish, sprinkle with grated parmesan, add the rest of the pasta, sprinkle with more cheese and brown in a hot oven.

LASAGNETTE WITH FONTINA **121**

1 lb. lasagnette
3 oz. butter

½ lb. fontina, sliced
grated parmesan

Cook the pasta and toss with half the butter, then line a greased baking dish with alternate layers of pasta and the sliced fontina. Make the last layer with pasta, dot it with butter, sprinkle over one tablespoon of parmesan and brown for a few minutes in a hot oven.

GNOCCHI AU GRATIN WITH FONTINA

2¾ lb. potatoes
½ lb. fontina, sliced
salt

10 oz. flour
3 oz. butter

This is a traditional and more elaborate version of the previous recipe. Peel, boil and sieve the potatoes, mix them with the flour and a pinch of salt. Make as many little cylinders as possible out of this mixture, then give them their concave gnocchi shape by pressing each dumpling against the inside prong of a fork with your forefinger. Cook in plenty of boiling, salted water and remove with a slotted spoon as they rise to the surface. Arrange in a well-greased oven-proof dish in alternate layers of gnocchi and the sliced fontina. The final layer of gnocchi should be dotted with butter. Brown in a hot oven.

LINGUINE OR FETTUCCINE WITH GRUYERE AND CREAM

1 lb. linguine or fettuccine
5 oz. gruyere, diced
pepper

2 oz. butter
6 oz. thick cream

Cook the pasta and toss with the butter, add the finely diced gruyere and then the cream. Mix quickly and gently with the hot pasta and serve, adding more grated gruyere to each serving and plenty of freshly ground pepper to taste. This is a popular Swiss recipe.

SPAGHETTI WITH CHEESE AND PEPPER

1 lb. spaghetti
pepper and salt

¼ lb. grated pecorino/romano

Originally a shepherds' dish from ancient Latium and the Abruzzi. Cook the pasta, but do not drain too thoroughly as the water left on the pasta helps to blend the cheese and pepper. Use plenty of coarsely grated pecorino/romano and mix it with the hot pasta; you can add an extra four tablespoons of the pasta water to mix with the cheese as it can only improve the flavour.

MALLOREDDUS WITH BUTTER AND PECORINO

12 oz. semolina flour	saffron
3 oz. butter	3 oz. grated pecorino/romano
pepper	nutmeg
salt	

Malloreddus are the famous Sardinian gnocchi, usually served with a meat sauce. This very rustic version has a delicious flavour. Make the gnocchi: work the flour with very little warm water and a pinch of saffron dissolved in it and a pinch of salt. Form this dough into small cylinders not more than ¼ inch thick and divide into pieces about ½ inch long. Press each piece against the fork, as in the previous recipe. Leave to dry for at least 12 hours, then cook in boiling salted water and remove with a slotted spoon as they float to the surface. Toss in butter, then add grated pecorino, plenty of coarsley ground pepper and a pinch of nutmeg.

MACARONI WITH PECORINO/ROMANO AND MINT 126

1 lb. macaroni (or zite, mezze zite, penne, etc.)	10 oz. sliced pecorino/romano
mint	olive oil

A simplified version of the famous su farru Sardinian dish. Put the finely sliced pecorino/romano in a pan with a little water and heat until it begins to melt. Discard the water and add some oil. Continue cooking over moderate heat without letting the oil sizzle; the cheese must cook without frying or burning. When it is almost completely melted and mixes with the oil to form a sauce add a little dried mint. Cook for a minute so the flavours mingle, then mix well with the hot pasta.

MACARONI WITH CHEESE, GARLIC AND PEPPER 127

1 lb. macaroni (zite, mezze zite, maniche, etc.)	6 tablespoons olive oil
3 cloves garlic	¼ lb. grated pecorino/romano
nutmeg	pepper

Heat the oil and cook the chopped garlic until it starts to brown, then pour over the hot pasta. Add the grated cheese, coarsely ground pepper and a pinch of nutmeg: stir well and serve.

MALLOREDDUS WITH
PECORINO/ROMANO AND TOMATO

128

1 lb. semolina flour	1 lb. tomatoes
¼ lb. pecorino/romano, sliced	olive oil
parsley	salt and pepper
basil	garlic

This is another Sardinian gnocchi dish. Work the flour with a pinch of salt and a few tablespoons of warm water. Make into little cylinders, then cut them into small pieces and shape as in recipe 125. Make the sauce: heat a little oil, add one or two cloves of chopped garlic, a few chopped basil leaves and some parsley, the pureed tomatoes. Cook the gnocchi in plenty of water and remove with a slotted spoon as they rise to the surface: toss in the garlic and tomato sauce, sprinkle with pepper and arrange in a greased ovenproof dish. Cover with slices of fresh pecorino/romano and bake in a hot oven until the cheese has melted.

TRENETTE WITH PESTO—I

129

1 lb. trenette	plenty of fresh basil (2 cups leaves)
3 or 4 cloves garlic	3 oz. grated pecorino/romano
coarse salt	olive oil
prescinseua (see note below)	pine nuts
parmesan	(parsley, walnuts)

Trenette are a commercial pasta rather like broad linguine, which are traditionally served with pesto. Pesto is more an unguent than a sauce, and as its name suggests (pestare: to pound) it is made by pounding all the ingredients in a mortar. The mortar should be stone or marble and the pestle boxwood or hardwood. There is a lot of argument about what goes to make a good pesto and it varies from one household to the next, most of all in its native Genoa. The most ancient and traditional recipes contain basil, garlic and Sardinian pecorino/romano. Basil rules supreme in Ligurian cooking, which is always well endowed with fresh herbs. It is claimed that sea breezes produce the finest basil, even the breezes blowing through the narrow streets or carrugi of Genoa, which nurture the little pots of basil growing on every windowsill. Garlic is the dominant flavour in the pesto; if you reduce the quantity the pesto is no longer genuine. All these are indisputable facts: the arguments begin when it comes to the cheese. Once only pecorino/romano was used, but gradually parmesan has crept into pesto. Some purists say to add even the smallest amount of parmesan is sacrilege, while others claim that a mixture of parmesan and pecorino/romano has been common for a long time since greater prosperity helped living standards to rise, and that the combination of flavours is a positive advantage. There is less argument about the fairly common custom of adding a few pine nuts, or about prescinseua—a soft whey that remains when milk has curdled—as it counteracts the strong flavour of the garlic and pecorino/romano. All are respectable alternatives, but the most authentic traditional recipe is the simplest of all and therefore perhaps the best. Remove the basil leaves from the stems and clean with a soft cloth. Break in pieces over the mortar, chop the garlic and start pounding them together in the mortar, gradually adding more garlic and basil and a little coarse salt. Only add more when you have obtained a good pulp, and when all the garlic and basil are incorporated continue pounding with a circular movement and start to add the grated pecorino/romano (or pecorino/romano and parmesan) so they all blend to form a fairly thick sauce. Dilute with a little olive oil, preferably a characteristic clear, light Ligurian variety. The pesto is then ready, although you can also add a few pine nuts at the end, or several tablespoons of prescinseua or whey, or some curdled milk, or failing these, a few tablespoons of the water the pasta is cooking in. Drain the trenette and serve with the pesto.

Variations 1. Add a little parsley with the basil.
2. Add finely chopped shelled walnuts instead of pine nuts.

TRENETTE WITH PESTO—II **130**

1 lb. trenette	36 basil leaves
3 cloves garlic	3 oz. grated pecorino/romano
3 oz. green beans, sliced	3 potatoes
olive oil	(pine nuts, parmesan, prescinseua—
salt	see recipe 129)

Peel the potatoes, cut them in pieces and cook with very young green beans in plenty of boiling salted water. When almost ready add the trenette, and when they are cooked al dente drain everything and mix with the pesto made as in the previous recipe.

Variations 1. Mix in some pine nuts at the end or a few tablespoons of prescinseua.
2. Serve with grated parmesan separately.

SPAGHETTI WITH GORGONZOLA AND RICOTTA

1 lb. spaghetti	3 oz. good strong gorgonzola cheese
6 oz. milk	½ lb. ricotta cheese
2 oz. butter	1 stick celery
½ onion	(paprika)
salt and pepper	

Put the gorgonzola and ricotta in the blender with about two tablespoons milk to make a fairly liquid puree. Transfer to a bowl, add the rest of the milk, the chopped onion, chopped celery, salt and pepper. Cook the pasta, toss in butter and add the gorgonzola mixture diluted just before adding with one or two tablespoons of the pasta water.

Variation Use paprika instead of pepper.

MACARONI WITH GRUYERE AND PARMESAN—I

1 lb. macaroni (or zite, mezze zite, rigatoni, etc.)	¼ lb. grated parmesan
2 oz. butter	¼ lb. grated gruyere
	salt and pepper

Cook the macaroni in lightly salted boiling water, drain well, toss in the butter and add the grated cheeses and freshly ground pepper.

MACARONI WITH GRUYERE AND PARMESAN—II

1 lb. macaroni (or zite, mezze zite, rigatoni, etc.)	¼ lb. grated parmesan
3 oz. butter	¼ lb. grated gruyere
	salt and pepper

Cook the macaroni in lightly salted boiling water, toss with the butter and put in layers in a greased ovenproof dish with the grated cheese in between. Dot the final layer of macaroni and cheese with butter and sprinkle with pepper, then brown in a hot oven.

MACARONI WITH CHEESE AND TOMATO   **134**

1 lb. macaroni (zite, mezze zite, maniche, rigatoni, etc.)
6 oz. thick cream
4 tablespoons olive oil
nutmeg
cloves

½ lb. grated gruyere
3 oz. grated parmesan
1 lb. tomatoes
onion
salt and pepper
butter

Cook the macaroni in plenty of boiling, salted water with a bit of butter, one chopped onion and one clove. Make the sauce with the cream, grated cheese, nutmeg and pepper. Make a tomato sauce with the oil and the pureed tomatoes (see recipe 15). Add the hot pasta to the cream and cheese sauce, cook for a minute stirring well, sprinkle with pepper; transfer to a deep serving dish and cover with the tomato sauce.

MACARONI WITH FONTINA AND PARMESAN   **135**

1 lb. macaroni (or zite, mezze zite, maniche, etc.)
6 oz. thick cream
salt and pepper

5 oz. fontina
¼ lb. grated parmesan
butter

Melt the diced fontina, some of the grated parmesan and the cream in an oven-proof dish, add the hot pasta, sprinkle with freshly ground pepper and the rest of the parmesan. Dot with butter and bake for a few minutes in a hot oven.

MACARONI WITH FOUR CHEESES   **136**

1 lb. macaroni (or perciatelli, zite, mezze zite, penne, rigatoni, etc.)
2 oz. grated gruyere cheese
2 oz. grated fontina cheese
salt and pepper

3 oz. butter
2 oz. grated parmesan cheese
2 oz. grated gouda cheese
parsley
(provolone cheese)

Cook the macaroni in lightly salted water, drain and toss in butter. Heat a greased ovenproof dish, add the macaroni and the grated cheeses, mix well, adding one or two tablespoons of the pasta water if it seems too dry. Season with pepper and a handful of chopped parsley. Bake in a hot oven until the cheese begins to melt.

Variation In southern Italy provolone is used instead of fontina and gives a stronger flavour to the sauce.

MACARONI WITH FIVE CHEESES 137

1 lb. macaroni (or perciatelli, zite, mezze zite, penne, rigatoni, etc.)
2 oz. fontina cheese
2 oz. grated parmesan cheese
3 oz. butter
2 oz. gruyere cheese
2 oz. provolone cheese
2 oz. gouda cheese
1 tablespoon flour

Cut the provolone, fontina, gouda cheese and gruyere in thin strips or julienne. Melt the butter, add the flour and then the cheese. As the cheese begins to melt add this mixture to the hot macaroni. Add grated parmesan and serve.

SPAGHETTI WITH PARSLEY, BASIL AND MOZZARELLA 138

1 lb. spaghetti
2 sprigs of basil
1 small piece of ginger
1 lb. tomatoes
salt and pepper
3 sprigs of parsley
2 cloves garlic
3 oz. butter
7 oz. mozzarella
(parmesan)

Chop the parsley (reserve some to sprinkle over at the end), the basil, garlic and ginger and cook gently in the butter. Add the skinned, chopped and seeded tomatoes and season with salt and pepper. Cook until nicely thickened and then add the hot pasta. Raise the heat, stir vigorously and add the diced mozzarella. Serve immediately with a final sprinkling of chopped parsley.

Variation Add a few tablespoons of grated parmesan with the mozzarella.

SPAGHETTI WITH BAY LEAVES—II 139

1 lb. spaghetti
2 tablespoons olive oil
1 lb. tomatoes
salt and pepper
1 oz. butter
2 onions
15-20 bay leaves
cinnamon
(sage, brandy, parmesan)

Heat the butter and oil, add the sliced onions and as soon as they begin to brown add the pureed tomatoes. Season with salt and pepper, add a pinch of cinnamon and the bay leaves—not crumbled or chopped, but just rubbed together a little to bring out the flavour. Cook for another ten minutes and then serve with the hot pasta.

Variations 1. Eliminate the cinnamon. However, it has a pleasantly sweet flavour that blends well with the bay leaves.
2. Add a few sage leaves to the sauce as well as the bay leaves.
3. Add one tablespoon brandy to the sauce.
4. Serve grated parmesan separately.

LINGUINE WITH SPINACH AND BECHAMEL **140**

1 lb. linguine	2 lb. spinach
2 oz. butter	3 tablespoons flour
18 oz. milk	salt
nutmeg	

Wash and pick over the spinach. Reserve a handful and put the rest in a saucepan, cover and cook over high heat for five minutes so the spinach cooks in its own steam. Chop finely and put aside. Make a thin bechamel with the butter, flour and milk, then dilute it with any spinach water in the pan. Season with salt, pepper and nutmeg. Add the chopped spinach, stir a little, then add the reserved uncooked spinach, which has been finely chopped to give the sauce an extra taste of freshness. Mix well and serve with the hot pasta.

MACARONI WITH BROCCOLI AND PECORINO/ROMANO **141**

1 lb. macaroni (zite, mezze zite, penne, etc.)	1 lb. broccoli spears (or cauliflower florets)
6 tablespoons olive oil	5 oz. grated pecorino/romano

Wash and chop the broccoli and fry in the olive oil. Cook the macaroni, drain well and toss in the oil used to cook the broccoli with half the grated pecorino/romano. Grease a mould, sprinkle with pecorino/romano and put in alternate layers of macaroni and broccoli spears. Sprinkle with the remaining pecorino/romano and brown for a few minutes in a hot oven.

LASAGNETTE RICCE WITH AUBERGINES/EGGPLANT AND PESTO

1 lb. lasagnette ricce
36 basil leaves
3 oz. grated pecorino/romano

3 aubergines/eggplant
3 cloves garlic
salt

Another Ligurian dish using pesto. Peel and slice the aubergines/eggplant and cook in plenty of salted water. When they start to soften, add the pasta and finish cooking together. Drain well and mix with a pesto sauce made as in recipe 129 by pounding basil, garlic and pecorino/romano in a mortar.

MACARONI WITH ONION AND AUBERGINES/EGGPLANT

1 lb. macaroni (or bucatini, mezze zite, etc.)
6 oz. butter
2 small onions
salt

2 firm, medium-sized aubergines/eggplant
1 clove garlic
(parmesan)

This recipe obviously has oriental origins. Heat three ounces butter in a pan, add the chopped garlic and finely sliced onion, then the peeled and diced aubergines/eggplant, first prepared by draining for a while under a lightly weighted plate. Cook over moderate heat until soft. Cook the pasta, toss in the remaining butter and add the vegetables and onion sauce.

Variation For a more Italian flavour serve grated parmesan separately.

MACARONI WITH AUBERGINES/EGGPLANT AND PARMESAN

10 oz. macaroni
2 lb. tomatoes
coarse and fine salt
parmesan
basil

6 aubergines/eggplant
½ lb. mozzarella
pepper
olive oil
(eggs)

This is a Neapolitan method of including the parmesan in the sauce. Slice the aubergines/eggplant and leave to drain sprinkled with coarse salt, under a lightly weighted plate for a few hours. Then fry in plenty of hot oil and drain on absorbent paper. Peel and chop one pound tomatoes, cook them slowly in their own liquid in the old Neapolitan way, with just a little basil, and then put through a food mill. Cover the bottom of a greased ovenproof dish with some of this tomato sauce, then add a layer of aubergines/eggplant with the slices slightly overlapping. Sprinkle with a little parmesan, make another layer of sliced mozzarella, add more sauce, aubergine/eggplant slices, parmesan and mozzarella, finishing with a layer of the vegetable topped with the remaining sauce and bake in a hot oven for 40 to 45 minutes. If you like you can also moisten each layer with a little beaten egg mixed with a few basil leaves. Put this parmesan and aubergine/eggplant mixture into a large saucepan containing a sauce made with the remaining pureed tomatoes, olive oil and a pinch of salt and pepper. Continue cooking for 15 minutes and moisten with a few tablespoons of warm water as necessary. Pour over the hot pasta in a large serving dish. Serve grated parmesan separately, or mix it with the hot pasta before adding the vegatables and parmesan sauce.

PASTICCIO OF MACCHERONI, AUBERGINES/EGGPLANT AND MOZZARELLA 145

1 lb. macaroni (or maccheroncelli, maniche, mèzze zite, etc.)	3 medium-sized aubergines/eggplant
	¾ lb. tomatoes
4 oz. butter	7 oz. mozzarella
salt and pepper	olive oil
basil	(caciocavallo cheese, garlic, onion)

Wash and slice the aubergines/eggplant, then sprinkle with coarse salt and leave to drain for a few hours under a lightly weighted plate. Make a tomato sauce with half the butter, the pureed tomatoes, a few basil leaves and salt and pepper. Cook the macaroni and mix with this sauce and a little extra butter. Grease a mould and fill with alternate layers of macaroni, aubergines/eggplant and finely sliced mozzarella, ending with mozzarella. Dot with butter and bake in a hot oven until the cheese has melted.

Variations 1. Use a soft caciocavallo cheese instead of mozzarella for a stronger flavour.
     2. When making the tomato sauce add half a finely sliced onion and a chopped clove of garlic to the oil (or a crushed clove to be discarded before serving).

¾ lb. macaroni 1¾ lb. courgettes/zucchini
2 lb. tomatoes 7 oz. mozzarella
olive oil basil
grated parmesan salt and pepper
pecorino/romano

A similar receipe to the previous one although the courgettes/zucchini have a milder flavour than the aubergines/eggplant, so the ingredients vary accordingly. Slice the courgettes/zucchini lengthwise and leave to dry for about one hour (in Naples the sun can be counted on to assist in this). Fry them, drain well and set aside. Chop half the tomatoes and cook without any liquid, but just a pinch of salt and some basil. Grease an ovenproof dish and put in a layer of tomato sauce, the vegetables, slices of mozzarella and grated parmesan, ending with the courgettes/zucchini covered with any remaining sauce, then bake at moderate heat until the vegetables are soft and the cheese melted—about 20 minutes. Make a sauce with the remaining pureed tomatoes, oil, salt and pepper and some basil; add the courgettes/zucchini and cheese mixture and mix well, so the sauce is well blended but not too thick. Cook for about ten minutes, adding a few tablespoons of warm water as necessary. Pour over the hot pasta in a large serving dish and serve grated pecorino/romano separately; or mix the hot pasta with grated pecorino/romano and then add the sauce for a slightly different flavour.

PASTA WITH LEEKS OR SHALLOTS **147**

1 lb. pasta ¾ lb. leeks or shallots
¾ lb. tomatoes (only the tender white
1 carrot part of the leeks)
1 stick celery 4 oz. butter
parsley salt and pepper
grated parmesan (thyme, marjoram)

Melt the butter in a pan, add the well-cleaned chopped leeks, the chopped carrot and celery, and when they begin to soften, add the pureed tomatoes. Season with salt and pepper and the chopped parsley. Add a little grated parmesan and mix with the hot pasta. Serve more grated parmesan separately.

Variation Add a little thyme or marjoram to the sauce.

BUCATINI WITH ONION SAUCE—I

1 lb. bucatini
olive oil
grated parmesan

6 medium-sized onions
2 tablespoons butter
pepper

Peel and finely slice the onions, then put them in a pan with enough oil to cover. Cook slowly over low heat so they soften without breaking up. Watch them carefully after the first ten minutes and stir with a wooden spatula. Cook the bucatini and toss in the butter, then mix in plenty of grated parmesan, and finally the onions. Serve with freshly ground black pepper. The ingredients are simple, but this is a really special dish.

Variation When you have mixed the pasta with the butter, cheese, onion and pepper, put it in a greased ovenproof dish and bake for a few minutes in a hot oven.

BUCATINI WITH ONION SAUCE—II

1 lb. bucatini
4 medium-sized onions
4 oz. butter

salt and pepper
(thyme, marjoram,
gruyere, parmesan)

Heat three-quarters of the butter, add the finely sliced or chopped onions and cook over low heat until soft. Season with salt and pepper. Cook the pasta, toss in the remaining butter and the onion sauce.

Variations 1. Add a little thyme and marjoram to the sauce.
2. Serve grated gruyere or parmesan separately.

PASTICCIO OF MACARONI AND ONIONS

1 lb. macaroni (maniche,
mezze zite, penne, etc.)
3 tablespoons flour
2 tablespoons white wine
salt and pepper
grated parmesan

12 onions
5 oz. butter
27 oz. milk
olive oil
(brandy)

Peel and chop the onions finely. Cook slowly in a little oil and butter, stirring so they soften evenly without browning. Add the wine and continue cooking until it evaporates. Make a thin bechamel with three ounces butter, three tablespoons flour and the milk. Cook the pasta and mix with half the bechamel, pepper and grated parmesan. Stir over the heat until well blended. Grease a large mould and fill with layers of macaroni and onions sprinkled with grated parmesan and dotted with butter, ending with a layer of pasta. Top with the bechamel and more grated parmesan and brown in a hot oven.

MACCHERONCINI WITH SWEET PEPPERS **152**

1 lb. maccheroncini
4 oz. butter
parsley
salt and pepper

2 sweet peppers (1 red, 1 yellow)
¾ lb. tomatoes
grated parmesan

Clean and chop the peppers and cook in a pan with half the butter. Add the pureed tomatoes, a handful of chopped parsley and salt and pepper. Cook the maccheroncini, toss in the remaing butter and mix with the peppers. Serve grated parmesan separately.

SPAGHETTI WITH TOMATO
AND SWEET PEPPER BLENDER SAUCE **151**

1 lb. spaghetti
1 sweet pepper
parsley
6 tablespoons milk
olive oil

3 tomatoes
salt and pepper
3 tablespoons grated parmesan
(garlic)

Put all the ingredients except the spaghetti and the oil in the blender and when you have a smooth sauce continue blending as you gradually incorporate a little oil to make it the required thickness. Serve with hot spaghetti.

Variation Add one clove garlic to the blender.

PASTA WITH ASPARAGUS TIPS **153**

1 lb. pasta
3 oz. butter

½ lb. asparagus tips
2 oz. grated gruyere

You can cut the asparagus tips from asparagus cooked in the usual way, or use tinned/canned ones if these are not available. Cook the pasta and toss with the butter and grated gruyere. Add the asparagus tips, mix together gently, add the remaining butter which you have melted until it begins to brown and serve immediately.

PASTA WITH ARTICHOKES AND PEAS **154**

1 lb. pasta	6 globe artichokes
½ lb. shelled peas	olive oil
4 oz. butter	lemon juice
parsley	salt and pepper
parmesan	

Remove the hearts from the artichokes, cut in strips and soak in lemon juice and water. Heat the butter and a little oil and cook the artichoke strips gently. Add the peas, season with salt and pepper and add a handful of chopped parsley. Cook the pasta, toss in a little butter then add the artichokes, peas and oil from the pan. Serve grated parmesan separately.

SPAGHETTI WITH CARROTS **155**

1 lb. spaghetti	¾ lb. carrots
4 oz. butter	parsley
grated parmesan	salt and pepper

Peel and chop the carrots and cook them in half the butter. Season with salt and pepper and a handful of chopped parsley. Cook the spaghetti in plenty of salted water, toss with the rest of the butter (melted previously if you like), add some grated parmesan and the carrots.

SPAGHETTI WITH POTATOES **156**

1 lb. spaghetti	3 large potatoes
4 oz. butter	olive oil
grated parmesan	parsley
salt and pepper	(milk)

Peel and chop the potatoes then cook them with half the butter and a little oil, salt and pepper and the chopped parsley. Cook the pasta, toss with the remaining butter and the grated parmesan, add the potatoes and serve.

Variation Add four tablespoons milk to the potatoes while they are cooking.

PASTA WITH PUMPKIN

1 lb. pasta
3 oz. butter
grated parmesan
salt and pepper

1 lb. pumpkin
olive oil
parsley

Dice the peeled pumpkin flesh, cook in butter and oil, season with salt and pepper and a little chopped parsley. Cook the pasta, toss with the remaining butter (melted if you like), some grated cheese and the pumpkin.

PENNE OR RIGATONI WITH BLACK OLIVES 158

1 lb. penne or rigatoni
4 tablespoons olive oil
½ lb. tomatoes
basil

3 oz. small black olives
½ onion
8 oz. thin cream
salt and pepper

Heat the oil and fry the finely sliced onion with a pinch of salt; add the seeded black olives and the pureed tomatoes. Stir well, then add the cream, plenty of pepper and a little basil and mix with the hot pasta.

PENNE OR RIGATONI WITH GREEN OLIVES 159

12 oz. rigatoni or penne
2 cloves garlic
2 tablespoons white wine
salt and pepper

3 oz. butter
½ lb. green olives
3 tomatoes
grated parmesan

Heat the butter and cook the finely sliced garlic. Add the peeled, seeded and chopped tomatoes, the seeded, chopped olives, moisten with white wine and cook until the olives are soft. Season with salt and pepper. Cook the pasta, toss in a little extra butter and parmesan and mix with the olives and tomatoes in the pan.

MINESTRONE WITH PESTO **160**

½ lb. short pasta
(tubetti, cannolicchi, etc.)
4 courgettes/zucchini
2 sticks celery
2 cloves garlic
30 basil leaves

3 onions
3 potatoes
2 aubergines/eggplant
olive oil
2 oz. grated pecorino/romano
(beans, peas)

Put the peeled, chopped potatoes in a pan and cook with plenty of water. After ½ hour add the chopped onions, courgettes/zucchini and celery, and the peeled and diced aubergines/eggplant. Cook until soft, then add a few tablespoons of olive oil, and finally the pasta. When the pasta is cooked stir in a few tablespoons of pesto, made as in recipe 129, with pounded basil, garlic and grated pecorino. This gives the minestrone a really delicious flavour.

Variation Add beans and peas in season.

TUBETTINI WITH CARROTS AND PEAS **161**

1 lb. tubettini
½ lb. shelled peas
parsley

6 carrots
4 oz. butter
salt and pepper

Finely slice or dice the carrots and cook gently until soft in the butter. Add the peas and season with salt and pepper. When they are cooked add a handful of chopped parsley. Cook the pasta, toss with a little butter and mix in the vegetables.

PASTA WITH VEGETABLES AND HERBS **162**

1 lb. pasta
cloves
peppercorns
nutmeg
parsley
flour

2 lb. vegetables (carrots,
onions, celery and others
according to taste)
thyme
butter
salt and pepper

This is based on one of the great French sauces. Make a vegetable broth with a few very finely chopped carrots, chopped onion, celery, parsley, some thyme and nutmeg, a few whole peppercorns and a couple of cloves (the quantities can be varied according to taste). When the vegetables are soft, put through a food mill together with any remaining cooking water and keep warm. Melt one tablespoon butter, add one tablespoon flour and then the vegetable puree and another chopped onion and carrot. Cook until the sauce thickens, season with salt and pepper and add a pinch of nutmeg and some cloves to taste. When very thick add more of the puree, more chopped onion, carrot and celery and more nutmeg and clove to taste. Continue cooking over low heat until the sauce is really thick and then mix with the hot pasta. Serve grated parmesan separately. For final perfection you can put the sauce through a food mill once more, return to the heat and add a further tablespoon of flour so it thickens. Cook just a few minutes longer, mix with the hot pasta and serve.

MACARONI WITH VEGETABLE BROTH   **163**

¾ lb. macaroni (rigatoni, zite, maniche, etc.)	1 onion
	2 aubergines/eggplant
1 sweet pepper	3 tomatoes
1 potato	2 cloves garlic
2 oz. butter	4 tablespoons olive oil
salt and pepper	nutmeg
oregano	basil

Heat the oil and butter in a large pan and add the finely chopped onion, then one of the aubergines/eggplant diced, but not skinned. Cook slowly, then add the seeded and chopped pepper, the skinned, chopped and seeded tomatoes and a pinch of nutmeg and oregano. Season with salt and pepper, add the peeled, grated potato and cook until all the ingredients are soft and well blended. Finely chop two cloves of garlic and plenty of basil, add to the rest of the ingredients and stir well. Add the uncooked pasta and let it cook gently in this sauce. Fry slices of the remaining aubergine/eggplant which you have previously left to drain sprinkled with coarse salt under a weighted plate. Put slices of aubergine/eggplant in each individual dish before serving the macaroni broth. It makes a substantial meal on its own.

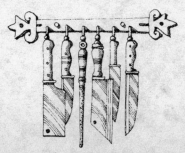

1 lb. bucatini
¾ lb. tomatoes
¼ lb. butter
grated parmesan

½ lb. mushrooms
parsley
salt and pepper
(onion, tomato puree, white wine)

Slice the mushrooms and cook in the melted butter; add the pureed tomatoes and season with salt and pepper and a handful of chopped parsley. Bring to a boil and cook with the lid on for 20 minutes. Cook the pasta, toss with butter, add the sauce and serve grated parmesan separately.

Variations 1. Lightly brown ½ chopped onion in the butter and then add the mushrooms and other ingredients.
2. Use one tablespoon of tomato puree diluted with a little water instead of the fresh tomatoes.
3. Add two tablespoons white wine to the mushrooms and let it cook a little before adding the tomato puree.

LASAGNETTE RICCE WITH
SPINACH AND MUSHROOMS
165

1 lb. lasagnette ricce
1 lb. spinach
salt and pepper

3 oz. mushrooms
4 oz. butter
parmesan

Cook the mushrooms until soft in a little butter and season with salt and pepper. Clean and cook the spinach in the usual way, drain very thoroughly, chop and add to the mushrooms with a little more salt and pepper. Cook the pasta, drain well, toss in butter and add to the spinach and mushroom in the pan. Stir for a few minutes over moderate heat and serve immediately. Serve grated parmesan separately.

TAGLIATELLE WITH MUSHROOMS **166**

¾ lb. tagliatelle
6 tomatoes
6 cloves garlic
2 tablespoons butter
olive oil
oregano
salt and pepper

3 onions
10 oz. mushrooms
2 oz. valgrana (sharp
Gorgonzola or
Roquefort cheese)
basil

Quarter the onions and fry over low heat in four tablespoons of oil and two tablespoons of butter. After 15 minutes add the skinned and chopped tomatoes. Cook for another five minutes, then add the sliced mushrooms, cook for ten minutes and season with chopped basil, oregano and salt and pepper. Lightly brown the garlic in more oil—use the full quantity of garlic or the flavour is less interesting—add the mushrooms, the grated cheese and cook for a few more minutes so the sauce is well blended. Add the hot tagliatelle, stir well and serve.

BUCATINI OR LASAGNETTE RICCE WITH MUSHROOM SAUCE **167**

1 lb. bucatini or lasagnette ricce
3 oz. spring onions/scallions
salt and pepper
thyme
grated parmesan

4 oz. fresh mushrooms
½ lb. tomatoes
parsley
bay leaf
(green olives)

Lightly brown the sliced onions in the butter and add the sliced mushrooms, salt and pepper and parsley. Add the pureed tomatoes with more butter, thyme and bay leaf, and cook for a few minutes longer. Cook the pasta, toss in butter and parmesan, add the sauce and serve.

Variation Add 12 seeded, chopped green olives to the sauce.

1 lb. bucatini or lasagnette ricce
4 oz. fresh mushrooms
1 onion
4 oz. butter
grated gruyere

2 aubergines/eggplant
½ lb. tomatoes
sage
olive oil
(parmesan)

Heat the oil and butter and cook the chopped onion with a sage leaf, then add the diced aubergines/eggplant. Season with salt and pepper and add the sliced mushrooms, then the peeled, seeded and chopped tomatoes. Cook for about 20 minutes. Cook the pasta, toss in butter and grated gruyere, add the mushroom sauce and serve.

Variations 1. Use parmesan instead of gruyere.
2. Put the pasta in a greased ovenproof dish with the sauce and bake for 15 minutes in a hot oven.

TAGLIATELLE WITH WHITE TRUFFLE **169**

1 lb. tagliatelle
6 tablespoons grated parmesan
white truffle
salt and pepper

3 oz. butter
white wine
(marsala, nutmeg)

Heat the butter in a small pan, add six tablespoons parmesan and moisten with about two tablespoons of white wine. Season with salt and pepper. Cook the pasta, toss in butter, then mix with this sauce and garnish with slices of white truffle.

Variations 1. Use a little marsala instead of white wine.
2. Add a pinch of nutmeg to the sauce.

DITALINI WITH LENTILS **170**

1 lb. ditalini (or any small
variety of pasta)
grated parmesan

½ lb. lentils
4 oz. butter
salt and pepper

Wash the lentils, cook until soft in water to cover. Drain and toss in some of the butter. Cook the pasta, toss in the remaining butter, add grated parmesan and pepper, mix with the lentils and serve.

1 lb. pasta
4 oz. butter
salt and pepper

½ lb. lentils
grated parmesan

Wash the lentils and cook until soft in boiling salted water to cover, drain, then pass through a food mill. Cook the pasta, toss in butter, add some parmesan and pepper, then mix with the lentil puree, and if necessary a little water, and serve.

Variation   Put the puree and butter in a pan, add the pasta and cook for a few minutes stirring continuously. Or put the pasta and puree mixture in an ovenproof dish, dot with butter and brown for 15 minutes in a moderate oven. In Apulia orecchiette are used with this dish.

PASTA WITH WALNUTS AND PECORINO/ROMANO 172

1 lb. pasta
4 oz. grated pecorino/romano
olive oil
salt

3 oz. shelled walnuts
basil
(garlic, parmesan,
large breadcrumbs, milk)

This recipe is similar to Genovese pesto, with the basic difference that walnuts are an essential ingredient, while they are only occasionally used in authentic pesto. Plunge the kernels in boiling water for a minute to remove the outer skin, then pound in a mortar with plenty of chopped basil and the pecorino/romano, and gradually add a little oil until it is the desired thickness. Serve with the hot pasta.

Variations   1.   Pound one or two cloves garlic with the other ingredients to give a more genuine pesto flavour.
2.   Use half pecorino/romano and half parmesan.
3.   A handful of large breadcrumbs soaked in milk gives a smoother and more delicate consistency to the sauce. Squeeze lightly, then pound with the other ingredients.

PASTA WITH WALNUTS AND CREAM 173

1 lb. pasta
6 oz. thin cream
breadcrumbs
marjoram
salt and pepper

4 oz. shelled walnuts
2 oz. butter
milk
grated parmesan

Pound the nuts well in a mortar, adding a handful of large breadcrumbs soaked in milk and squeezed out. Transfer to a bowl, add the cream and mix with salt and pepper and marjoram. Cook the pasta, toss in butter and parmesan, mix well with the walnut sauce and serve.

PASTA WITH WALNUTS AND AUBERGINES/EGGPLANT 174

1 lb. pasta
2 aubergines/eggplant
4 oz. pecorino/romano
olive oil
milk
salt and pepper

3 oz. shelled walnuts
1 lb. tomatoes
2 oz. butter
handful of large breadcrumbs
breadcrumbs, fine

Chop the peeled aubergines/eggplant and leave to drain for a few hours sprinkled with coarse salt under a lightly weighted plate; then fry in plenty of hot oil. Pound the nuts well in a mortar with a handful of large breadcrumbs soaked in milk and then squeezed lightly. Heat four tablespoons oil, add the pureed tomatoes (or the equivalent amount of concentrated tomato puree diluted with warm water), the fried aubergines/eggplant and the pounded nuts and mix well. Cook the pasta, toss in butter, add freshly ground pepper and then the sauce, reserving four tablespoonsful. Put the pasta in a greased oven-proof dish, cover with the rest of the sauce and the finely sliced cheese, dot with butter, sprinkle with the fine breadcrumbs and brown in a hot oven.

MACARONI WITH HONEY 175

¾ lb. flour
cinnamon

honey
salt

Make the pasta with the flour, a pinch of salt and some water. Roll the dough out thinly, cut in strips, then use a very ancient technique to form the macaroni. Roll the strips round a floured knitting needle (a sorghum stalk was used originally) to make small macaroni tubes. Cook in plenty of boiling salted water and serve with honey melted with a little of the pasta water and some cinnamon. A sort of molasses rather thinner than honey was probably used originally and did not need to be diluted.

Variation You can use commercial macaroni, but it has none of the flavour of fresh macaroni and honey. If you make the pasta dough you can just cut it in strips without rolling them, but this spoils the special feature of the macroni tubes, which absorb the honey better.

MACARONI WITH MILK AND HONEY **176**

1 lb. flour
54 oz. milk
6 tablespoons honey

salt
(sugar, candied fruit, cinnamon)

Make the macaroni as in the previous recipe. Cook them in the milk over moderate heat so the liquid reduces a little, and before it has been completely absorbed remove a little to dilute the honey. This makes a thick, sweet sauce to serve with the macaroni, as near as can be to the way it was eaten in the Middle Ages.

Variations 1. Use commercial macaroni.
2. Use sugar instead of honey and sprinkle it directly over the macaroni instead of diluting it with milk, although it is not as tasty as the honey and macaroni.
3. Add diced candied orange and lemon peel after adding the honey and serve as a dessert.
4. Add a pinch of cinnamon to the sauce.

MACARONI WITH WALNUTS AND ALMONDS **177**

1 lb. macaroni
3 oz. walnuts, shelled
6 tablespoons milk
nutmeg

3 oz. almonds, shelled
4 tablespoons olive oil
salt

Pound the almonds and walnuts in a mortar, transfer to a bowl and gradually work in the oil, then the milk, to make a smooth, well-blended sauce. Season with a pinch of salt and nutmeg. Dilute with a couple of tablespoons of the water in which the pasta is cooking and serve with the hot pasta.

MACARONI WITH PRUNES   **178**

1 lb. macaroni
½ lb. prunes
4 oz. butter
2 oz. sugar

cloves (or ½ teaspoon
powdered cloves)
cinnamon
(pepper and salt)

Soak the prunes in hot water for one hour. Seed, chop, and finish cooking in the butter. Add the sugar, cinnamon and a few cloves, or the powdered cloves. Cook the pasta and dilute the prune sauce with a few tablespoons of the pasta water.

Variation This is an ancient recipe with a definite central European flavour. Originally salt and pepper were included.

MACARONI WITH SWEET CHERRIES   **179**

1 lb. macaroni
3 oz. almonds
2 oz. sugar
cloves

½ lb. seeded sweet cherries
4 oz. butter
cinnamon
(walnuts, apricots)

Sprinkle the cherries with sugar and leave to marinate for a few hours. Cook the pasta, toss in butter and mix with the cherries. Add the chopped, toasted almonds and some cinnamon and mix well, then transfer to a greased oven-proof dish, sprinkle with grated cheese, dot with butter and brown for a few minutes in a hot oven.

Variations 1. Use walnuts instead of almonds and remove the outer skins.
2. Use apricots instead of cherries.

MACARONI WITH BANANAS   **180**

1 lb. macaroni
5 oz. butter
3 bananas
sugar

3 oz. strong grated cheese
(parmesan or pecorino/romano)
hot red pepper, a few grains

Peel and slice the bananas, fry quickly in very hot butter (they must not get mushy) and sprinkle with sugar. Cook the pasta, toss with butter, the grated cheese and red pepper, top with fried banana and serve. If the strong contrast of sweet and hot flavours does not appeal you can omit the cheese and hot pepper. However, this is a tropical recipe and has a typically colourful flavour.

III
PASTA WITH VEGETABLES, DAIRY PRODUCTS AND EGGS

1 lb. flour
54 oz. milk
salt

4 eggs
(pepper, parmesan, sugar)

Lagane is the ancient name for fettucine and lasagne, derived from the Greek, laganon and the Latin laganum, which still survive in other words like laganaturo (rolling pin), or laganelle (tagliatelle). Make the egg pasta dough: put the flour in a mound on a pastry board or working surface, break the eggs in the middle and work lightly with the fingers to draw in all the flour gradually; then knead more thoroughly adding one pinch salt. When you have a smooth, elastic dough let it rest for a few minutes. Roll out not too thinly, and finally roll up the sheet of pasta loosely on your rolling pin. Remove the rolling pin and cut strips of pasta about ¼ inch thick from the roll for traditional fettuccine. For lasagne, roll the dough out more finely and cut into broader strips. Cook in boiling milk with a little salt until they are suitably al dente, and most of the milk has been absorbed.

Variations 1. Add pepper and grated parmesan.
              2. Add a few tablespoons of sugar when cooked.

1 lb. flour
½ lb. butter
salt and pepper

4 eggs
½ lb. grated parmesan

A Roman dish requiring plenty of butter. Make an egg pasta dough, as in the previous recipe, with the flour, eggs and salt. Leave to rest, roll out not too thinly, roll up loosely on the rolling pin and cut in strips about ½ inch wide. Cook the fettuccine and put in the serving dish with two tablespoons of the cooking water and the grated parmesan. Add the softened butter, mix gently and serve with a generous sprinkling of freshly ground black pepper.

FETTUCCINE WITH BUTTER AND CREAM — **183**

1 lb. flour
4 oz. butter
6 tablespoons thick cream

4 eggs
4 oz. grated parmesan
salt and pepper

Make the fettuccine with the flour and eggs (see recipe 181). Melt the butter in a large pan, season with salt and then add three tablespoons of the water you are cooking the fettuccine in. When it is ready (firm, rather than tender), drain and add to the butter in the pan. Mix well, adding the grated parmesan and cream. In Rome the fettuccine are deftly handled with two forks and served on really hot plates with freshly ground black pepper.

TAGLIATELLE WITH BUTTER AND MILK — **184**

1 lb. flour
4 oz. butter
4 oz. grated parmesan
salt and pepper

4 eggs
6 tablespoons milk
nutmeg

Melt the butter without letting it brown, then add the milk and parmesan, stirring until it is a creamy mixture. Season with salt and pepper and a pinch of nutmeg. Keep the heat low so the sauce thickens slowly without getting lumpy. Make the tagliatelle with an egg pasta dough cut into strips slightly less than ¼ inch thick, cook them in plenty of salted water so they are ready at just the same time as the sauce.

FETTUCCINE WITH RICOTTA — **185**

1 lb. flour
10 oz. ricotta
salt and pepper

4 eggs
olive oil

Prepare the fettuccine with the flour and eggs (see recipe 181). Sieve the ricotta and work three tablespoons oil into it and a few tablespoons of the water in which you are cooking the pasta. Add plenty of freshly ground black pepper and serve with the hot pasta.

Variation Roman cooks sometimes add a little oil when mixing the egg pasta dough.

TAGLIOLINI WITH GARLIC, OIL AND ROSEMARY 186

1 lb. flour	4 eggs
4 tablespoons olive oil	2 cloves garlic
rosemary	salt and pepper

Another very basic sauce that is a delicious accompaniment with fresh egg pasta. Make the tagliolini with an egg pasta dough (see recipe 181) made with flour, eggs, a pinch of salt and one or two tablespoons of warm water as necessary. Roll the dough out not too thinly and cut in strips about ⅛ inch wide. Make the sauce: heat the oil in a pan, add two cloves garlic crushed to bring out their flavour (to be discarded before serving), and two small sprigs of rosemary. Add two tablespoons of the water in which the pasta is cooking. Season with salt. Remove the garlic and rosemary, add freshly ground pepper and serve with the hot pasta.

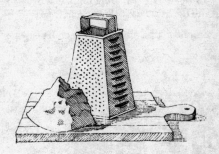

COLD TAGLIOLINI WITH OIL AND TOMATOES 187

1 lb. flour	5 eggs
2 lb. tomatoes	2 cloves garlic
olive oil	parsley
salt and pepper	

Make the tagliolini with the eggs and flour as in recipe 181, cutting the dough into strips ⅛ inch wide. Cook the in boiling salted water and drain. Mix gently with five tablespoons oil, the chopped garlic and plenty of chopped parsley. Leave in an open serving dish so the pasta is well spread out and cannot stick together. Do not put in the refrigerator or it may gel, but leave in a cool place. Make a simple tomato sauce with the pureed tomatoes and oil (see recipe 15), add salt and pepper and serve with the cold tagliolini.

1 lb. flour	5 eggs
2 cloves garlic	2 lb. tomatoes
olive oil	parsley
salt	(pepper)
hot chili pepper	

Make the tagliolini with an egg pasta dough (see recipe 181) rolled out rather more finely than usual and cut into strips ⅛ inch wide. Heat four tablespoons olive oil, add the chopped garlic (or crushed cloves to be discarded before serving) and one or two pieces of hot chili pepper (also to be discarded before serving). Add the pureed tomatoes (or an equivalent quantity of tomato puree diluted with water), and season with salt. Add plenty of chopped parsley and cook over moderate heat. Cook the tagliolini, mix with the sauce and leave to cool. This delicious recipe represents a combination of Italian and Jewish traditions; a type of pasta closely resembling tagliatelle was common in the Mediterranean region and the Middle East in ancient times.

Variation Use freshly ground pepper instead of hot chili pepper.

TAGLIATELLE WITH LETTUCE AND PEAS 189

1 lb. flour	4 eggs
½ lb. shelled peas	large head of lettuce
½ onion	4 oz. butter
salt and pepper	

Prepare the tagliatelle as in recipe 181. Wash the lettuce and cut it in strips. Heat half the butter in a large pan, add the chopped onion, the lettuce and the peas. Continue cooking for about ½ hour, adding a few tablespoons of warm water if it seems too dry. Season with salt and pepper and mix with the hot pasta.

1 lb. flour	4 eggs
4 globe artichokes (use only	1 lb. tomatoes
small young ones)	2 oz. butter
olive oil	basil
salt and pepper	garlic

Franzini was a famous Italian chef at the turn of the century. Make the tagliatelle as in recipe 181 with the flour and eggs. Prepare the artichokes, trimming the leaves far down, and cut in quarters. Cook in the butter and two tablespoons oil, until quite tender. Add the pureed, tomatoes and a crushed clove of garlic (to be discarded before serving) and a little basil. Cook until soft and well blended and pour over the hot tagliatelle.

TAGLIATELLE VERDI WITH BUTTER AND PARMESAN
191

1 lb. flour	¾ lb. spinach
3 eggs	4 oz. butter
parmesan	salt and pepper

The spinach gives colour and flavour to the pasta: it is important to get the proportions right. Put the flour in a mound on a pastry board or working surface, but reserve a few tablespoons. Put the eggs in the well and add the spinach which you have cooked, drained and put through a food mill. Follow this Emilian method of preparing the spinach: wash carefully, cook in very little boiling water. Drain and squeeze out the remaining water first by hand, then in a dishcloth. When you have put the spinach through the food mill you will be able to tell if it was well drained: the puree should be thick and bright green and the success of your tagliatelle verdi depends on this. Do not use more than three eggs to make the dough or it will be too soft: gradually add the flour with your fingertips (see recipe 181) and then knead thoroughly, adding the puree to make a smooth firm dough. If it seems too soft add a little of the extra flour. Roll out and cut into strips ½ inch or ⅜ inch wide. Cook in lightly salted boiling water and serve with butter, freshly ground pepper and parmesan.

1 lb. flour
3 eggs
3 tablespoons flour
grated parmesan
salt and pepper

1¼ lb. spinach
4 oz. butter
18 oz. milk
(nutmeg)

Make the tagliatelle verdi as in the previous recipe, with the flour, eggs and pureed spinach. Make a bechamel in the usual way with half the butter, the flour and milk. Cook the tagliatelle, drain well and put half of them in a greased ovenproof dish. Cover with a layer of bechamel, sprinkle with parmesan, dot with butter; make a second layer of tagliatelle, cover with the rest of the bechamel, sprinkle with more parmesan, dot with the rest of the butter and brown in a hot oven.

Variation Add a pinch of nutmeg to the bechamel.

1 lb. flour
4 oz. fresh mushrooms
6 oz. milk
4 oz. grated parmesan
salt and pepper

5 eggs
2 oz. large breadcrumbs
6 tablespoons butter
parsley

Make the tagliatelle with the flour, two eggs, a pinch of salt and a little warm water if necessary (see recipe 181). Clean and chop the mushrooms, then cook them in two ounces of the butter with a handful of chopped parsley. Soak the bread in the milk, drain slightly and mix with the yolks of three eggs, the mushrooms and a pinch of salt and pepper. Beat the egg whites until stiff and fold into this mixture. Cook the tagliatelle in plenty of salted water, drain, then put a layer of tagliatelle on the bottom of a greased ovenproof dish. Add a layer of the sauce, sprinkle with grated parmesan, add another layer of tagliatelle, and so on until all the ingredients are finished. Dot the final layer with butter, sprinkle with parmesan and brown for a few minutes in a hot oven.

1 lb. flour	10 oz. spinach
3 eggs	10 oz. mushrooms
1¼ lb. tomatoes	4 oz. butter
2 cloves garlic	olive oil
parsley	salt and pepper
6 tablespoons white wine	(parmesan)

One of the most inspired of the delicious recipes from the rich Emilian cooking tradition, which has a perfect combination of flavours. Make the tagliatelle in the usual way with the flour, eggs and spinach (see recipe 191). Make the sauce: heat half the butter, a little oil and the sliced garlic (or crushed cloves to be discarded before serving). Cook until brown, add the sliced mushrooms, season with salt and pepper, add the wine and cook until it evaporates a little. Add the pureed tomatoes, or peeled, seeded, chopped tomatoes, and continue cooking until you have a thick sauce. Add a handful of chopped parsley and remove from the heat. Toss the hot tagliatelle in butter then mix with the sauce. Serve grated parmesan separately.

SFOGLIATELLE ROSA WITH ASPARAGUS TIPS **195**

1 lb. flour	6 eggs
2 tomatoes	10 oz. asparagus tips
½ lb. mascarpone cheese	6 tablespoons thick cream
salt	

Put the tomatoes through a food mill. Gently cook the asparagus, remove the most tender tips and put them through a food mill reserving about 2 ounces whole tips. Put the flour on a pastry board or working surface, make a well and add the eggs (the larger quantity is justified by the other ingredients). Add four tablespoons of tomato puree, one tablespoon of the pureed asparagus, a pinch of salt, and if necessary one or two tablespoons of warm water. Mix in the flour, knead well; the dough will be quite soft so you will not be able to roll it out very thinly. Roll it up loosely and cut into fairly broad strips, as for lasagne or pappardelle (about ⅝ inch wide). Cook this pasta very carefully, only putting the strips a few at a time in the boiling water so they do not stick together. Remove gently with a slotted spoon. Meanwhile make the sauce by melting the mascarpone cheese with the cream and the remaining asparagus puree, then carefully add the remaining whole asparagus tips. Season with salt and pepper and serve with the hot pasta. This dish has a most attractive colour and flavour.

1 lb. flour	3 eggs
2 lb. tomatoes	4 tablespoons olive oil
salt and pepper	grated pecorino/romano

Commercial fusilli can be used but it has a much less interesting flavour. For homemade fusilli: make a pasta dough with the flour, eggs and a pinch of salt (see recipe 181). Let the dough rest and roll out not too finely, then cut in strips about ¼ inch to ½ inch wide. Wrap each strip round a floured knitting needle to make spirals. Cook in plenty of boiling salted water and serve with a simple tomato sauce made with the oil and pureed tomatoes (see recipe 15). Serve grated pecorino/romano separately. Any sauce can be served with this pasta.

PICAGGE WITH GARLIC AND PARSLEY **197**

1 lb. flour	2 eggs
3 cloves garlic	parsley
6 tablespoons olive oil	(parmesan, pecorino/romano, basil)
salt	

Picagge is a rustic form of lasagne made in Liguria. Make the pasta dough in the normal way (see recipe 181), but with only two eggs to one pound flour. Cut strips about ½ inch thick from the rolled out dough and cook in boiling salted water, adding only a few picagge at a time to prevent them from sticking together. Pound the garlic and some parsley in a mortar, heat briefly in hot oil and mix with the pasta. Serve grated pecorino/romano separately.

Variation Picagge can also be served with a traditional Genovese pesto (see recipe 129).

LASAGNE WITH POPPY SEEDS **198**

1 lb. flour	4 eggs
4 oz. butter	2 oz. sugar
1 oz. poppy seeds	salt

Make an egg pasta dough (see recipe 181) and cut into the classic lasagne strips about ¾ inch wide. Pound the poppy seeds and sugar. Melt the butter in a pan while you cook the lasagne in plenty of boiling, salted water. Toss them in the butter until well coated, then add the poppy seed mixture, stir well and serve. This dish is still made in Trieste, but it really comes from the Danube region, where it is called Mohnnudeln.

1 lb. flour	4 eggs
1 lb. chick peas	4 cloves garlic
2 bay leaves	6 oz. olive oil
2 sprigs rosemary	salt

An ancient Florentine dish. The day before soak the chick peas in water to cover with one tablespoon coarse salt, two crushed cloves of garlic and a few bay leaves. Make the strisce like lasange with an egg pasta dough (see recipe 181). The dough will be fairly soft: roll it out not too thinly and cut in strips about ¾ inch wide. Set aside to dry. Heat the oil (use a good clear light Tuscan oil) and add two crushed cloves of garlic and a couple of sprigs of rosemary and cook over low heat. The chick peas should be drained and cooked in boiling water with a pinch of salt until really soft. Drain them, reserve two tablespoons of chick peas and put the rest through a food mill. Return the puree to the pan with a few tablespoons of the water they were cooked in. Bring to a boil, add the strisce immediately. When it is al dente continue cooking a little with the whole chick peas you have reserved, and the garlic and rosemary-flavoured oil (strained to remove the garlic and rosemary), then serve immediately.

TAGLIATELLE WITH WALNUT AND TOMATO   **200**

1 lb. flour	4 eggs
12 shelled walnuts	6 tablespoons butter
10 oz. tomatoes	olive oil
4 oz. grated parmesan	salt and pepper

Make the tagliatelle in the normal way (see recipe 182) with the flour, eggs and salt, and cut the dough in ¼ inch strips. Make the sauce: heat two tablespoons oil, add the nuts which have been coarsely pounded in a mortar, season with salt and pepper, then add the butter and a sauce made with oil and the pureed tomatoes (see recipe 15). Bring to a boil, dilute with one tablespoon of the pasta cooking water and cook a little longer over low heat. Mix with the hot pasta and serve grated parmesan separately.

DANTESCHE WITH MUSHROOMS

1 lb. flour	4 eggs
4 oz. mushrooms	5 oz. tomatoes
4 oz. butter	4 oz. grated parmesan
salt	(fontina cheese)

Make an egg pasta dough with the flour, eggs and salt (see recipe 181). Roll out and cut in rectangles about two by four inches. Cook in boiling, salted water until al dente. Drain well and arrange in a greased ovenproof dish. Spread with butter, slices of gently fried mushrooms and sliced fresh tomatoes, sprinkle with grated cheese and brown in a hot oven.

LASAGNE WITH RICOTTA, AUBERGINES/EGGPLANT AND WALNUTS

1 lb. flour	4 eggs
2 aubergines/eggplant	½ lb. ricotta
6 oz. tomatoes	12 shelled walnuts
6 tablespoons olive oil	grated parmesan
salt and pepper	

Make the lasagne in the usual way with the flour, eggs and salt (see recipe 181). Cut the dough in strips about ¾ inch wide. Make a sauce with the pureed tomatoes, oil and salt and pepper. Plunge the walnuts in boiling water for a moment to remove the outer skins, then pound them in a mortar. Slice the peeled aubergines/eggplant and leave to drain sprinkled with coarse salt and covered with a weighted plate for an hour. Fry in hot oil, drain on absorbent paper and chop roughly. Cook the lasagne. Make a sauce with the aubergine/eggplant, walnut pulp and crumbled ricotta, diluted with two tablespoons of the pasta cooking water. Mix about three-quarters of this sauce with the hot lasagne, cover with the remaining ricotta and the tomato sauce, sprinkle with grated cheese and brown in a hot oven.

DUMPLINGS WITH BUTTER AND CHEESE

1 lb. flour	10 oz. milk
3 eggs	5 oz. butter
4 oz. grated parmesan	salt

A German form of gnocchi from the Danube area, where they are called spatzle. They are served as an accompaniment for meat and gravy, but are also pleasant as a dish on their own. Make a dough with the flour, milk, eggs and a pinch of salt (see recipe 181). Knead until it is smooth and slightly bubbly. Form into tiny balls and drop these into boiling water, removing them as they rise to the surface with a slotted spoon. Put in an ovenproof dish dotted with half the butter, then add the rest of the melted butter and sprinkle with grated cheese. Brown for a few minutes in a hot oven.

GNOCCHETTI WITH BUTTER AND PARMESAN 204

3 oz. flour
½ lb. grated parmesan
salt and pepper

6 eggs
4 oz. butter
(gravy)

Beat the eggs in a bowl and gradually beat in six ounces of the parmesan, then enough flour to make a soft dough which you can moisten if necessary with a few tablespoons of warm water. Season with salt and pepper. Make gnocchi by taking small balls of the dough and dropping them, about two dozen at a time, into plenty of boiling salted water. They are cooked when they rise to the surface—in about ten minutes—and can be removed with a slotted spoon. Serve with the rest of the grated parmesan and the melted butter.

Variation Serve with meat gravy instead of butter.

RICOTTA GNOCCHI 205

1 lb. ricotta
7 oz. grated parmesan
3 egg whites
salt and pepper

6 oz. flour
6 eggs
nutmeg

This is a recipe from Padua. Mix the ricotta with the flour in a bowl and work well together; the ricotta needs to be quite watery or it will be difficult to mix. Add three ounces of the grated parmesan, salt and pepper and the beaten eggs. When the dough is smooth add the beaten egg whites to lighten the mixture, together with a pinch of nutmeg. Work together thoroughly, then divide the mixture into little cork-shaped pieces and cook them in unsalted boiling water. As they float to the surface after about two or three minutes, remove them with a slotted spoon. Put in a flat serving dish, cover with melted butter and grated parmesan and they are ready to serve.

1¾ lb. spinach	¾ lb. ricotta
½ lb. flour	1 egg
1 egg yolk	4 oz. butter
4 oz. grated parmesan	(beef stock, gravy)
salt and pepper	

Cook the spinach and drain very thoroughly, then pass through a food mill. Work the spinach puree together with the ricotta, flour, eggs and salt and pepper to make a smooth dough. Form into little cork-shaped pieces and cook in plenty of boiling water. Remove with a slotted spoon as they float to the surface. Serve with melted butter and grated parmesan.

Variations 1. Cook the gnocchi in beef stock instead of water.
2. Serve with meat gravy instead of butter and cheese.

10 oz. flour	2 lb. potatoes
5 oz. butter	5 oz. grated parmesan
salt	(gravy)

The simplest form of gnocchi, known also as gnocchi alla piemontese, all'emiliana or alla romana. Cook the potatoes, remove the skin and put through a sieve. Mix the potato puree with ½ pound flour, adding more as necessary to obtain a soft, smooth dough. Potatoes vary enormously in their moisture content, so you may need to vary the quantities used. Make up into little cylinders and press against the prongs of a fork if you want them grooved, or against the edge of the pastry board. Cook them in boiling, salted water and when they rise to the surface let them cook another minute, then remove with a slotted spoon. Serve with melted butter and grated parmesan.

Variation Serve with meat gravy instead of butter.

1 lb. flour	2 lb. potatoes
2 lb. tomatoes	4 tablespoons olive oil
basil	salt and pepper
3 oz. grated parmesan	

The colourful Italian name of this dish: strangolapreti or choke a priest, may come from the fact that it is so filling and delicious that it has dire effects on those who gobble it up too fast. Cook the potatoes, peel and put through a sieve quickly so they stay as hot as possible. Gradually add the flour to this puree until it forms a large ball. The potatoes must absorb the flour (the quantity given is the maximum you should need) to form a smooth, soft paste. Add a pinch of salt and then make into little cylinders as thick as your finger, cut them in one inch pieces and roll each one on a floured board, pressing down the ends or pressing them against the prongs of a fork to make gnocchi. Leave to rest on a flour-sprinkled cloth to prevent them sticking, then cook in plenty of boiling, salted water. Remove with a slotted spoon as they rise to the surface, arrange carefully in a serving dish and cover with a tomato sauce made in the usual way by heating the oil, adding the pureed fresh tomatoes, and cooking for a minute with fresh basil and salt and pepper.

POTATO GNOCCHI WITH EGG   **209**

½ lb. flour	2 lb. potatoes
4 oz. butter	1 egg
salt	grated parmesan
brandy	(gravy)

Cook the potatoes, peel and put them through a sieve, then mix the puree with the flour, egg and one tablespoon brandy and one tablespoon butter, to obtain a smooth, soft dough. Divide into long cylinders, then cut off one inch pieces to make gnocchi; press the ends down with your thumb, or against the prongs of a fork. Cook in plenty of salted water and serve with melted butter and parmesan.

Variations   1. Use two eggs.
           2. Use two egg yolks only.
           3. Serve with gravy instead of melted butter.

½ lb. flour	2 lb. potatoes
1 egg	salt and pepper
olive oil	4 oz. butter
2 cloves garlic	(brandy, sage)

This is a dish from Piacenza. Cook, peel and sieve the potatoes, then add the flour, one egg and a pinch of salt to the puree. Work to obtain a smooth, pliable dough. Add a couple of tablespoons of oil if it seems too dry. Divide into little cylinders and cut these into pieces about one inch long, then press them against a fork, or the edge of a pastry board to give them the traditional gnocchi shape. Cook in boiling salted water and remove with a slotted spoon as they rise to the surface. Serve with the melted butter and the finely chopped garlic.

Variations   1. Add one tablespoon brandy to the dough.
                   2. Add some sage leaves instead of garlic and serve with grated parmesan.

10 oz. flour	1¼ lb. potatoes
10 oz. spinach	2 eggs
4 tablespoons butter	2 lb. tomatoes
1 onion	1 clove garlic
celery	carrot
parsley	3 bay leaves
2 teaspoons sugar	16 oz. thick cream
4 oz. grated parmesan	salt

Boil the potatoes, peel and sieve them. Knead with the flour, eggs and the cooked, finely chopped spinach until you have a light, soft dough. Divide into cylinders and cut these into one inch pieces, without pressing down the ends as for real gnocchi. Make the sauce: put the tomatoes through a food mill, then cook them in butter with the chopped garlic, celery, carrot and parsley. Add one bay leaf, the sugar, and a pinch of salt. Bring to a boil. Meanwhile cook the gnocchi in boiling, salted water. As they rise to the surface remove with a slotted spoon, add to the sauce and cook for a few more minutes. Add the cream and finally the grated parmesan.

10 oz. flour	2 lb. potatoes
4 oz. butter	1 egg
4 tablespoons milk	plums or apricots
sugar	breadcrumbs
cinnamon	(prunes or dried apricots)
salt	

A recipe from Trieste. Cook the potatoes, peel and sieve them. Knead with the flour, egg, salt and one tablespoon of butter to make a smooth dough. Take large round pieces of dough and wrap around a small plum or apricot (choose a good dark variety of plum or the small highly flavoured apricots). Carefully seed the fruit first and fill with sugar. Cook the gnocchi with their fruit filling in plenty of salted water. Drain well, roll in breadcrumbs lightly fried in butter, dust with sugar and cinnamon and serve.

Variation   Use prunes or dried apricots. Soak them in warm water, seed, chop, and mix with the sugar. Put small mounds of this mixture on the circles of dough and make them into a ball. Cook and serve in the same way as for the fresh fruit.

SEMOLINA GNOCCHI—I   **213**

10 oz. semolina flour	36 oz. milk
5 oz. butter	2 eggs
4 oz. grated parmesan	nutmeg
salt and pepper	(saffron)

Melt four tablespoons of the butter, add the milk, season with salt and pepper and a pinch of nutmeg. Bring to a boil, pour in all the semolina and stir vigorously to prevent sticking or lumps. When well mixed, remove from the heat, add the eggs, three ounces of grated parmesan and stir well. Spread this mixture on a marble slab or a piece of aluminium foil so it is about ½ inch thick. Leave to cool, then cut in circles with a pastry cutter or a glass about two inches in diameter. Arrange these gnocchi in a greased ovenproof dish so they overlap slightly. Sprinkle with grated parmesan, dot with butter and brown for a few minutes in a hot oven.

Variations   1. Use four eggs instead of two. Do not add the parmesan to the semolina mixture but just sprinkle it over the finished gnocchi.
2. Instead of nutmeg add a pinch of saffron diluted in one tablespoon warm water after pouring in the semolina.

10 oz. semolina flour
4 oz. butter
4 oz. grated parmesan
salt and pepper

27 oz. milk
2 eggs
nutmeg

The ingredients are the same as the previous recipe, but they are mixed differently. Put the semolina in a mound on the pastry board and make a well in the middle. Beat the eggs, put in the well and gradually incorporate all the semolina; mixing vigorously pour in the milk gradually, together with salt, nutmeg and the grated cheese. Spread out and make into gnocchi as in the previous recipe. Serve with melted butter and grated parmesan.

LIGHT GNOCCHI WITH EGGS **215**

10 oz. semolina flour
12 eggs
grated parmesan
salt

35 oz. milk
2 oz. grated gruyere cheese
butter

Heat the milk, pour in the semolina with a pinch of salt and stir quickly until well mixed and smooth. Cook until all the milk has been absorbed. Remove from the heat and add the yolks and grated parmesan. Fold in the beaten egg whites. Work until well mixed and pour into a greased ovenproof dish sprinkled with grated gruyere. Bake in a moderate oven for about ½ hour or until thoroughly set in a bain-marie (water bath). Cut the pasta into circles or diamonds, return to a greased ovenproof dish, cover with melted butter and grated parmesan and brown in a hot oven.

GNOCCHI WITH TOMATO **216**

10 oz. semolina flour
2 lb. tomatoes
4 oz. grated parmesan

4 eggs
4 oz. butter
salt

Make a sauce with the pureed tomatoes and two ounces butter. Mix the semolina on a pastry board with five tablespoons of this sauce, a pinch of salt and a few tablespoons of warm water as necessary. Mix the dough well, then transfer to a saucepan and cook, stirring continuously. Beat the eggs with a pinch of salt; remove the semolina from the heat, add the eggs and mix well.

Drop small spoonfuls of this batter into boiling salted water and remove as they rise to the surface with a slotted spoon. Arrange on a serving dish and cover with the remaining sauce and grated parmesan.

SPINACH SEMOLINA GNOCCHI   **217**

10 oz. spinach	10 oz. semolina flour
5 oz. butter	4 oz. grated parmesan
4 eggs	flour
salt	(milk, nutmeg)

Cook the spinach, drain well and put through a food mill. Mix the semolina with the beaten eggs, ½ ounce softened butter and one teaspoon flour, adding a few tablespoons warm water if the dough seems too hard and sticky, then add the spinach puree and mix well. Drop small spoonfuls of this mixture into boiling, salted water and remove as they float to the surface with a slotted spoon. Serve with melted butter and grated parmesan.

Variation   Reserve four ounces of the spinach before it is cooked, chop finely, mix with a thin bechamel sauce made with four tablespoons butter and two tablespoons flour and about 16 ounces milk. Serve with the gnocchi and serve grated parmesan separately.

GNOCCHI WITH CHEESE AND TOMATO   **218**

10 oz. semolina flour	35 oz. milk
4 eggs	2 oz. grated parmesan cheese
2 oz. grated gruyere cheese	2 large peeled tomatoes
3 oz. mozzarella cheese	2 cloves garlic
breadcrumbs	oregano
olive oil	salt and pepper
nutmeg	

Bring the milk to a boil with a pinch each of salt and nutmeg, then pour in the semolina. Add the beaten eggs and grated cheeses, and stir vigorously to remove any lumps. Pour onto a marble slab or piece of aluminum foil and cool. Cut in circles or diamonds and arrange in slightly overlapping lines in a greased ovenproof dish. Cover with sliced tomatoes and mozzarella, sprinkle with breadcrumbs and oregano, a little chopped garlic and some pepper. Pour over about four tablespoons olive oil and brown in a hot oven.

Variation   Substitute boiling water for milk.

SEMOLINA GNOCCHI WITH RICOTTA **219**

10 oz. semolina	35 oz. milk
5 oz. butter	4 eggs
4 egg yolks	6 oz. grated parmesan
7 oz. ricotta	flour
salt	nutmeg

Bring the milk to a boil, pour in the semolina, add one tablespoon butter, a pinch of salt and a pinch of nutmeg. Stir until smoothly blended, then put on a marble slab or pastry board and gradually work in the four eggs and four yolks with your fingertips. Add three ounces of the grated parmesan and all of the crumbled ricotta. Mix well to obtain a smooth, soft dough. Divide into pieces about ¾ inch long and ½ inch wide. Roll in flour and cook in boiling water. Remove as they float to the surface with a slotted spoon. Serve with melted butter and more grated parmesan.

GNOCCHI WITH RICOTTA AND ALMONDS **220**

10 oz. semolina flour	35 oz. milk
5 oz. butter	4 eggs
4 egg yolks	6 oz. grated parmesan
5 oz. ricotta	4 tablespoons blanched almonds
salt	nutmeg
flour	

Bring the milk to a boil, pour in the semolina, add one tablespoon butter and a pinch each of salt and nutmeg. Stir until smooth, then pour onto a marble slab or pastry board. Add the eggs and the yolks and work together with three ounces of the parmesan, the ricotta and finely chopped almonds. Make into gnocchi about ¾ inch long and ½ inch wide. Cook in boiling water, removing with a slotted spoon as they rise to the surface. Serve with grated parmesan and melted butter.

5 oz. stale bread	4 oz. dried mushrooms
4 eggs	6 oz. milk
½ lb. butter	3 oz. flour
garlic	grated parmesan
parsley	salt and pepper

A recipe from the Alto Adige. Cube the crustless bread; mix the eggs with the milk and a pinch of salt and pour over the bread in a bowl. Soak for a few hours. Soak the mushrooms separately in warm water, drain well and pat with a cloth to remove the moisture. Cut in pieces and cook with a small piece of butter, a sliced clove of garlic and salt and pepper. Put the bread through a sieve or food mill, add the mushrooms and butter and three ounces extra softened butter and the flour. Knead well and make into cylinders about ¾ inch long. Cook in boiling salted water, removing with a slotted spoon as they rise to the surface. Serve with melted butter and freshly chopped parsley. Serve grated parmesan separately.

DUMPLINGS   **222**

1 lb. stale bread	3 oz. flour
4 eggs	1 onion
2 oz. butter	6 oz. milk
parsley	salt

Another dish from the Alto Adige (called Fastenknodel in German), which was served during the Lenten fast. Cube the bread. Brown the chopped onion lightly in the butter and pour over the bread in a bowl. Add the eggs beaten with the milk and some finely chopped parsley. Soak for about one hour, then transfer to a pastry board. Work with enough flour to make a fairly firm dough and form into dumplings slightly larger than a ping-pong ball. Leave to rest a little, then drop into gently boiling water and remove from the water with a slotted spoon as they rise to the surface. Serve with sauerkraut or meat, or in a vegetable soup (in which case you can cook them in a vegetable stock).

Variation Fry the bread in butter before soaking.

PASTINA WITH EGG **223**

10 oz. pastina (peperini,
farfalline, etc.)
salt and pepper

54 oz. milk
4 eggs
4 oz. grated parmesan

Cook the pastina very slowly in the milk so all the liquid is gradually absorbed. Beat the eggs with salt and pepper and grated cheese. Pour over the pastina and hot milk, stir so they blend well and serve.

PASTA WITH PUREED ARTICHOKES **224**

1 lb. short pasta (ditalini or
farfalline, etc.)
6 egg yolks
4 oz. grated parmesan
salt and pepper
4 oz. butter

10 or 12 globe artichokes (use
only small young ones)
½ onion
parsley
(cream)

Trim and cook the artichokes, remove the hearts and put them through a food mill (you should have about 12 ounces puree). Heat the butter and cook the finely sliced onion, season with salt and pepper, add the puree and the beaten egg yolks and some chopped parsley. Stir well; the sauce should be quite liquid, so add a few tablespoons of warm water as necessary. Serve with the hot pasta and grated parmesan.

Variation Add a few tablespoons cream for an even more delicate sauce.

PASTA WITH PUREED ASPARAGUS **225**

1 lb. short pasta
4 egg yolks
4 oz. grated parmesan
salt and pepper

10 oz. cooked asparagus tips
4 oz. butter
½ onion

Similar to the previous recipe, except that you do not need to put the asparagus through a food mill. Cook them gently in butter until soft, add the chopped onion, egg yolks and parmesan; stir well, season with salt and pepper and serve with the hot pasta. Reserve a few asparagus tips to garnish the pasta before serving.

COLD PASTINA, ARTICHOKES AND EGGS

10 oz. pastina (peperini,
farfalline, etc.)
12 oz. olive oil
lemon juice
salt and pepper

6 globe artichokes
2 hard-boiled eggs
2 egg yolks
(½ tablespoon tomato puree)

Cook the artichokes, remove the hearts and slice finely. Thinly slice the hard-boiled eggs. Make a mayonnaise with the egg yolks, a few drops of lemon juice and the olive oil. Add more lemon juice and oil if necessary to get the desired consistency of mayonnaise. Cook the pasta, drain thoroughly and put in a serving dish. Add the artichokes, eggs and the mayonnaise, sprinkle with pepper, mix well and serve cold.

Variation Add a tomato sauce made with a little oil and the tomato puree diluted with one teaspoon water.

TUBETTI WITH EGGS AND CHEESE

1 lb. tubetti
4 oz. grated parmesan
parsley

5 egg yolks
salt and pepper

Cook the pasta, drain well and put in a very hot serving dish; add the beaten egg yolks and cheese, mix quickly together and serve with freshly gound black pepper and a handful of chopped parsley.

MACCHERONCINI WITH FRIED EGGS

1 lb. maccheroncini
6 oz. butter
salt and pepper

6 eggs
4 oz. grated parmesan

Cook the maccheroncini, drain well and add half the butter, the parmesan and some pepper. Fry the eggs in the rest of the butter. Put the pasta into individual dishes, top with a fried egg and a little of the butter from the pan.

COLD PASTINA, ARTICHOKES AND EGGS **229**

10 oz. pastina (peperini,
farfalline, etc.)
12 oz. olive oil
lemon juice
salt and pepper

6 globe artichokes
2 hard-boiled eggs
2 egg yolks
(½ tablespoon tomato puree)

Cook the artichokes, remove the hearts and slice finely. Thinly slice the hard-boiled eggs. Make a mayonnaise with the egg yolks, a few drops of lemon juice and the olive oil. Add more lemon juice and oil if necessary to get the desired consistency of mayonnaise. Cook the pasta, drain thoroughly and put in a serving dish. Add the artichokes, eggs and the mayonnaise, sprinkle with pepper, mix well and serve cold.

Variation Add a tomato sauce made with a little oil and the tomato puree
diluted with one teaspoon water.

TUBETTI WITH EGGS AND CHEESE **230**

1 lb. tubetti
4 oz. grated parmesan
parsley

5 egg yolks
salt and pepper

Cook the pasta, drain well and put in a very hot serving dish; add the beaten egg yolks and cheese, mix quickly together and serve with freshly gound black pepper and a handful of chopped parsley.

MACCHERONCINI WITH FRIED EGGS **231**

1 lb. maccheroncini
6 oz. butter
salt and pepper

6 eggs
4 oz. grated parmesan

Cook the maccheroncini, drain well and add half the butter, the parmesan and some pepper. Fry the eggs in the rest of the butter. Put the pasta into individual dishes, top with a fried egg and a little of the butter from the pan.

1 lb. pasta
2 hard-boiled egg yolks
1 lb. tomatoes
6 tablespoons olive oil

1 very large aubergine/eggplant or
2 medium ones
12 shelled walnuts, ground
salt and pepper

Roast the aubergine/eggplant in the oven until the skin is black. Remove the softened flesh and work in a bowl with the two egg yolks. Add a little salt and pepper and the nuts. Make a sauce with oil and the pureed tomatoes, add the nut and aubergine/eggplant mixture. Season with salt and pepper and cook for a few minutes until slightly thickened, then serve with the hot pasta.

SPAGHETTI WITH WALNUTS AND EGGS **233**

1 lb. spaghetti
3 oz. butter
3 oz. grated parmesan
salt

4 egg yolks
12 shelled walnuts, ground
(cream)

Work the butter and egg yolks together. Add the parmesan, nuts and a few tablespoons of the water in which the spaghetti is cooking. Mix well and serve with the hot pasta.

Variation Six ounces thin cream added to the sauce instead of water gives it a very pleasant, delicate flavour.

TUBETTINI WITH PARMESAN AND EGGS **234**

1 lb. tubettini
3 eggs
3 oz. grated parmesan

2 onions
3 oz. butter
salt and pepper

Melt the butter in a large pan over low heat. Cook the chopped onion until transparent, but without browning. Season with salt and pepper. Add the beaten eggs, stir well and remove from the heat. Cook the pasta, drain and add to the pan with the grated parmesan. Stir well and serve.

RIGATONI WITH EGGS AND CREAM 235

1 lb. rigatoni	3 oz. butter
10 oz. thick cream	3 egg yolks
3 oz. grated parmesan	salt and pepper

Melt the butter over low heat, add the cream and egg yolks mixed with the salt and the grated cheese. Cook the rigatoni, drain well and serve with the sauce and freshly ground black pepper.

MACCHERONCINI WITH RICOTTA AND SPINACH 236

1 lb. maccheroncini	3 oz. butter
10 oz. ricotta	3 egg yolks
10 oz. spinach	milk
salt and pepper	

Melt the butter in a large pan. Add the ricotta and some salt and pepper and cook gently over low heat to melt. If the mixture seems too dry to make a good sauce, add a little milk. Remove from the heat, add the egg yolks and mix well. Boil the spinach in very little water just long enough for it to become limp, drain well and chop finely. Cook the pasta, drain well and add to the spinach in the pan, stir together for a minute over the heat and then serve with the ricotta sauce.

TAGLIATELLE WITH EGGS AND WHISKY 237

1 lb. flour	4 eggs
3 egg yolks	3 apples
6 tablespoons butter	2 oz. raisins
16 oz. thick cream	6 tablespoons whisky
salt	

Make the tagliatelle with the flour, four eggs and a pinch of salt (see recipe 181). Peel and dice the apples, cook in one tablespoon butter together with the raisins soaked in whisky. When the apple begins to brown, add the cream, mix well, add three egg yolks and stir to blend. Cook the tagliatelle, drain and put in a pan with a little butter and the rest of the whisky. Cook until it evaporates a little, add the sauce, stir gently and serve.

1 lb. tubettini	18 oz. milk
2 eggs	½ lb. grated gruyere
2 oz. butter	salt and pepper
breadcrumbs	(parmesan)

Beat the eggs with the milk and pour into a greased ovenproof dish. Add the hot tubettini, grated gruyere and some salt and pepper. Sprinkle with bread-crumbs, dot with butter and brown for just a few minutes in a hot oven.

Variation Use half gruyere and half parmesan.

MACCHERONCINI WITH CHEESE AND EGGS **239**

1 lb. maccheroncini	3 oz. butter
3 oz. grated parmesan	2 eggs
6 oz. milk	nutmeg
salt and pepper	(fontina, gruyere, caciocavallo)

Cook the pasta and drain well. Add the butter and grated cheese, a little pepper and a pinch of nutmeg. Put in a greased ovenproof dish, pour over the eggs beaten with the milk and bake in a hot oven until well browned.

Variation Use a mixture of grated cheeses such as parmesan and gruyere, caciocavallo or fontina, or any of these on their own.

BUCATINI WITH POACHED EGGS **240**

1 lb. bucatini	5 oz. butter
4 oz. grated parmesan	4 oz. mozzarella
9 oz. milk	6 eggs
salt and pepper	

Break the bucatini into fairly small pieces and cook only until a little firmer than al dente. Drain and mix with three ounces melted butter and three ounces parmesan and put in a greased ovenproof dish. Sprinkle with pepper, add the thinly sliced mozzarella and a little parmesan. Pour over the milk and bake for about 15 minutes at 375 °F. Meanwhile prepare the poached eggs; break them carefully into boiling water and remove when cooked with a slotted spoon. Arrange in a circle on the pasta, pour over more melted butter and serve so each person has a helping of egg and pasta.

1 lb. flour	4 eggs
4 egg yolks	7 oz. butter
3 oz. grated gruyere	18 oz. milk
6 oz. thick cream	onion
salt and pepper	breadcrumbs

A recipe from France with a richly blended sauce. Make the tagliatelle in the usual way with one pound flour, four eggs and a pinch of salt (see recipe 181). Make a bechamel with four tablespoons butter, four tablespoons flour and about 18 ounces milk. Add half the finely chopped onion and season with salt and pepper. Add the cream and more softened butter to make a good rich cream sauce. Cook the tagliatelle in boiling, salted water, drain and put in a greased ovenproof dish. Toss with the beaten egg yolks and the grated gruyere; dot with butter, sprinkle with breadcrumbs and brown for a few minutes in a hot oven. Serve the cream sauce separately.

TAGLIATELLE SOUFFLE **242**

¾ lb. flour	6 eggs
3 egg whites	3 oz. butter
9 oz. milk	salt and pepper
2 oz. grated parmesan	(margarine, gruyere)
nutmeg	

Make the taligatelle with ten ounces flour, three eggs and a pinch of salt (see recipe 181). Set aside to dry a little. Melt the butter, stir in the flour and cook for two minutes. Add the warm milk and stir well until the sauce is thick and creamy. Remove from the heat and stir in the grated cheese. Cool a little then add the yolks of three eggs and mix well. Cook the tagliatelle until rather firmer than al dente and add to the sauce mixture. Cool a little then carefully fold in the six firmly beaten egg whites. Put in a greased souffle dish, leaving about ¼ inch at the top for the souffle to rise. Cook in a moderate oven for about ½ hour until the top has risen and is golden brown.

Variations 1. Use margarine instead of butter.
2. Use gruyere instead of parmesan.

PASTA AND VEGETABLE PIE

10 oz. macaroni	2 aubergines/eggplant
½ lb. tomatoes	or ½ lb. shelled peas
1 clove garlic	olive oil
2 oz. grated parmesan	basil
½ lb. flour	7 oz. butter
salt and pepper	1 egg

Make the pastry: put the flour in a mound on a pastry board and rub in three ounces softened butter, the egg and a pinch of salt until you have a crumbly dough. Gradually add about one tablespoon warm water to make the dough hold together, although it does not have to be smooth like a pasta dough. Wrap in a cloth or a piece of plastic wrap and set aside to rest for about one hour in a cool place so it loses some of its elasticity. Roll out about ¼ inch thick on a floured board. Cut two circles, one to line a pie dish and the other for a top crust. Butter a deep pie dish, line it with the larger circle of pastry so it comes up the sides. Cover with greaseproof or waxed paper weighted with dried beans or peas to prevent the pastry from bubbling. Put the other circle of pastry on a greased baking sheet and bake them both at 375 °F. until firm, but not brown (about ten minutes). Cool, then very carefully remove the pastry from the pie dish and baking sheet and keep on one side. Cook the pasta. Make the sauce: heat four tablespoons olive oil in a pan with a crushed clove of garlic (to be discarded). Add the pureed tomatoes and season with salt and pepper. Prepare the aubergines/eggplant: peel, slice and leave to drain sprinkled with coarse salt under a lightly weighted plate, then fry in hot, salted oil. If using peas, cook them very quickly until just tender; toss with butter, the tomato sauce and a few basil leaves and mix in the hot pasta. Put half this mixture in the bottom pastry crust, cover with a layer of fried aubergine/eggplant, then add the rest of the pasta and cover with the pastry lid. Bake at 400 °F. for about ten minutes. You can put as many layers of pasta and vegetable as you want, depending on the size of the pastry case.

TAGLIATELLE PIE

2 lb. flour	6 eggs
4 egg yolks	18 oz. milk
4 oz. lard or vegetable shortening	7 oz. butter
salt and pepper	grated parmesan

Make the tagliatelle with one pound flour, four eggs and a pinch of salt (see recipe 181). Put the rest of the flour minus three tablespoons on a pastry board, make a well in the middle and mix in the three egg yolks, the shortening cut in pieces and a pinch of salt. Work gently with a little warm water if necessary to obtain a soft, crumbly dough. Roll out and cut into one large circle to line the bottom of a deep pie dish and one smaller one for the top crust. Make a bechamel sauce with two ounces butter, three tablespoons flour and the milk. Cook the tagliatelle in boiling, salted water, drain, then toss with butter and two beaten eggs. Add pepper, grated parmesan and the bechamel. Grease the pie dish and line with the larger pastry circle so it goes up the edges, then put in the tagliatelle mixture and cover with the top crust, pressing the edges together firmly. Brush with beaten egg yolk and bake at 375 °F. until the pastry is firm and golden, about thirty minutes.

Variation You can use butter instead of lard to make the pastry, but the flavour won't be as good.

PASTICCIO OF MACARONI—I   **245**

¾ lb. macaroni
3 hard-boiled eggs
7 oz. provolone cheese
1 lb. flour
4 oz. lard
or vegetable shortening

72 oz. milk
7 egg yolks
4 oz. grated parmesan
salt and pepper
(raisins, pine nuts,
scamorza cheeze, mozzarella)

Make the pastry as in the previous recipe with the flour, shortening, three egg yolks and a pinch of salt and line the pie dish with the pastry in the same way. Cook the macaroni until half done, drain well and finish cooking in the milk. Do not drain, and remove from the heat still well covered with the milk. Add three egg yolks, pepper, salt and most of the parmesan and mix well. Put a layer of this macaroni and egg mixture in the pastry case, then a layer of provolone and sliced hard-boiled eggs and sprinkle with parmesan. Continue filling the pie in this way, ending with a layer of macaroni. Cover with the top crust, press the edges together, brush with beaten egg yolk and bake until firm and golden at 350 °F. for about 40 minutes.

Variations 1. Put a few handfuls of raisins and pine nuts between the layers of macaroni.
2. Use scamorza cheese or mozzarella instead of provolone.
3. Use water instead of egg yolks to make the pastry. It is then more a shortcrust pastry.

1 lb. macaroni	72 oz. milk
3 oz. white truffle	3 oz. mushrooms
2 aubergines/eggplant	4 oz. grated parmesan
8 shelled walnuts	¾ lb. flour
6 oz. lard	3 oz. sugar
or vegetable shortening	4 egg yolks
2 oz. butter	olive oil
nutmeg	salt and pepper

Make the pastry: put the flour on a pastry board, make a well in the middle and put in the shortening cut in small pieces, the sugar, three egg yolks and a pinch of salt. Work as little as possible to incorporate all the ingredients, just adding warm water as necessary so the dough is well mixed but still crumbly. Form into a ball and fold it over several times, then wrap in a cloth or plastic wrapping and leave to rest, preferably for the whole day, but a few hours will do. Prepare a bechamel with one ounce butter, one tablespoon flour, ten ounces milk, salt, pepper and nutmeg. Slice and peel the aubergines/eggplant, sprinkle with coarse salt and leave to drain under a lightly weighted plate. Fry in plenty of hot, salted oil, then chop with the mushroom and truffle, adding the ground nuts and some pepper. Half cook the macaroni, drain well and finish cooking it in the milk. Drain to remove any remaining milk when the macaroni is al dente. Grease a pie dish and line it with a large circle cut from the pastry (see preceding recipes). Fill with layers of macaroni, then a mixture of truffle, mushrooms, aubergines/eggplant and walnuts, a little grated parmesan, the bechamel and small pieces of butter. Finish with a layer of macaroni, cover with the remaining pastry and press the edges of the top and bottom crust well together. Brush with beaten egg yolk and bake at 350°F. until firm and golden or about 40 minutes.

Variations 1. Use butter instead of lard to make the pastry.
2. Eliminate the sugar.

1 lb. pasta	5 oz. butter
6 oz. grated parmesan	3 eggs
parsley	(tomatoes, olive oil)
salt and pepper	

This Neapolitan dish is a sumptuous way of using up cooked pasta leftovers. If you have no leftovers, cook one pound macaroni or spaghetti and drain well. Toss whatever pasta you are using in four ounces butter and four ounces parmesan and leave to cool. Beat the eggs and then coat the pasta very gently with the egg, more parmesan, a handful of chopped parsley and a little pepper, using two forks. Heat one tablespoon butter in a heavy frying pan (cast iron is best), add the pasta and form into a round pancake. Tip the pan as the pasta cooks so the heat is evenly distributed and add more butter so it never dries out completely. When the underneath is brown slide the pancake gently onto a wide plate and then return to the pan uncooked side down after adding another ½ ounce of butter (too much butter put in at the beginning makes the pasta rather oily). Cook in the same way and then serve warm or cold.

Variations 1. Mix tomato or any other sauce with the pasta before frying it.
2. Use a little olive oil to fry the pasta instead of butter.

SMALL PASTA PANCAKES **248**

1 lb. thin pasta	5 oz. butter
4 oz. grated parmesan	3 eggs
4 oz. black olives	(nutmeg, chicken stock)
salt and pepper	

A similar recipe to the previous one, but the pasta is divided into smaller pancakes and served in a different way. Use pasta leftovers or cook some fresh pasta. Toss with three ounces butter and the grated parmesan. Add the eggs, the seeded, chopped olives and season with salt and pepper. Form into small pancakes and cook them gently in butter.

Variations 1. Add a little nutmeg to the sauce.
2. Cook the pasta in chicken stock.

1 lb. macaroni
1 tablespoon flour
5 egg yolks
2 oz. grated gruyere
olive oil

60 oz. milk
2 oz. butter
2 oz. grated parmesan
breadcrumbs

Half cook the macaroni, drain and finish cooking in 48 oz. milk. When cooked, drain by tipping the pan to remove any remaining milk. Cool the pasta and chop it in small pieces. Add one tablespoon flour to two ounces butter and slowly add the remaining 12 ounces milk. Stir as the mixture thickens. Remove from the heat, add the chopped macaroni, three egg yolks, the parmesan, gruyere and pepper and mix well. Pour onto a marble slab or pastry board and divide into large croquettes. Dip these in beaten egg yolk and then breadcrumbs. Fry until golden in hot oil.

RAVIOLI WITH RICOTTA **250**

1 lb. flour
½ lb. ricotta
4 oz. butter
salt and pepper

6 eggs
6 oz. grated parmesan
sage
(olive oil, nutmeg, cinnamon)

This recipe can be varied to suit other ingredients. Ravioli are of course a round or square sort of stuffed pasta. Make the pasta dough as for tagliatelle, but it should be a little firmer; mix one pound flour with three eggs and a pinch of salt and only a very little warm water (see recipe 181). Leave the dough to rest, covered with a cloth or wrapped in plastic film. Sieve the ricotta to make the stuffing, add two beaten eggs, two ounces parmesan, salt and pepper, and mix well to form a smooth paste. Divide the dough for the ravioli and roll out into two equal sheets. Brush one sheet with egg beaten with water, then place equal sized mounds of the stuffing at regular intervals on the dough, about 1½-2 inches apart. Cover with the second sheet of dough and press this down between the stuffing to make the two layers of pasta dough stick together. Use a pastry wheel to divide these mounds into squares of ravioli. Cook them in boiling salted water. As they rise to the surface remove with a slotted spoon and put in a hot serving dish. Pour a little melted butter (heated until golden with a few sage leaves) over the first layer of ravioli and sprinkle with parmesan. Continue in this way until all the ravioli are used up, then leave to stand two or three minutes before serving.

Variations 1. Roman cooks add one teaspoon oil to the pasta dough.
2. In Emilia a pinch of nutmeg or cinnamon is added to the ricotta filling. The pasta dough is made with one egg for every three ounces flour.

RAVIOLI WITH RICOTTA AND CHEESE 251

1 lb. flour
½ lb. ricotta
4 oz. butter
salt and pepper

6 eggs
3 oz. soft cheese (caciotta)
4 oz. grated parmesan

Make the pasta dough with the flour, three eggs and a pinch of salt, adding more water as necessary (see recipe 181). Make the stuffing: sieve the ricotta, mix with the chopped soft cheese, two beaten eggs and salt and pepper. Roll the pasta dough into two equal sheets and brush one with beaten egg and water. Place equal sized mounds of the filling at regular intervals on the dough 1½-2 inches apart, and then cover with the second sheet of dough, as in the previous recipe. Cut out the ravioli with the pastry wheel and cook them in boiling salted water. Remove them with a slotted spoons as they float to the surface and put in a serving dish with melted butter and grated parmesan. Leave to stand for two or three minutes before serving.

RAVIOLI WITH SPINACH 252

1 lb. flour
1¾ lb. spinach
3 egg yolks
6 tablespoons cream

4 eggs
4 oz. butter
5 oz. grated parmesan
salt and pepper

Make the ravioli dough with the flour, three eggs, salt and a little water (see recipe 181) so it is firmer than a tagliatelle dough. Cook the spinach and drain very thoroughly, squeezing out extra moisture with your hands. Put it through a food mill and mix with ½ ounce butter. Sieve the ricotta and mix with the spinach puree, add half the grated parmesan, the beaten egg yolks and salt and pepper. Roll out the pasta into two sheets as in recipe 250 and make ravioli in the usual way with the spinach and ricotta filling. Cook in boiling, salted water. Melt the butter and scald the cream. As the ravioli rise to the surface remove them with a slotted spoon and put in a dish in layers with melted butter, hot cream and grated parmesan.

Variation Finely chop the spinach instead of putting it through a food mill: or puree one half and chop the rest.

RAVIOLI WITH RAISINS   **253**

1 lb. flour	6 eggs
9 oz. ricotta	3 oz. raisins
2 tablespoons breadcrumbs	salt
nutmeg	4 oz. butter
parsley	4 oz. grated parmesan

Make the ravioli dough as in preceding recipes with the flour, three eggs, a pinch of salt and as much water as necessary. Make the filling with the sieved ricotta, the raisins (soaked in warm water then diced or chopped), the breadcrumbs, two beaten eggs, the salt, nutmeg and a handful of chopped parsley. Roll out the pasta dough and make the ravoili with this filling in the usual way (see recipe 250). Cook the ravioli and serve with melted butter and grated parmesan.

TORTELLI WITH RICOTTA   **254**

1 lb. flour	6 eggs
10 oz. ricotta	5 oz. grated parmesan
4 oz. butter	nutmeg
parsley	(garlic, tomato)
salt and pepper	

These tortelli are very similar to the ravioli in the preceding recipe, but the filling differs slightly. Make a fairly firm dough (see recipe 181) and set aside to rest. Make the filling: sieve the ricotta, add half the parmesan, two eggs, plenty of chopped parsley, salt, pepper and nutmeg. Roll the dough out quite thinly and cut into little circles about 2½-3 inches in diameter. Place a mound of filling in the middle of each circle, fold them over and press the edges together gently. Remember to keep the pasta covered with a cloth while you are working so it does not dry out. Cook the tortelli in boiling water and remove with a slotted spoon as they rise to the surface. Put them in a heated serving dish with melted butter and grated parmesan.

Variations 1. In certain parts of Emilia a little finely chopped garlic is added to the stuffing.
2. The tortelli are sometimes served with tomato sauce.

1 lb. flour
1¾ lb. spinach
5 oz. grated parmesan
salt and pepper

5 eggs
9 oz. ricotta
4 oz. butter
nutmeg

Make the pasta dough with the flour, three eggs, a pinch of salt and some warm water (see recipe 181). Prepare the filling: cook the spinach and drain very well, squeezing out excess moisture with your hands. Put through a food mill, then mix with the ricotta, half the parmesan, two beaten eggs, nutmeg, salt and pepper. Roll out the dough and cut into circles 2½ inches in diameter, and put a mound of the filling on each circle as in the previous recipe. Cook these tortelli until they float to the surface, remove with a slotted spoon and serve with melted butter and grated parmesan. For tortelloni: cut the pasta circles a bit larger (3½ inches). In Parma these are called maltagliati, and are square instead of round.

TORTELLI WITH PUMPKIN **256**

10 oz. flour
5 lb. pumpkin
½ lb. grated parmesan
salt

2 eggs
4 oz. butter
nutmeg

Choose a good firm pumpkin; a soft watery one has no flavour. Cut in slices and bake until soft, then remove the flesh and mix with the parmesan and a pinch each of salt and nutmeg. Make the pasta dough with the flour, eggs, a pinch of salt and warm water as necessary (see recipe 181). Roll out and cut into large circles about three inches in diameter. Put a little of the stuffing on each circle, fold over and press the opposite edges well together. Cook the tortelli in boiling water and serve with melted butter and parmesan.

1 lb. flour
1¾ lb. potatoes
5 oz. ricotta
salt and pepper
4 oz. butter

6 eggs
7 oz. grated parmesan
nutmeg
1 tablespoon brandy

One of the most frugal and yet delicious recipes ever, from the region between Reggio and Modena, in the Emilian Apennines. Mix the flour with four eggs, a pinch of salt and warm water to make the pasta dough (see recipe 181). Cook, peel and put the potatoes through a food mill, then mix the puree with the ricotta, two eggs, three ounces grated parmesan, salt and pepper, nutmeg and brandy. Work well until the mixture is smooth. Roll out the dough and cut into circles about 2½ inches in diameter. Put a mound of filling on each circle, fold over and press the opposite edges together well, then cook the tortelli until they rise to the surface of the water. Remove with a slotted spoon and serve with melted butter and grated parmesan.

TORTELLI WITH BEETROOT/BEETS AND POTATO **258**

1 lb. flour
1¼ lb. raw beetroot/beets
7 oz. butter
olive oil
4 oz. grated parmesan

4 eggs
½ lb. potatoes
2 tablespoons flour
milk
salt and pepper

A dish from the Cortina d'Ampezzo region. Make the filling the day before: cook the beetroot/beets and potato, put through a food mill, add a little oil, salt and pepper then fry in ½ ounce butter. Add two tablespoons flour and cook a little longer until it starts to brown. Put in the refrigerator to cool. Make the pasta dough with one pound flour, the eggs, a pinch of salt and a little warm water (see recipe 181). Cut into circles about two inches in diameter and put a little of the filling on each circle. Fold over, pressing the opposite edges well together, then cook in boiling salted water. Toss with melted butter and grated cheese. If you can obtain stagionato cheese from the Ampezzo area this gives a more authentic flavour than the parmesan.

1 lb. semolina flour
7 oz. ricotta
1 onion
1 lb. tomatoes
2 eggs
parsley
saffron
parmesan

2 aubergines/eggplant
2 oz. grated pecorino/romano
salt and pepper
8 shelled walnuts
basil
sage
olive oil

Make the pasta dough without eggs, but just with a pinch of salt dissolved in a little warm water and add more warm water as necessary. Chop the peeled aubergines/eggplant and leave to drain sprinkled with coarse salt under a lightly weighted plate. Fry the aubergines/eggplant and chopped onion and mix with the ricotta and grated pecorino/romano, the ground nuts, chopped parsley, sage and basil and the beaten eggs. Season with salt and pepper. Roll out the dough and brush the bottom sheet with beaten egg. Put mounds of the filling at regular intervals 1½-2 inches apart and place the second sheet of dough on top. Press down the dough between the filling and cut into little squares, as for ravioli, with a pastry wheel. Set aside to dry for 40 minutes, then cook in boiling salted water. Put in layers in a serving dish with a sauce of pureed tomatoes cooked with a little oil and garlic, and sprinkle with grated parmesan.

1 lb. flour
5 lb. pumpkin
7 oz. grated parmesan
nutmeg

6 eggs
4 oz. butter
breadcrumbs
salt

These are a form of tortelli from Ferrara. Make the pasta dough with the flour, four eggs, a pinch of salt and warm water as necessary (see recipe 181). Roll out not too thinly and cut into strips three inches wide, then divide these into squares. Make the filling: slice the pumpkin and bake in the oven on a baking sheet. When the flesh is soft, pound and mix with two beaten eggs, two ounces grated parmesan, enough breadcrumbs to bind and a little nutmeg. Put mounds of this filling on the squares, fold over and press the edges together to make rather thick tortelli. The edges should be slightly crinkly like the brim of a hat (cappellacci means little hats). Cook in boiling salted water, put in layers in a serving dish with melted butter and parmesan.

1 lb. flour	4 eggs
3 egg yolks	7 oz. butter
6 oz. grated parmesan	2 oz. grated emmenthal cheese
6 tablespoons flour	42 oz. milk
nutmeg	salt and pepper
olive oil	(fontina cheese)

Make the pasta dough with one pound flour, four eggs, a pinch of salt and as much warm water as necessary (see recipe 181). Set aside for an hour, then roll out and cut into four inch squares and cook for just one minute in boiling, salted water with a few tablespoons olive oil (this makes the pasta easier to handle). Drain well and leave on a cloth. Make the filling: melt four ounces of butter, add six tablespoons flour and gradually add the milk, nutmeg, salt and pepper, stirring constantly to obtain a smooth bechamel sauce. Reserve a little less than half this sauce and return the rest to the heat. Stir in two ounces each of grated parmesan and emmenthal and one tablespoon butter. Remove from the heat and add the lightly beaten egg yolks. Distribute this filling between the squares of pasta. Roll them up to make cannelloni and press the ends together gently so the stuffing does not come out. Arrange in a greased ovenproof dish, not too closely packed, cover with the remaining bechamel sauce, sprinkle with grated parmesan, dot with butter and brown in a hot oven.

Variation Use fontina cheese instead of emmenthal.

PANCAKES WITH CHEESE—I **262**

4 oz. flour	7 oz. ricotta
6 eggs	2 oz. grated parmesan
6 oz. milk	4 oz. mozzarella
olive oil	10 oz. tomatoes
2 tablespoons butter	parsley
salt and pepper	

Make a fairly thin batter with the flour, milk and eggs, add the grated cheese and some salt and pepper. Heat a little oil in a heavy pan and use two tablespoons batter to make quite soft, large pancakes. Drain on absorbent paper and reserve. Make the filling; sieve the ricotta and mix with the chopped mozzarella, chopped parsley and enough parmesan to bind. Divide the stuffing between the pancakes, roll them up and arrange in a greased ovenproof dish so they do not overlap; pour over tomato sauce made with the pureed tomatoes and oil (see recipe 15) and heat for about 15 minutes at 400 °F.

4 oz. flour	8 eggs
6 oz. milk	3 oz. butter
7 oz. mozzarella	1 lb. tomatoes
olive oil	1 onion
salt and pepper	oregano
basil	

Make a batter with the flour, milk and lightly beaten eggs, add three ounces melted butter and set aside for one hour. Fry the pancakes using two tablespoons batter for each one; tip the pan well so they are quite thin. Drain on absorbent paper and put a large thin slice of mozzarella on each pancake. Roll them up and arrange in a greased ovenproof dish so they do not overlap Make a sauce with the pureed tomatoes, one chopped onion and salt and pepper and basil, pour over the crespelle or pancakes, sprinkle with a little oregano and brown for 10-15 minutes in a hot oven.

PANCAKES WITH CHEESE AND SWISS CHARD **264**

¾ lb. flour	3 eggs
4 egg yolks	54 oz. milk
10 oz. ricotta	3 oz. Swiss chard
3 oz. grated parmesan	5 oz. butter
salt	nutmeg

A Tuscan recipe: the Swiss chard gives it a very special flavour, but you can use spinach instead. Make a smooth batter with the egg yolks, one whole egg, a pinch salt and about ten ounces milk. Use two tablespoons of the batter at a time to make thin pancakes, then leave them to cool. Make the filling: cook the Swiss chard or spinach, drain well and put through a food mill. Mix with the ricotta, the parmesan, two whole eggs, the nutmeg and the salt. Spread this filling no more than ½ inch thick on each pancake so it does not come right to the edges, then roll up into cannelloni. Arrange them close together but not overlapping in a greased ovenproof dish. Cover with a bechamel sauce made from four ounces butter, three ounces flour and 44 ounces milk. Brown for a few minutes at 400°F.

1 lb. flour	5 eggs
10 oz. ricotta	parsley
olive oil	salt

Make the pasta dough with the flour and three eggs in the normal way (see recipe 181). Cut it into four inch squares. Spread the squares with a filling made with the sieved ricotta, two beaten eggs, salt and chopped parsley. Fold the pasta in half to make large ravioli, then fry them in plenty of hot oil.

IV
PASTA WITH FISH

PASTA WITH ANCHOVIES

1 lb. pasta
6 tablespoons olive oil
salt and pepper

8 salt-cured anchovy fillets
parsley

This is one of the simplest and most delicious ways of serving pasta. Wash the anchovy fillets to remove the salt, chop roughly and cook in the olive oil over low heat until soft, then add plenty of coarsely chopped parsley. Serve with the hot pasta and plenty of freshly ground pepper.

Variation Sprinkle chopped parsley on each individual serving.

VERMICELLI OR BUCATINI WITH BREADCRUMBS

1 lb. vermicelli or bucatini
3 oz. or 2 slices
stale white bread

6 tablespoons olive oil
6 salt-cured anchovy fillets

A recipe with Greek origins. Wash the anchovies well to remove the salt, chop roughly and cook over very low heat with half the oil until quite soft. Cook the pasta and when it is almost ready lightly brown the crumbled crustless bread in the remaining oil in another pan. Have the pasta and the breadcrumbs ready at the same time. Drain the pasta well, put in a hot serving dish and pour over the breadcrumbs, anchovies and oil. Serve with plenty of freshly ground pepper.

LINGUINE OR VERMICELLI WITH GARLIC, OIL AND ANCHOVIES

1 lb. linguine or vermicelli
2 cloves garlic
parsley

6 salt-cured anchovy fillets
6 tablespoons olive oil
salt and pepper

Similar to the classic aglio e olio (garlic and oil) recipe, but the anchovy alters the dominant flavour of the garlic. Heat the oil and lightly brown the garlic over medium heat, then discard the garlic. Wash the anchovies to remove the salt, chop finely and cook in the oil until soft, adding pepper and a good handful of chopped parsley. Cook the pasta and drain it, leaving a little water on it to dilute the anchovy sauce, as this gives an even better flavour.

Variation Cook the sauce in a large pan and add the hot pasta so they cook together for a minute before serving.

FRIED PASTA WITH ANCHOVIES

1 lb. pasta
(preferably a thin variety)
2 cloves garlic
salt and pepper

6 salt-cured anchovy fillets
4 tablespoons olive oil
parsley

Heat the oil in a large, heavy pan and add the crushed cloves of garlic. Cook until lightly browned, then remove the garlic and add the roughly chopped and washed anchovy fillets. Cook until soft and add a handful of parsley and some pepper. Cook the pasta so that it is still firm in plenty of lightly salted boiling water. Drain well, pour into the frying pan and toss with the sauce. Shape the pasta into a flat pancake with a fork. Cook until brown underneath, then turn it over and brown the other side. It should be crisp and brown on the outside and soft inside.

PASTA WITH ANCHOVY AND GARLIC

1 lb. pasta
6 salt-cured anchovy fillets
3 oz. or 2 slices stale bread
hot chili pepper

6 tablespoons olive oil
2 cloves garlic
parsley
salt

This is a pasta and breadcrumb mixture with a difference. Brown the crushed garlic in four tablespoons olive oil, remove from the pan and add the well-washed, chopped anchovy fillets. Cook until soft, then add the crumbled, crustless bread and brown for a minute in the remaining oil. Add a piece of hot chili pepper (remove before serving) and a good handful of coarsely chopped parsley. Serve with hot pasta.

VERMICELLI WITH OIL, GARLIC AND ANCHOVY

1 lb. vermicelli
6 salt-cured anchovy fillets
4 oz. or 3 slices stale bread
hot chili pepper

6 tablespoons olive oil
2 cloves garlic
parsley
salt

This is a frugal but richly flavoured dish. Heat the oil and brown two crushed cloves of garlic. Remove from the pan and add the diced or chopped bread. Brown lightly and add the anchovy fillets, which you have washed to remove the salt and chopped roughly. Cook until soft. The bread absorbs the flavour from the anchovy and this is the key to the dish. Add a piece of hot chili pepper (discard before serving) and plenty of chopped parsley. Serve with the hot pasta.

BIGOLI WITH ANCHOVIES AND ONION $\qquad$ **272**

1 lb. bigoli
3 medium onions
salt and pepper

6 tablespoons olive oil
6 salt-cured anchovy fillets

You may use any sort of pasta instead of the famous bigoli, which are a pasta made from whole wheat flour in the Veneto; linguine do very well. Heat half the oil and cook the sliced onion until lightly browned, then add a few tablespoons warm water and continue cooking gently until the onion softens. Keep the pan covered, stirring the onion from time to time to prevent it from sticking. When almost cooked add the washed and roughly chopped anchovy fillets; cook until soft, then add the remaining oil. Stir well and serve with the hot pasta and a little pepper freshly ground over each serving.

SPAGHETTI WITH TOMATOES AND ANCHOVIES $\qquad$ **273**

1 lb. spaghetti
6 tablespoons olive oil
2 cloves garlic
parsley
salt

1 lb. tomatoes
6 salt-cured anchovy fillets
1 hot chili pepper
(pepper, capers)

The tomatoes give a quite different flavour to the anchovy sauce. Brown the crushed clove of garlic in the oil, then discard; add the washed and chopped anchovy fillets. Choose small plum tomatoes, peel and chop them. Add to the pan with the hot chili pepper, broken in pieces (remember to discard it before serving), and finally a good handful of chopped parsley. Serve with the hot pasta.

Variations 1. Put the potatoes in before the anchovies to obtain a milder flavoured sauce.
2. Use pureed tomatoes or tinned/canned peeled tomatoes instead of fresh.
3. Add freshly ground pepper.
4. Add a heaped tablespoon of capers to the sauce, but wash them first to remove the salt.

1 lb. vermicelli
6 salt-cured anchovy fillets
2 cloves garlic
1 heaped tablespoon capers
parsley

1 lb. tomatoes
6 tablespoons olive oil
3 oz. black olives
1 hot chili pepper
oregano

A recipe from Ischia. Heat the oil with the chopped or crushed garlic (to be discarded). When it browns add the chopped, peeled and seeded tomatoes. Cook for a few minutes and add a chopped hot chili pepper (to be discarded), and the capers. Add the seeded olives, whole or chopped as you prefer. Cook for a few minutes so the sauce thickens and add the washed and chopped anchovy fillets. Let these soften a little, add a good handful of chopped parsley and serve with the hot pasta.

Variations 1. Add the anchovies to the pan before the tomatoes to obtain a milder flavour.
2. Use a little concentrated tomato puree diluted with warm water instead of fresh tomatoes.

1 lb. pasta
8 salt-cured fillets of anchovy
3 oz. or 2 slices stale bread
parsley
2½ lb. tomatoes

6 tablespoons olive oil
2 cloves garlic
salt and pepper
(onion, celery, hot chili pepper)

A grand combination of many flavours: heat four tablespoons oil, add the crushed garlic (to be discarded) and when it starts to brown add the washed, chopped anchovies. While they are cooking add the tomatoes (skinned, seeded and chopped). Season with pepper and plenty of chopped parsley. While it is cooking lightly brown the crumbled crustless bread in the remaining oil. Cook the pasta and toss first in the anchovy sauce, then with the breadcrumbs.

Variations 1. Omit the garlic from the sauce, adding instead half an onion, chopped or finely sliced, and a stick of chopped celery.
2. Cook a piece of hot chili pepper in the oil before the garlic and discard before serving. Omit the fresh pepper.

SPAGHETTI WITH TOMATOES, ANCHOVIES AND ONIONS
276

1 lb. spaghetti
6 salt-cured anchovy fillets
1 stick celery
4 tablespoons olive oil
parsley

2¾ lb. tomatoes
1 onion
1 carrot
2 cloves garlic
salt and pepper

Wash the anchovy fillets to remove the salt and pound to a paste in a mortar with the garlic and a good handful of chopped parsley. Heat the oil, add the anchovy paste and cook over very low heat until the sauce thickens. Remove from the heat. Meanwhile cook the skinned, chopped tomatoes and the finely chopped celery, carrot and onion in their own water with just a little salt and pepper. When soft put through a food mill and return to the heat in a clean pan. Add the anchovy sauce and cook for 15 minutes. Serve with the hot pasta.

SPAGHETTI WITH COLD ANCHOVY SAUCE **277**

1 lb. spaghetti
6 tomatoes
1 red or yellow sweet pepper
(or ½ yellow and ½ red sweet pepper)
worcestershire sauce
salt and pepper

6 salt-cured anchovy fillets
2 cloves garlic
6 tablespoons olive oil
basil
parsley

Roast the pepper under the grill, moisten your fingers and remove the skin carefully, then chop the pepper in strips. Skin the tomatoes, seed and cut in strips. Chop the garlic, parsley and basil. Wash the anchovies and pound to a paste in a mortar, then set aside in a cool place with the oil for an hour or more. Add the peppers, tomatoes, oil, parsley and basil and mix well together. Finally add one teaspoon worcestershire sauce and a pinch of pepper. Mix with the hot pasta and leave to stand at least 30 minutes before serving.

SWEET PEPPERS STUFFED WITH SPAGHETTINI

10 oz. spaghettini	6 peppers
1 large tomato	2 oz. black olives
6 salt-cured anchovy fillets	1 tablespoon capers
1 clove garlic	olive oil
oregano	parsley
salt and pepper	

Roast the peppers under the grill, moisten your fingers and carefully remove the outer skin, then remove the ribs and seeds. Brown a crushed clove of garlic in six tablespoons olive oil and discard the garlic. Add the chopped tomato and cook for ten minutes, then add the washed capers and seeded olives broken into small pieces. Cook for another few minutes, remove from the heat and mix in the washed, chopped anchovy fillets, some oregano, pepper and chopped parsley. Mix the hot pasta with this sauce, then stuff the peppers with the mixture. Cover each pepper with its own top, pack them tightly in a well-greased ovenproof dish and moisten with a little oil. Bake in a moderate oven for about 40 minutes or until the peppers are soft.

BUCATINI WITH AUBERGINES/EGGPLANT AND ANCHOVY

1 lb. bucatini	3 large aubergines/eggplant
1½ lb. tomatoes	6 salt-cured anchovy fillets
2 oz. capers	2 oz. black olives
olive oil	1 clove garlic
basil	salt and pepper

Peel the aubergines/eggplant and cut into narrow strips. Sprinkle with coarse salt and leave for a few hours under a lightly weighted plate. Wash and dry the aubergines/eggplant, fry in hot oil and set aside. Put two tablespoons of the oil in which you have fried the vegetables in a pan, add the crushed garlic (to be discarded) and the skinned, chopped tomatoes and a few basil leaves. Cook for a few minutes, add the washed capers, seeded olives and the aubergines/eggplant and season with salt and pepper. Cook over low heat for ten minutes and add the washed, chopped anchovy fillets. Cook until soft and serve with the hot pasta.

BUCATINI WITH STUFFED TOMATOES 280

1 lb. bucatini
6 tablespoons olive oil
2 oz. capers
parsley
breadcrumbs

6 large, ripe tomatoes
6 salt-cured anchovy fillets
4 cloves garlic
oregano
salt and pepper

Cut the tomatoes in half and remove the seeds and excess juice. Wash the anchovies and chop in small pieces. Wash the capers. Chop two cloves garlic and a good handful of parsley. Mix well together, adding a pinch of oregano, pepper, and enough breadcrumbs to bind. Stuff the tomatoes with the mixture, put in a greased ovenproof dish, moisten with a little olive oil and bake in a hot oven for 30 minutes or until soft and brown. Meanwhile prepare a sauce with three tablespoons olive oil and the two remaining cloves of garlic. Cook the pasta and mix with the olive and garlic sauce. Put a serving of pasta in each dish and top with a cooked stuffed tomato.

PASTA WITH CAULIFLOWER OR BROCCOLI AND ANCHOVIES 281

1 lb. long pasta
1 large cauliflower or
1¾ lb. broccoli spears
olive oil

6 salt-cured anchovy fillets
2 cloves garlic
salt
hot chili pepper

Use tender young broccoli tips, or if using cauliflower, only the florets and tender part of the stalks. Cook until tender and reserve the water. Make the usual sauce with the oil, garlic, hot chili pepper (to be discarded) and washed anchovy fillets. Cook the pasta in the vegetable water. Mix the vegetables with the hot pasta, pour over the sauce and serve immediately.

1 lb. pasta
1 onion
6 salt-cured anchovy fillets
2 oz. pine nuts
basil
saffron
salt and pepper

1 cauliflower
4 tablespoons olive oil
2 oz. raisins
1 tablespoon concentrated tomato puree
(broccoli spears, fresh tomatoes)

Cook the cauliflower in boiling, salted water and drain while still firm, using just the most tender parts. Brown the sliced onion in a little oil, add the tomato puree diluted in a little warm water. Add the cauliflower and cook altogether for a few minutes with a pinch of saffron. Wash the anchovies, cut in small pieces, and soften in a pan with the rest of the oil. Add the tomato and cauliflower sauce and the pine nuts and raisins soaked in warm water. Mix well and serve with the hot pasta and a few coarsely chopped basil leaves.

Variations 1. Use broccoli tips instead of cauliflower.
2. Use tomatoes instead of concentrated tomato puree.
3. Omit the saffron.

1 lb. short pasta such as ditalini
4 tablespoons olive oil
12 black olives
2 oz. or 1 slice stale white bread
parsley

¾ lb. broccoli spears
4 salt-cured anchovy fillets
1 tablespoon white wine
1 clove garlic
salt

According to the name of this recipe it was used by Sicilian cooks when the weather was bad (ro malu tempu) and the fisherman could not bring back fresh fish, so salt-cured anchovy fillets were used instead. Rub the bottom of the pan with the crushed clove of garlic then heat the oil with it. When the garlic browns remove from the pan and add the washed, chopped anchovies. Cook until soft and add a handful of chopped parsley, then moisten with a little white wine. Stir until the wine has been absorbed, add the broccoli spears, using only very young tips and leaves—if the flowers have opened too much the best of the flavour has gone. Lightly brown the breadcrumbs in very little oil. Seed and chop the olives. Cook the pasta so it is ready at the same time as the other ingredients, and serve with the broccoli, chopped olives and breadcrumbs.

BUCATINI WITH TURNIPS AND ANCHOVIES

1 lb. bucatini	3 white turnips
8 tablespoons olive oil	6 salt-cured anchovy fillets
parsley	salt and pepper

Wash the turnips, cook until soft and put through a food mill. Heat the oil and add the washed, chopped anchovies, cook until soft and add the turnip puree. Stir well, then serve with the hot pasta, some freshly ground pepper and a handful of chopped parsley.

MACCHERONCINI WITH SPINACH, ONION AND ANCHOVY

1 lb. maccheroncini	1 lb. spinach
4 onions	4 tablespoons olive oil
8 salt-cured anchovy fillets	(Swiss chard)
salt and pepper	

Wash and cook the spinach, then chop finely. Clean, boil and chop the onions. Wash and chop the anchovy fillets. Heat the oil, add the anchovies and when soft add the spinach and onion. Continue cooking until the sauce is thick and well blended, adding a few tablespoons of warm water if it seems too dry, then serve with the hot pasta and sprinkle with freshly ground pepper.

Variation Use Swiss chard instead of spinach.

FARFALLE WITH ASPARAGUS AND ANCHOVIES

1 lb. farfalle	6 tablespoons olive oil
1 clove garlic	4 salt-cured anchovy fillets
¾ lb. asparagus tips	hot chili pepper
salt	

Heat the oil with a crushed clove of garlic and a piece of hot chili pepper (to be discarded). When the garlic starts to brown add the washed and chopped anchovy fillets. Cook until soft, add the asparagus tips and cook until tender. Serve with the hot pasta.

MACCHERONCINI WITH GLOBE ARTICHOKES, OLIVES AND ANCHOVIES

1 lb. maccheroncini	8 tablespoons olive oil
10 young, tender globe artichokes	lemon juice
2 cloves garlic	3 oz. black olives
1 tablespoon capers	4 salt-cured anchovy fillets
parsley	salt and pepper

Clean the artichokes and cut in pieces, then leave for about an hour in cold water and lemon juice. Heat the oil with the chopped garlic and cook the washed, chopped anchovy fillets. Add the artichokes and cook for a few minutes over a high heat, then add the washed capers and seeded chopped olives. Cover the pan and cook for another 30 minutes, then add a generous handful of chopped parsley and some freshly ground pepper. Cook the pasta until still firm, drain, add to the pan with the artichokes and cook for another two minutes. If the sauce seems too dry add a little of the pasta cooking water.

PASTICCIO OF MACARONI, SWEET PEPPER AND ANCHOVY

1 lb. macaroni	2 lb. sweet peppers
10 salt-cured anchovy fillets	8 tablespoons olive oil
1 lb. tomatoes	2 oz. seeded black olives
1 tablespoon capers	basil
oregano	2 cloves garlic
breadcrumbs	salt and pepper

Roast the peppers under the grill, moisten your fingers and carefully remove the skin. Heat four tablespoons of the oil with a crushed clove of garlic (to be discarded), add the pureed tomatoes, basil, oregano and salt and pepper. Make another sauce in a pan with four tablespoons olive oil, one crushed clove of garlic and a good handful of breadcrumbs. Add the capers, olives and washed, chopped anchovies and cook until soft. Cook the macaroni until still slightly firm and mix with the tomato sauce, and then the anchovy sauce. Pour half this mixture into a greased ovenproof dish, put the peppers in the middle and moisten with a little oil. Cover with the rest of the macaroni, sprinkle with breadcrumbs, moisten with more oil and bake for 30 minutes in a moderate oven or until the peppers are soft.

Variation Line the greased ovenproof dish with a sheet of buttered greaseproof/waxed paper, put some of the peppers on it, then add some macaroni, cover with another layer of peppers, macaroni, breadcrumbs and a little more oil, and then another sheet of greaseproof/waxed paper. Bake until the peppers are done, then turn out onto a plate: the coloured peppers will be on top.

1¼ lb. vegetables in season,   1 lb. pasta
including onions, celery, artichokes,   6 tablespoons olive oil
broccoli, carrots, beetroot/beets   6 salt-cured anchovy fillets
salt and pepper   (gruyere)

Lightly cook the chopped vegetables and washed, chopped anchovies in the oil until soft. Add salt and a little pepper. Pour over the hot pasta. Mix well and serve.

Variation   Serve with grated gruyere.

SPAGHETTI WITH GRAPEVINE LEAVES AND ANCHOVIES   **290**

1 lb. spaghetti   6 young grapevine leaves
peel of 2 lemons   olive oil
4 salt-cured anchovy fillets   1 tablespoon capers
1 tablespoon pine nuts   breadcrumbs
1 tablespoon sugar   nutmeg
vinegar   salt and pepper

Use only very young grapevine leaves and remove any tough ribs. Put in a bowl with the grated lemon peel, a handful of well-drained breadcrumbs which have been soaked in vinegar, the chopped, washed anchovy fillets, pine nuts and capers, one tablespoon sugar and a little pepper. Pound in a mortar until you have a smooth paste, then thin with a little olive oil until the right consistency for a sauce. Serve with the hot pasta.

BUCATINI WITH MUSHROOMS AND ANCHOVIES   **291**

1 lb. bucatini   4 tablespoons olive oil
¾ lb. tomatoes   2 cloves garlic
3 salt-cured anchovy fillets   10 oz. fresh mushrooms
1 tablespoon Worcestershire sauce   oregano
parsley   pepper

Heat the oil with the crushed cloves of garlic (to be discarded). Add the washed, chopped anchovies and cook until soft, then add the pureed tomatoes. Stir well, then add the chopped mushrooms and cook for 20 minutes with some pepper, a pinch of oregano and the Worcestershire sauce. Add a handful of chopped parsley and a little more pepper and serve with the hot pasta, or cook them together for a couple of minutes over low heat so the pasta absorbs even more flavour.

PASTICCIO OF BUCATINI WITH ANCHOVIES AND MUSHROOMS 292

1 lb. bucatini	3 oz. fresh mushrooms
4 tablespoons olive oil	6 salt-cured anchovy fillets
2 cloves garlic	2 oz. or 2 slices stale white bread
parsley	salt and pepper

Wash and slice the mushrooms and cook gently in a little oil with a pinch of salt for about 15 minutes, adding a little water if they seem too dry. Wash the anchovy fillets cut in small pieces, then mix with the mushrooms away from the heat. Chop finely together or put in the blender. Heat four tablespoons oil with the crushed garlic and brown for a few minutes; discard the garlic and add the anchovy and mushroom mixture. Cook for a few more minutes, stirring so the sauce is thick and well blended. Cook the breadcrumbs in one tablespoon oil until brown. Have the pasta and the other ingredients ready at the same time; drain the pasta, toss with the mushroom and anchovy sauce, add chopped parsley and plenty of freshly ground pepper. Sprinkle with the breadcrumbs and brown in a hot oven.

COLD SPAGHETTI WITH ANCHOVIES 293

1 lb. spaghetti	6 tablespoons olive oil
3 cloves garlic	3 tablespoons lemon juice
12 black olives	4 anchovy fillets in oil
3 oz. button mushrooms in oil	mint
salt and pepper	(orange juice)

Heat the oil and warm the chopped garlic, but do not let it cook. Put the oil in a large serving dish with the garlic, anchovies and chopped mushrooms, lemon juice, seeded chopped olives, chopped mint and freshly ground pepper. Mix with the hot pasta and leave until cold.

Variation Use about six tablespoons orange juice instead of the lemon juice.

SPAGHETTI WITH BLACK TRUFFLES

1 lb. spaghetti	3 oz. black truffles
3 salt-cured anchovy fillets	parsley
olive oil	salt

This is probably the simplest and most ancient version of a classic Umbrian dish—really a speciality of Norcia, where the best truffles are found. You can use tinned/canned truffles, but they don't have the flavour of the fresh ones that are in season from December to February. Clean the truffles with a small brush (never wash them) and chop in small pieces. Wash and chop the anchovy, gradually adding a little oil to make a smooth sauce, then a pinch of salt. This dark glossy sauce looks wonderful served with the hot pasta and a handful of chopped parsley.

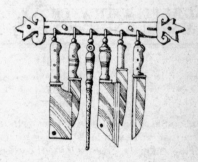

PASTA AND CHICK PEA SOUP

½ lb. avemarie (cannolicchi)	10 oz. dried chick peas
4 tablespoons olive oil	3 salt-cured anchovy fillets
2 cloves garlic	2 sprigs rosemary
salt and pepper	

Wash the chick peas and soak overnight, then cook them in a large pan (preferably an earthenware pot), with plenty of water, a sprig of rosemary, a pinch of salt and plenty of pepper. Cover the pan and cook for at least two hours. When almost cooked heat the oil with two crushed cloves of garlic and another sprig of rosemary. When the garlic is brown remove the oil from the heat and discard the garlic and rosemary. Add the washed, chopped and pounded anchovy fillets: the hot oil will soften them enough without further cooking. Add to the chick peas in the pan, mix well together, then cook the pasta with all these other ingredients in the pan, and serve when it is al dente.

LASAGNETTE RICCE WITH TOMATO AND ANCHOVY SAUCE

1 lb. lasagnette ricce
4 tablespoons olive oil
3 oz. or 2 slices stale white bread
6 salt-cured anchovy fillets

2 lb. tomatoes
½ onion
2 oz. blanched almonds
salt and pepper

Heat half the oil with the chopped onion, add the skinned, chopped tomatoes and some freshly ground pepper, and cook over moderate heat. Meanwhile, brown the diced bread in the remaining oil, remove from the heat and add the washed and pounded anchovy fillets and the chopped almonds. Mix well—the heat from the pan should dissolve the anchovies. Cook the lasagnette in lightly salted water, drain well and toss with the tomato sauce, and then the fried bread and anchovy sauce.

SPAGHETTI WITH ANCHOVY, GARLIC AND ONIONS

1 lb. spaghetti
6 salt-cured anchovy fillets
2 cloves garlic
parsley

3 oz. butter
4 tablespoons olive oil
½ lb. tomatoes
salt and pepper

Wash and finely chop the anchovy fillets and mix with the softened butter to form a smooth paste that can be kept in the refrigerator until used. Heat the oil with the crushed cloves of garlic. Discard the garlic when brown and add the pureed tomatoes. Cook for a few minutes until thick, then remove from the heat and season with salt and pepper and a good handful of chopped parsley. Meanwhile cook the spaghetti. Put the butter and anchovy mixture on the bottom of a hot serving dish, add the hot pasta, pour over the tomato sauce, then mix well and serve.

PASTA WITH MUSHROOMS AND ANCHOVIES

1 lb. spaghetti
3 oz. mushrooms
½ lb. tomatoes
1½ tablespoons pine nuts
salt and pepper

2 oz. butter
6 salt-cured anchovy fillets
½ onion
flour

This Emilian recipe is adapted from one of the great Artusi's collection of recipes. Lightly brown the pine nuts in ½ ounce butter, then pound in a mortar with a little flour. Brown a little chopped onion in the remaining butter and add the peeled and chopped tomatoes. Season with salt and pepper. When the tomatoes are cooked put them through a food mill and return to the pan. Add the finely chopped mushrooms, the pounded pine nuts, and the remaining butter and cook for about half an hour, adding a few tablespoons of warm water as necessary to obtain a fairly liquid sauce. Take a little of this sauce and put in a separate pan to cook the anchovies, which have been washed and chopped. Add the anchovy sauce to the tomatoes and mushrooms, cook for a few minutes more and serve with the hot pasta.

FETTUCCINE WITH BUTTER AND ANCHOVIES   299

1 lb. flour	4 eggs
4 oz. butter	6 salt-cured anchovy fillets
salt and pepper	(pecorino/romano, parsley)

Make the fettuccine in the usual way (see recipe 181) with the flour, eggs, a pinch of salt and a little warm water if necessary. Roll out fairly thinly and cut into strips about ¼ inch wide. Wash the anchovy fillets, chop them and cook in the butter until they dissolve. Boil the fettuccine in plenty of water and drain well, then mix with this deliciously simple sauce and serve with freshly ground black pepper.

Variations 1. In Rome this recipe is served with grated pecorino/romano.
2. Serve with a handful of chopped parsley as well as pepper.

PASTA WITH WHITE WINE AND ANCHOVIES   300

1 lb. pasta	6 salt-cured anchovy fillets
2 hard-boiled egg yolks	olive oil
white wine	salt and pepper

Wash the anchovies to remove the salt. Pound the egg yolks and anchovies to make a smooth paste. Moisten with a little oil and work together, adding a little white wine, and when that is well absorbed, a little more oil. Add some freshly ground pepper and serve with the hot pasta.

Variation For a less piquant flavour use anchovy fillets in oil.

FETTUCCINE WITH MOZZARELLA, EGGS AND ANCHOVIES

1 lb. flour   4 eggs
3 hard-boiled egg yolks   5 oz. mozzarella
4 salt-cured anchovy fillets   2½ oz. butter
salt and pepper   (anchovies in oil)

Make the fettuccine in the usual way (see recipe 181) with the flour, eggs, warm water and salt. Roll out fairly thin and cut into strips about ¼-½ inch wide. Mix the cubed mozzarella, the washed, chopped anchovies, the chopped egg yolks and a little pepper in a large bowl. Heat the butter over low heat, add the hot fettuccine, adding a little of the pasta cooking water if it seems too dry. Add the mozzarella, egg and anchovies and stir over the heat until the mozzarella melts and forms threads.

Variation Use anchovies in oil for a milder flavour.

VERMICELLI, EGG AND ANCHOVY PANCAKES

1 lb. vermicelli   5 eggs
6 salt-cured anchovy fillets   olive oil
salt and pepper

Wash the anchovies to remove the salt and pound to a paste in the mortar. Put in a large bowl with the beaten eggs, a pinch of salt and enough oil to bind the sauce. Cook the pasta until still firm, drain well and mix with the other ingredients in the bowl. Make this mixture into flat pancakes about three or four inches in diameter. Fry in plenty of oil so they are brown and crisp on the outside and soft inside.

SALAD OF CONCHIGLIE AND TUNNY/TUNA FISH

¾ lb. conchiglie   7 oz. tin can tunny/tuna fish
4 oz. onion   juice of 1 lemon
olive oil   salt and pepper

Parboil the onion, chop them and put in a serving dish with the mashed fish. Add the cooked pasta, mix well, sprinkle with oil, lemon juice and salt and pepper. Mix well and serve cold.

MACCHERONCINI OR LINGUINE WITH TUNNY/TUNA FISH

1 lb. maccheroncini or linguine
4 tablespoons olive oil
2 cloves garlic
salt and pepper

7 oz. tin/can tunny/tuna fish
1 tablespoon capers
parsley

Heat the oil with the chopped garlic, or whole crushed cloves of garlic (to be discarded). When the garlic is brown, add the mashed fish, stir, add the washed capers and the pepper, then plenty of chopped parsley. Cook the pasta, drain well and serve with the sauce.

MACCHERONCINI OR LINGUINE WITH TOMATOES AND TUNNY/TUNA FISH

1 lb. maccheroncini or linguine
4 tablespoons olive oil
1 tablespoon capers
parsley
salt and pepper

7 oz. tin/can tunny/tuna fish
1¼ lb. tomatoes
2 cloves garlic
(basil)

Make a tomato sauce: heat the oil with the chopped garlic, or whole crushed cloves of garlic (to be discarded), add the pureed tomatoes. Cook for a few minutes, then add the mashed fish, the capers, a little pepper and a handful of chopped parsley. Heat and serve with the hot pasta.

PASTA WITH ARTICHOKES AND TUNNY/TUNA FISH

1 lb. pasta
6 globe artichokes (only use very young, tender ones)
6 tablespoons white wine
parsley

7 oz tin/can tunny/tuna fish
4 tablespoons olive oil
1 tablespoon tomato puree
1 clove garlic
salt

Heat the oil with the chopped garlic, a pinch of chopped parsley and the finely sliced artichoke hearts. Cook until the artichokes are golden brown, then add the tomato puree. Let the sauce thicken, add the wine and cook a few minutes and add the mashed fish. Cook for another 15 minutes, adding a few tablespoons of warm water as necessary, then mix with the hot pasta.

SPAGHETTI OR BUCATINI WITH TUNNY/TUNA FISH AND MUSHROOMS

1 lb. spaghetti or bucatini	3 oz. tin/can tunny/tuna fish
½ lb. mushrooms	6 tablespoons olive oil
1¼ lb. tomatoes	3 cloves garlic
salt and pepper	parsley

Clean the mushrooms with a brush, rather than in water, then cut into slices and cook with about two tablespoons oil (add the mushrooms to the pan when the oil is very hot). As soon as they are soft add the mashed fish, season with pepper and cook for a few minutes, stirring gently. Heat the remaining oil with the chopped garlic, or crushed cloves of garlic (to be discarded). Add the pureed tomato, season with salt and pepper and cook until thickened. Mix the hot pasta with these sauces, and serve immediately.

MACCHERONCINI WITH TUNNY/TUNA FISH AND RICOTTA

1 lb. maccheroncini	3 oz. tin can tunny/tuna fish
6 oz. ricotta	½ onion
4 tablespoons olive oil	parsley
salt and pepper	

Mash the fish with the ricotta, gradually adding the olive oil and chopped onion. Season with salt and pepper, and continue adding oil until you have a fairly thin sauce. Serve with the hot pasta and plenty of chopped parsley.

VERMICELLI WITH ANCHOVY AND TUNNY/TUNA FISH

1 lb. vermicelli	4 oz. salt-cured anchovy fillets
7 oz. tin/can tunny/tuna fish	6 oz. meat stock
3 oz. butter	3 tablespoons olive oil
parsley	hot chili pepper

A classic Neapolitan recipe. Wash the anchovies and chop in small pieces. Mash the fish, put through a food mill or blender with the chopped anchovies, then cook in butter and stock over low heat with a little hot chili pepper (to be discarded). Mix the hot pasta with the butter and oil, add plenty of chopped parsley and serve with the fish and anchovy mixture.

SPAGHETTI WITH TUNNY/TUNA FISH, TOMATO AND ANCHOVY **310**

1 lb. spaghetti
1 tablespoon capers
4 salt-cured anchovy fillets
6 oz. olive oil
1 onion
parsley

4 oz. tin can tunny/tuna fish
1¾ lb. tomatoes
1 oz. butter
1 oz. almonds
1 clove garlic
salt and pepper

Heat the oil with the chopped garlic and onion and when they are just beginning to brown add the pureed tomatoes. Cook until soft and well blended, season with salt and pepper and a pinch of chopped parsley. Melt the butter in another pan, add the mashed fish, the washed capers, and the washed, chopped anchovy fillets. Cook until soft, add the tomato sauce and cook until thickened again. Blanch the almonds and chop roughly. Serve the hot pasta with the tomato and fish sauce and sprinkle with the chopped almonds.

TUNNY/TUNA AND ANCHOVY ROLL **311**

3 oz. flour
4 egg whites
salt
3 oz. tin/can tunny/tuna fish
2 oz. butter

2 eggs
olive oil
a few leaves lettuce
4 salt-cured anchovy fillets

Make a very soft pasta dough with the eggs, flour, stiffly beaten egg whites and a pinch of salt. Roll out very thin (⅛ inch) on foil placed on a greased baking sheet. Bake in a hot oven for five or six minutes. Cover with a layer of fresh lettuce, then a layer of the fish pounded with the anchovy and butter. Roll up the pasta, wrap in a cloth and keep in the refrigerator. Cut in slices and serve.

PASTA AND BROCCOLI WITH TUNNY/TUNA FISH

1 lb. pasta
1¼ lb. tomatoes
2 cloves garlic
3 oz. olive oil
salt and pepper

1 large cabbage
4 salt-cured anchovy fillets
3 oz. tin/can tunny/tuna fish
parsley

Wash the cabbage, shred and cook in lightly salted boiling water for about two minutes. Add the pasta. Make the sauce: heat the oil, add the chopped garlic and the pureed tomatoes, then the washed, chopped anchovy fillets, and the mashed fish. Cook until soft and serve with plenty of freshly ground pepper and chopped parsley.

SPAGHETTI WITH HERRINGS

1 lb. spaghetti
3 cloves garlic
hot chili pepper

6 tablespoons olive oil
4 oz. herrings in oil
salt and pepper

Heat the oil, add the chopped garlic and cook until just brown. Add the chopped hot chili pepper (to be discarded) and the mashed herrings. Stir well and moisten with one or two tablespoons water to make a good sauce. Serve with the hot pasta.

PASTA WITH HERRINGS

1 lb. pasta
3 oz. herrings in oil
1 onion
salt and pepper

6 oz. butter
olive oil
1 lemon

Soften half the butter and pound with the herring, gradually adding the lemon juice, onion juice and a little pepper, then enough olive oil to make a good, fairly liquid sauce. Serve with the hot pasta.

SPAGHETTI WITH SMOKED SALMON

1 lb. spaghetti	4 tablespoons olive oil
2 cloves garlic	4 oz. smoked salmon
2 oz. black olives	8 oz. cream
½ lb. tomatoes	dried mint
oregano	salt

Cook the garlic in the oil and when it is just beginning to brown add the smoked salmon, cut into thin strips or julienne. Stir gently, add the seeded, chopped olives and the cream to make a sauce. Add the pureed tomatoes (this gives the sauce a beautiful colour) and season with chopped mint, oregano and a little salt. Simmer for a few minutes and serve with the hot pasta.

PASTICCIO OF SALMON AND PASTA BEKENDORF

1 lb. long pasta	4 oz. smoked salmon
5 oz. butter	3 tablespoons flour
18 oz. milk	nutmeg
salt	grated parmesan

Bekendorf was chef to the last Czar just before the Russian Revolution. Cook the pasta until still quite firm, drain well and toss with two ounces butter. Put half of the pasta on the bottom of a greased mould. Cover with a layer of salmon cut into thin strips, then with some bechamel sauce made with the remaining butter, the flour, milk, nutmeg and salt. Sprinkle with grated parmesan, cover with the remaining pasta and then the rest of the bechamel. Sprinkle with more parmesan, dot with butter and brown for a few minutes in a hot oven.

SPAGHETTI WITH ROE

1 lb. spaghetti	4 tablespoons olive oil
2 cloves garlic	½ lb. fish roe
salt	parsley
6 tablespoons cream	paprika
fish stock	

Use large roe, such as cod or herring roe. Heat the oil with the crushed cloves of garlic and the chopped parsley. Remove the garlic when brown and add the roe. Stir well and add six tablespoons thin cream and a pinch of paprika. Cook for a few minutes, add a couple of tablespoons fish stock (you can make this from the fish used to obtain the roe). Add salt to taste and cook until some of the liquid has evaporated. Crush the roe with a fork, or if they are large put through the food mill, and serve the sauce with the hot pasta.

SPAGHETTI WITH CAVIAR **318**

1 lb. spaghetti	2 oz. caviar
4 tablespoons butter	6 tablespoons cream
salt and pepper	(gravy, parmesan)

Melt the butter in a large pan, add the cream, a pinch of salt and some freshly ground pepper. Cook until thickened and add the caviar. Stir very gently and fold in the hot pasta. You can of course use any of the caviar substitutes, such as lumpfish roe, for this recipe.

Variation Add one tablespoon thin meat gravy to the sauce and a few tablespoons parmesan.

SPAGHETTI AND SALT COD PANCAKES **319**

1 lb. spaghetti	1 lb. filleted salt cod
olive oil	butter
salt and pepper	breadcrumbs

Soak the salt cod in cold water for at least eight hours. Change the water frequently. Bring to a boil in clean water and cook until tender. Cook the pasta in lightly salted boiling water until still quite firm, then mix with the mashed, cooked salt cod, a little butter and some pepper. Form this mixture into small pancakes, dip them in softened butter, then breadcrumbs, and fry in plenty of hot oil.

¾ lb. pasta	3 lb. assorted fish—white fish such as
onion	halibut, bass and brill or
celery	red snapper and a little dark fish
rosemary	such as eel or mackerel
parsley	10 oz. dry white wine
lemon	olive oil
salt and pepper	(marsala)

There are various ways of making a good fish soup, starting with the fish you use. Don't be afraid to experiment with any really fresh fish that is obtainable; clean them and put in a large pan with some chopped celery and onion, slices of lemon, parsley, rosemary, salt and pepper. Cover with plenty of cold water and cook over medium heat until the fish are soft and the stock well flavoured. Add the wine, cook for a little longer, then put the soup through a food mill for a thick broth. Cook the pasta in this broth with a few tablespoons of oil and salt and pepper to taste.

Variations 1. Instead of cooking whole fish, use just the heads, bones and tails, and reserve the flesh for another dish. This still gives a good flavour to the stock.
      2. Cook the fish whole until the flesh is falling off the bones, then remove it to use in another dish.
      3. Use marsala instead of white wine.

PASTA IN FISH SOUP—II **321**

¾ lb. pasta	3 lb. assorted fish (see recipe 320)
4 salt-cured anchovy fillets	4 tablespoons olive oil
2 cloves garlic	celery
bay leaves	parsley
salt and pepper	(tomatoes, fat salt pork)

Use the whole fish, or just the heads, tails and bones as in the previous recipe. Heat the oil in a pan or fish kettle and brown the crushed cloves of garlic, then discard them. Add the washed, chopped anchovy fillets and cook until soft. Add the fish, chopped celery, a few bay leaves and some parsley and reduce the heat so that the soup cooks very slowly for about an hour. Put through the food mill, then cook the pasta in the resulting thick broth, together with some extra salt and pepper.

Variations 1. Add nine ounces pureed tomatoes before adding the fish to the pan.

2. Pound the garlic with a little bacon fat or salt pork and add this to the oil before cooking the anchovies. It gives a very piquant flavour, so omit the other strong flavours such as the celery and bay leaves and use just the onion and less tomato.

PASTA WITH MUSHROOMS IN FISH SOUP 322

¾ lb. pasta
3 oz. fresh mushrooms
onion
celery
parsley
salt and pepper

1 lb. assorted fish (see recipe 320)
3 oz. or 2 slices stale white bread
carrot
bay leaves
olive oil

Clean and slice the mushrooms and cook in six ounces fish stock, made from about 1½ pounds of assorted fish, as in the previous recipes. Add one chopped onion, one carrot, one chopped stick celery, a few bay leaves and some chopped parsley. Cook slowly over low heat, season with salt and pepper and pass through a food mill. Crumble the bread and lightly brown in a little oil. Add to the mushroom and onion puree, then mix with the hot pasta and a little extra oil.

MACCHERONCINI WITH SARDINES 323

1 lb. maccheroncini
6 tablespoons olive oil
2 oz. pine nuts
2 oz. breadcrumbs

½ lb. fresh sardines
2 oz. raisins
2 cloves garlic
salt and pepper

This is a shorter version of the famous Palermitan recipe for pasta and sardines which comes next. Clean the sardines and remove the heads and tails. Put in a pan, cover with cold water and boil just enough for the flesh to cook but remain firm. Soak the raisins in water. Brown the breadcrumbs and pine nuts in a little oil. Brown the garlic in the remaining oil, then discard it; add the filleted sardines, season with salt and pepper and cook for a few minutes over low heat. Add the raisins, pine nuts and breadcrumbs, mix well and serve with the hot pasta.

1 lb. bucatini	1 lb. fresh sardines
1 lb. wild fennel	4 tablespoons olive oil
4 salt-cured anchovy fillets	1 oz. raisins
1 oz. pine nuts	1 onion
saffron	flour
salt and pepper	(butter, breadcrumbs)

There are many versions of this famous Palermitan recipe from other parts of western Sicily, but the most important and authentic ingredient is the wild fennel that grows on the Sicilian hillsides. Some Sicilians even go so far as to have it flown in fresh to America for special occasions. However you can use a cultivated variety of fennel. Soak the raisins for two hours in warm water and brown the pine nuts in a little oil. Chop the onion and cook in four tablespoons olive oil, then add the washed, chopped anchovy fillets, the raisins, pine nuts and a little pepper. Wash the fennel well and cook in plenty of boiling, salted water. Drain when still quite firm and reserve the water. Choose small sardines, as they have a better flavour and are easier to prepare. Split open the sardines, remove the heads, bones and tails. Toss them in a little flour and fry in the remaining oil with a pinch of saffron over low heat; remove from the pan and sprinkle with salt. Cook the pasta in the fennel water to give it added flavour, then drain and mix with the sauce, add the chopped fennel and finally the fried sardines, stirring them in gently so they do not break apart. Pile the pasta in a mound on a plate and leave to stand a few minutes before serving. It is considered a heresy to add garlic or parsley to this magnificent dish.

Variation The pasta mixed with the other ingredients can be baked for a few minutes in the oven in a greased ovenproof dish. This brings out the flavours and makes it less greasy.

1 lb. bucatini	1 lb. fresh sardines
4 salt-cured anchovy fillets	1 onion
6 tablespoons concentrated	1 oz. raisins
tomato puree	olive oil
1 oz. pine nuts	flour
sugar	salt and pepper

This is a way of making pasta with sardines in the Palermitan manner when wild fennel is not in season. Clean the sardines, remove the heads, tails and bones and flatten the fillets, then flour lightly and fry in a little oil until soft. Remove from the heat and add the washed, chopped anchovy fillets, which have been cooked over low heat until they soften. Return to the heat with a little water to prevent the sauce from sticking and add the concentrated tomato puree. Stir this to dissolve, then add the pine nuts and raisins (both soaked in warm water) and cook a little longer, adding warm water as necessary to make a fairly thick sauce. Season with salt and pepper and a teaspoon of sugar. Add the sardines and their cooking oil and mix carefully so they do not disintegrate. Cook the pasta, drain well and mix carefully with half this sauce, then spoon the remaining sauce over the individual servings.

BUCATINI WITH MUSHROOMS AND SARDINES

326

1 lb. bucatini	¾ lb. fresh sardines
¼ lb. fresh mushrooms	1 lb. tomatoes
4 tablespoons olive oil	4 salt-cured anchovy fillets
2 oz. black olives	2 cloves garlic
1 oz. capers	1 oz. breadcrumbs
parsley	salt and pepper
flour	

Clean the sardines, remove the heads, tails and bones. Flour lightly and fry gently in a little oil so the flesh softens. Add the washed, chopped anchovy fillets and cook until they soften, then add the cleaned, sliced mushrooms. Cook for a few minutes and add the pureed tomatoes. Cook a little longer, then add the washed, chopped capers and the seeded olives. Season with salt and pepper and a good handful of chopped parsley and cook a few minutes longer. Toss the hot pasta in half this sauce, then put some of the pasta in a greased ovenproof dish, cover with a layer of sardines and a little more sauce, then add a further layer of pasta. Sprinkle with breadcrumbs and moisten with fresh oil. Brown for a few minutes in a hot oven.

Variations 1. Omit the tomatoes.
               2. Omit the tomatoes, capers and olives from the sauce and put them chopped in small pieces between the pasta and the sardines in the ovenproof dish. Let the dish brown at least 15 minutes in this case.

LASAGNETTE RICCE WITH MACKEREL   **327**

1 lb. lasagnette ricce	1 lb. mackerel
2 lb. tomatoes	6 tablespoons olive oil
½ onion	flour
milk	(garlic)
salt and pepper	

Fillet the mackerel and chop into large pieces. Soak in milk for about ten minutes. Drain, flour lightly and fry in plenty of oil, using more than for sardines and anchovies, as the flesh is quite different. Prepare the sauce in a large saucepan: lightly brown the chopped onion in four tablespoons oil, add the pureed tomatoes and season with salt and pepper. Mix in the fried mackerel and then the hot pasta, heat for a minute together, and serve.

Variations 1. Instead of adding the mackerel to the sauce add them to the hot pasta and then pour over the sauce.
               2. Put a little chopped garlic in the oil as well as the onion.

PASTA WITH FRESH TUNNY/TUNA FISH STEW   **328**

1 lb. pasta	2 lb. fresh tunny/ tuna fish
6 tablespoons olive oil	8 oz. concentrated tomato puree
1 onion	2 cloves garlic
6 oz. dry white wine	mint
sugar	(caciocavallo cheese,
salt and pepper	courgettes/zucchini)

This is like a French pot-au-feu, using fish not meat. The fish is served as a separate dish and the pasta and soup are served together. Choose a large, regular-shaped piece of fish; leave it under running water to remove the blood. Pound chopped garlic and mint with some salt and pepper. Drain the fish, wipe it dry, pierce the flesh and make small incisions in it with a skewer or knife. Stuff these incisions with the garlic and mint mixture. Fry the fish in three tablespoons oil and fry the thinly sliced onion in another pan in the remaining oil. Add the tomato puree to the onion and cook for a few minutes, then add the white wine and a few tablespoons warm water to make a fairly liquid sauce. Season with salt and pepper and one tablespoon sugar. Add the fish and cook for about one hour, until the fish is soft and full of flavour. Scrape the garlic off the fish and stir into the sauce in the pan. Serve the sauce with the hot pasta. Slice the fish and serve separately.

Variation Serve the pasta and fish sauce with fried sliced courgettes/zucchini and grated caciocavallo cheese.

SPAGHETTI WITH SEA BASS   329

1 lb. spaghetti	1 bass (or brill, turbot,
4 tablespoons olive oil	halibut etc. weighing about 1½-2 lb.)
1 onion	1 carrot
1 celery heart	6 small tomatoes
basil	oregano
6 oz. white wine	salt and pepper

Make a sauce with any whole white fish you can find. Clean the fish, fillet and chop the fillets in small pieces. Brown the finely sliced onion in the oil, add the carrot and the celery heart cut in thin strips or finely chopped. Cook for a few minutes, until the vegetables are soft and add the peeled, chopped tomatoes. Season with salt and pepper, a pinch of oregano and a few basil leaves. When the sauce is thick, add the fish and cook over low heat for about one hour, until the fish flakes. Add the wine, let it cook a little over moderate heat and serve with the hot pasta.

COLD CONCHIGLIE WITH FISH   330

1 lb. conchiglie	1 white fish, weighing about 1½-2 lb.
2 egg yolks	olive oil
parsley	1 lemon
salt and pepper	

Any white fish will do for this recipe. Clean, fillet and cook the fish, then chop in pieces and mix with the hot pasta and a little oil to moisten (be careful not to make it too greasy), salt and pepper and the chopped parsley. Set aside to cool and serve with a mayonnaise made with two egg yolks, oil, salt and pepper and lemon juice.

1 lb. flour
2 large sole
5 tablespoons olive oil
1 large tomato
bay leaf
brandy

4 eggs
1 onion
6 tablespoons thick cream
thyme
salt and pepper

Make the tagliatelle in the usual way with the flour, eggs, a pinch of salt and a little warm water; knead well and roll out thinly, then cut in thin strips about ¼-½ inch wide (see recipe 181). Clean and fillet the sole and cut into small pieces. Heat the oil, add a finely sliced onion, a couple of chopped bay leaves, thyme and a few peppercorns. Add the pieces of sole and brown very lightly. Moisten with a little brandy, simmer a few moments and add the cream. Stir gently and add the pureed tomatoes. Bind the sauce with one teaspoon flour and cook for another five minutes. Remove from the heat, pass through a food mill, then toss with the hot tagliatelle. Put in a greased ovenproof dish and brown in a hot oven.

LINGUINE WITH EEL STEW 332

1 lb. linguine
5 tablespoons olive oil
¾ lb. tomatoes
basil
salt and pepper

1 eel, or a piece of eel
weighing about ½ lb.
garlic
(parsley)

A Puglian dish, usually made with freshly made lasagnette. Fry the onion and chopped garlic, add the pureed tomatoes, a little basil and some salt and pepper. Cook until the sauce is thick, then add the skinned, chopped eel and cook until soft. Serve with the hot pasta.

1 lb. linguine
2 eggs
3 oz. or about 2 slices white bread
3 tablespoons olive oil
¾ lb. tomatoes
3 oz. grated parmesan

1¾ lb. pike, or any similar fish
2 oz. butter
milk
1 onion
salt and pepper

Cook the fish, remove the flesh and pound with the egg yolks, softened butter, pieces of bread soaked in milk and squeezed gently, a pinch each of salt and pepper, and finally the beaten egg whites. Make into little balls about as big as a walnut. Heat the oil with the chopped onion, add the pureed tomatoes and the fish balls, cook for a few minutes and serve with the hot pasta. Serve grated parmesan separately, but don't use too much or it will spoil the flavour of the fish.

PASTICCIO OF VERMICELLI AND FISH BALLS **334**

1 lb. vermicelli
5 oz. olive oil
4 salt-cured anchovy fillets
1 tablespoon capers
1 tablespoon pine nuts
3 oz. breadcrumbs
1 onion
1 stick celery
1 clove garlic
pork fat

2 lb. fish with plenty of flesh
(e.g. bass, mullet, brill,
halibut, etc.)
2 oz. black olives
parsley
3 oz. mushrooms
1 carrot
flour
(tomatoes, butter)

Fillet the fish, then pound the flesh with the capers, seeded olives, pine nuts, a good handful of parsley, a little salt and pepper and enough breadcrumbs to give a smooth, fairly thick mixture. Form into small balls. Flour the balls lightly, fry in plenty of oil and set aside. Return the bones, heads, tails and skins of the fish to the pan with plenty of salted water, one onion, one carrot and a stick of celery. Cook for at least two hours, put through a food mill, then cook the chopped mushrooms in the fish broth until the liquid has reduced by half. Heat half the oil in a pan with the chopped garlic, add the washed, chopped anchovies and cook until soft. Cook the pasta until still quite firm, drain well and mix with the anchovy sauce. Grease an ovenproof dish, sprinkle with breadcrumbs and line with half the pasta, then a layer of fish balls. Press them down into the pasta, add the mushrooms and their liquid, the rest of the pasta, sprinkle with more breadcrumbs, dot with pork fat and brown in a hot oven.

Variations 1. When you have fried the fish balls, put them in a pan to cook for a few minutes with an oil and tomato sauce, made in the usual way (see recipe 15).
2. Dot the finished dish with butter instead of pork fat.

SPAGHETTI WITH SQUID 335

1 lb. spaghetti
5 tablespoons olive oil
parsley
1 onion
salt and pepper

1¼ lb. squid
(white or red wine, tomatoes, garlic, rosemary, carrots, celery, stock, pork fat)

You really need tiny Adriatic squid, but larger ones taste very good if they are cooked long enough to make them tender. Clean the squid well, removing the spine, the outside skin, eyes, ink bags and tentacles. Chop the tentacles into short pieces, slice the bodies. Heat the oil with the chopped onion, then add the tentacles, cook until tender, then add the rest of the squid and season with salt and pepper. Cook very slowly for about 1½ hours until soft, adding a few tablespoons of warm water if it seems too dry. When cooked, add a handful of chopped parsley, toss with the hot pasta and serve.

Variations 1. Fry a little celery, carrot and a sprig of rosemary with the onion.
2. Flavour the oil with two crushed cloves of garlic, then discard them. Omit the onion, according to taste.
3. Add some pureed tomato to the sauce immediately after adding the squid.
4. When the squid is cooked add six ounces white wine to the sauce. Use red wine to give a rather different flavour, and include the tomato puree.
5. For a more liquid sauce use stock instead of water, which gives an added flavour to the dish.
6. Use a mixture of oil and pork fat to fry the onion.

1 lb. spaghetti	1 lb. squid
½ lb. shelled peas	5 tablespoons olive oil
1 onion	white wine
salt and pepper	(tomatoes)

Use small, tender squid if possible. Clean them as in the previous recipe; chop the tentacles and cut the bodies into rings. Heat the oil with the chopped onion and the tentacles, then the rest of the squid and the peas. Season with salt and pepper and moisten with a little white wine; cook until it has partially evaporated and serve with the hot pasta.

Variations   1.   Add a little tomato sauce (see recipe 15) to the sauce.
                2.   If you can obtain really small, tender squid, cook them whole in the sauce and serve separately.

MACCHERONCINI WITH SQUID AND AUBERGINES/EGGPLANT   **337**

1 lb. maccheroncini	1 lb. squid
2 cloves garlic	1 large aubergine/eggplant or
6 tablespoons olive oil	2 smaller ones
4 large tomatoes	18 oz. fish stock
white wine	hot chili pepper
parsley	(meat stock)
salt	

Clean and chop the squid as in recipe 335. Dice the aubergines/eggplant and fry in three tablespoons olive oil. Heat the rest of the oil in a pan with the chopped garlic, or crushed cloves of garlic (to be discarded), a handful of parsley and a chopped hot chili pepper. When the garlic browns add the tentacles, cook for a few minutes, then add the sliced squid, the peeled, chopped tomatoes and the fried aubergines/eggplant. Moisten with wine, stir well, remove the crushed garlic or sweet pepper, cover with fish stock (see recipe 320). Season with salt and pepper and cook until the squid is soft, then serve with the hot pasta.

Variation   In certain parts of southern Italy a light meat stock is used instead of fish stock, and this gives a really delicious flavour.

1 lb. spaghetti
1 lb. tomatoes
2 oz. or about 2 slices white bread
parsley
salt and pepper

6 squid
5 tablespoons olive oil
1 onion
18 oz. fish stock

Choose tender squid large enough to take a stuffing. Clean well, as in recipe 335; chop the tentacles and put them in a bowl with the finely chopped garlic and parsley, the crumbled bread (discard the crust) and a pinch each of salt and pepper. Mix well and stuff the squid, sew up the top and bottom with thread. Heat the remaining oil in a pan with the chopped onion, and when it browns add the skinned, chopped tomatoes. Season with salt and pepper and cook for 15 minutes, then pack the stuffed squid loosely in the same pan, pour over the fish broth (made as in recipe 320) and cook uncovered over low heat for at least two hours, so the squid are well flavoured. Cook the pasta, drain well and toss in the sauce in which the squid have cooked. Serve a stuffed squid on each helping of pasta, or arrange them on top of the pasta in one big dish.

BUCATINI WITH SHRIMPS — **339**

1 lb. bucatini
4 oz. butter
1 large tomato
salt and pepper

½ lb. shelled shrimps
3 cloves garlic
parsley
(basil)

Melt the butter and brown the finely chopped garlic. Add the chopped shrimps. Season with salt and pepper and cook for a few minutes, then add the seeded, chopped tomatoes and a handful of chopped parsley. Meanwhile, cook the pasta, drain well, add to the sauce in the pan, stir well for a few minutes, then serve.

Variation Add a little basil to the sauce, either instead of or with the parsley.

1 lb. macaroni
½ lb. butter
9 oz. milk
4 oz. grated parmesan
nutmeg

5 oz. whole shelled prawns/scampi
4 tablespoons flour
5 oz. fresh mushrooms
salt and pepper

A recipe named after the famous Cardinal Alberoni of Piacenza, who gave famous banquets and set the fashion at the Spanish Court in the 18th century. It has been only slightly modernized; make a bechamel with one ounce butter, the flour and the milk, and season with salt, pepper and nutmeg. Clean the mushrooms, slice or chop them and cook with one ounce butter, salt and pepper. Pound the prawns/scampi then cook the puree in butter until it reduces a little. Mix in a bowl with the bechamel, mushrooms and half the grated parmesan. Cook the pasta, drain well and mix with the sauce, then arrange in a greased ovenproof dish and pour melted butter and a little grated cheese over. Brown in a hot oven.

1 lb. flour
1 lb. shelled shrimps
lemon
salt and pepper

4 eggs
olive oil
basil
(parsley)

Make the pasta dough with the flour, eggs, a pinch of salt and warm water in the usual way (see recipe 181). Roll out not too finely and cut in very thin strips, slightly less than ¼-inch wide. Cook the tagliolini, drain when still quite firm, cool, then mix with the boiled, shelled shrimps. Add some oil, lemon juice, chopped basil and salt and pepper.

Variation Use parsley instead of basil.

FRIED TAGLIATELLE WITH MUSHROOMS AND SHRIMPS

1 lb. flour	2 eggs
4 oz. mushrooms	½ lb. shrimps
3 oz. bamboo shoots	3 oz. savoy cabbage
2 tablespoons soy sauce	1 tablespoon cornflour/cornstarch
ginger	6 oz. rice wine
salt	(or sherry or marsala)

Make the dough for the tagliatelle with the eggs, flour, a pinch of salt and warm water as necessary (see recipe 181). Lightly brown the finely chopped bamboo shoots in two tablespoons oil with the finely chopped cabbage and mushrooms and a pinch of salt. Remove from the pan, then put another tablespoon of oil in the same pan and cook the diced shrimps with the soy sauce, cornflour/cornstarch, a pinch of ginger, and the rice wine. Cook for a few minutes, then add the mushrooms, bamboo shoots and cabbage. Heat the remaining oil and fry the tagliatelle, then add the vegetables, shrimps and sauce from the pan. Stir over moderate heat and serve.

MACARONI WITH CURRIED PRAWNS/SCAMPI

1 lb. macaroni	4 oz. shelled prawns/scampi
4 oz. butter	3 oz. grated parmesan
2 eggs	2 egg yolks
9 oz. fish stock	3 oz. white wine
curry powder	salt

Cook the prawns/scampi in ½ ounce butter, add the fish stock (see recipe 320) and season with salt. When the liquid has absorbed, add the wine, let this absorb a little, then add a large pinch of curry powder. Cook for a few minutes until thickened. Cook the pasta, drain well, toss in the remaining butter, the parmesan, the beaten eggs and egg yolks. Put the mixture in a greased ovenproof dish and cook for ½ hour in a bain-marie (hot water bath) in a moderate oven about 20 minutes or until slightly set. Pour over the prawn/scampi sauce and serve.

PASTICCIO OF TAGLIATELLE WITH PRAWNS/SCAMPI

1 lb. flour
36 oz. milk
3 eggs
breadcrumbs

4 eggs
¾ lb. shelled prawns/scampi
½ lb. butter
salt and pepper

Make the tagliatelle in the usual way with the flour, eggs, a pinch of salt and some water as necessary (see recipe 181). Pound the prawns/scampi to a puree (or put in the blender). Reserve five tablespoons of the puree and pound the rest with the softened butter. Cook the pasta until still quite firm, drain well and toss in the shellfish butter paste (reserving two tablespoons of the paste) and the previously reserved five tablespoons of prawn/scampi puree. Put in a greased ovenproof dish, sprinkle with breadcrumbs and some freshly ground pepper, dot with the reserved tablespoons shellfish butter paste, and brown in a hot oven.

MACCHERONCINI WITH PRAWNS/SCAMPI 345

1 lb. maccheroncini
3 oz. butter
paprika
1 tablespoon marsala

¾ lb. shelled prawns/scampi
1 lb. tomatoes
salt

Chop the prawns/scampi, cook them in butter and a little marsala, add the pureed tomatoes and a pinch each of salt and paprika. Cook for a few minutes and serve with the hot pasta.

TAGLIATELLE WITH PRAWNS/SCAMPI AND MUSHROOMS 346

1 lb. flour
6 large prawns/scampi
½ lb. spinach
3 tablespoons vegetable oil
candied lemon peel

4 eggs
1 oz. dried mushrooms
1 tablespoon soy sauce
sugar
salt

Boil the prawns/scampi for about three minutes until still firm, then cool under cold running water. Shell and wash them and remove the vein. Parboil the spinach and chop. Soak the mushrooms for one hour in warm water, put the liquid in a pan and bring to a boil. Add a pinch of sugar, one tablespoon soy sauce; reduce the heat and cook for at least 20 minutes until part of the liquid has evaporated. Heat two tablespoons oil, fry two of the eggs and cut them in strips (the yolks must be firm) on absorbent paper. Make the tagliatelle with the flour, 2 eggs, a pinch of salt and warm water as necessary (see recipe 181) and cook in plenty of boiling water. Drain when still quite firm and toss with the mushroom sauce. Serve with a little fried egg, a handful of chopped spinach and a prawn/scampi on each helping. Grate some candied lemon peel on top.

FARFALLE WITH LOBSTER 347

1 lb. farfalle	¾ lb. shelled, cooked lobster
1 egg yolk	olive oil
lemon juice	vinegar
paprika	salt

Make a mayonnaise with the egg yolk, about six to eight tablespoons olive oil, some lemon juice and a little salt. Dice the lobster flesh. Cook the pasta, drain well and cool. Mix with the lobster in a serving dish, adding the mayonnaise, a little more oil and vinegar and salt and paprika. Leave to stand in a cool place before serving.

MACCHERONCINI WITH MUSHROOMS AND LOBSTER 348

1 lb. maccheroncini	1 oz. dried mushrooms (soaked in warm water)
½ lb. cooked, shelled lobster	
6 tablespoons butter	(truffle)
salt and pepper	

Heat the butter and cook the chopped mushrooms. Season with salt and pepper and moisten with one or two tablespoons of the water the mushrooms have soaked in. Add the diced lobster, cook for a few minutes, then mix with the hot pasta.

Variations 1. Cut the lobster flesh in round discs and serve these on top of the pasta.
2. Add sliced or crumbled truffle to the sauce.

PANCAKES OF CAPELLI D'ANGELO AND LOBSTER

1 lb. capelli d'angelo
½ lb. cooked, shelled lobster
salt and pepper

4 eggs
olive oil

Cook the pasta, drain well and put in a bowl. Beat the eggs, and add to the pasta. Finely chop the lobster flesh and mix well with the pasta with a pinch of salt and pepper. Make into little round pancakes and fry in deep oil.

VERMICELLI WITH MUSSELS—I

1 lb. vermicelli
3 tablespoons olive oil
parsley

2½ lb. mussels
garlic
salt and pepper

One of the most ancient ways of cooking pasta and mussels. Make sure the mussels are very fresh, then clean well by scrubbing the shells with a hard brush to remove sand, seaweed, etc. Put in a pan over high heat without any extra liquid; as they open the mussels produce their own. You can wash them again in salt water, but in this way they lose the liquid they have produced. Remove from the heat quickly when the shells open. Cook the pasta, drain well and put in a serving dish with the mussel liquid sieved through a muslin cloth. Remove the mussels from their shells and add to the pasta with some olive oil, garlic and freshly ground pepper to taste.

VERMICELLI WITH MUSSELS—II

1 lb. vermicelli
5 tablespoons olive oil
parsley
salt and pepper

2½ lb. mussels
2 cloves garlic
(lemon peel, hot chili pepper)

Another classic recipe. Choose good, fresh mussels and scrub well with a hard brush. Cook without any additional liquid, but shake the pan frequently so the mussel liquid covers the bottom. When all the mussels are open, drain the liquid through a muslin cloth and reserve, then remove the shells, put the mussels back in the pan with the oil, chopped garlic (or crushed garlic, to be discarded later), and cook gently. Meanwhile cook the pasta, drain well and toss in a serving dish with the heated mussel liquid. Add the mussels and oil, sprinkle with plenty of coarsely chopped parsley and freshly ground black pepper.

1. Add a little grated lemon peel to the oil and mussels.
2. Add a piece of hot chili pepper to the oil with the garlic and discard before serving.
3. Add the parsley and hot chili pepper (to be discarded) to the mussels when they are cooking.

VERMICELLI WITH MUSSELS AND TOMATOES   352

1 lb. vermicelli
6 tablespoons olive oil
1 lb. peeled tomatoes
salt and pepper

2 lb. mussels
2 cloves garlic
parsley

A Neapolitan recipe. Use large mussels; scrub them with a hard brush under running water. Put them in a colander with chopped parsley and the tomatoes and set aside. Heat the oil with the finely chopped garlic over low heat. As soon as the garlic browns add the mussels, tomatoes and parsley. Stir with a fork as the mussels cook and remove from their shells as they open, then return them to the sauce at the end and serve with the hot pasta. Alternatively, serve the sauce with the pasta and the mussels separately, so each person can help himself to them individually.

TAGLIATELLE VERDI WITH MUSSELS   353

1 lb. flour
1 lb. spinach
1 onion
1 carrot
½ lb. tomatoes
1 clove garlic
salt and pepper

3 eggs
2¼ lb. mussels
1 stick celery
12 oz. dry white wine
5 tablespoons olive oil
basil

Clean the mussels well with a hard brush and cook with the onion, celery, sliced carrot and half the wine. Remove the mussels as they open; strain all the liquid, bring to a boil and reduce by about a half. Heat the oil with the chopped garlic, salt and pepper, then add the mussel liquid. Add the pureed tomatoes and cook until thick. Add more wine and let this cook until the sauce has again thickened. Add the mussels and stir well. Cook the tagliatelle, made in the usual way with the flour, spinach puree, eggs, and a pinch of salt and some warm water (see recipe 191), drain well and serve with the mussel sauce.

MACCHERONCINI WITH MUSSELS AND TOMATOES

1 lb. maccheroncini
3 oz. butter
1 tablespoon flour
onion

2¾ lb. mussels
½ lb. tomatoes
salt and pepper

Clean the mussels and cook without any extra liquid, then remove from the pan as they open. Strain their liquid and reserve. Heat the butter in another pan and cook the chopped onion, then add the mussel liquid and the flour to thicken the sauce. Add the mussels and the pureed tomatoes. Season with salt and pepper and cook for a few minutes, then serve with the hot pasta.

PASTA WITH STUFFED MUSSELS

1 lb. linguine
3 eggs
4 oz. grated pecorino/romano
½ lb. tomatoes
parlsey

1¾ lb. mussels
2 oz. or 2 slices white bread
5 tablespoons olive oil
3 cloves garlic
salt and pepper

Clean the mussels well with a hard brush and open with the point of a strong knife. Clean inside the shell under running water to remove all impurities. Stuff the half-opened shells with a firm mixture made from the bread soaked in water and well drained, the beaten egg, grated pecorino/romano, finely chopped garlic, parsley and salt and pepper. Pack the mixture in firmly so it won't come out while the mussels are cooking. Heat the oil, add the pureed tomatoes and the stuffed mussels and cook until the mussels are ready to serve. Mix the hot pasta with the sauce from the pan and serve some stuffed mussels on each individual helping.

VERMICELLI WITH CLAMS—I

1 lb. vermicelli
5 tablespoons olive oil
2 cloves garlic
salt and pepper

2 lb. small clams or
8 oz. cooked, shelled cockles
parsley

Clams in their shells should be cooked and washed like mussels (see recipe 350). Cook them without any extra liquid until they open, remove from the shells, strain the liquid through a fine cloth, return to the pan and boil for a couple of minutes. Cook the pasta, drain well and serve with about six tablespoons of the mussel liquid, a little oil, some finely chopped garlic and parsley, pepper and the clams.

VERMICELLI WITH CLAMS—II **357**

1 lb. vermicelli
6 tablespoons olive oil
2 cloves garlic
salt and pepper

2 lb. small clams or
8 oz. shelled, cooked cockles
parsley

Neapolitans use rather larger clams for this recipe, but any clam will do as well. Scrub the clams well and cook until they open in their own liquid. Remove from their shells and continue cooking in another pan with the oil and chopped garlic. Strain the clam liquid well and bring to a boil. Cook the pasta, drain and toss with the clam liquid, the clams and their sauce, freshly ground black pepper and chopped parsley.

VERMICELLI WITH CLAMS AND TOMATOES **358**

1 lb. vermicelli
5 tablespoons olive oil
2 lb. tomatoes
parsley

2 lb. small clams or
8 oz. shelled, cooked cockles
2 cloves garlic
salt and pepper

Use small, tender clams. Wash thoroughly and cook over moderate heat until they open. Remove from the shells and strain the liquid well. Heat the oil in another pan with the chopped garlic, add the pureed tomatoes, stir to thicken, add the clam liquid and reduce over moderate heat. Return the clams to the pan and add plenty of chopped parsley and freshly ground pepper, then serve with the hot pasta.

VERMICELLI WITH MUSSELS AND CLAMS **359**

1 lb. vermicelli
1¼ lb. clams or
4 oz. shelled, cooked cockles
1 lb. tomatoes
parsley

1¼ lb. mussels
6 tablespoons olive oil
2 cloves garlic
hot chili pepper
basil

The Neapolitans often clean mussels and clams by leaving them to soak for 24 hours in clean sea water, or for 12 hours in salted water. This recipe also comes from Naples. Brown two finely sliced cloves of garlic in the oil and add the skinned, seeded and chopped tomatoes and a few basil leaves and make a tomato sauce in the usual way (see recipe 15). Brown a crushed clove of garlic in one tablespoon oil in another pan and add a few pieces of hot chili pepper, then discard. Add the cleaned mussels and clams, cook until they open, remove from their shells and let the sauce reduce a bit until thick. Add the tomato sauce, mix well and serve with the mussels and clams, the chopped parsley and freshly ground black pepper.

PASTICCIO OF MACCHERONCINI WITH MUSSELS, CLAMS AND EGGS — **360**

1 lb. maccheroncini	4 oz. butter
4 eggs	2 egg yolks
1 lb. mussels	1 lb. small clams or
breadcrumbs	8 oz. cooked, shelled cockles
parsley	(tomatoes, grated parmesan)
salt and pepper	

An ancient Neapolitan recipe that combines an unusual, but delicious variety of ingredients. Clean the mussels and clams and cook until open, then remove from the shells and strain the liquid well. Return the clams and mussels to the heat with ½ ounce butter, a few tablespoons of the strained liquid and allow to reduce a little. Add the two egg yolks, mix well and season with salt and pepper and chopped parsley. Remove from the heat. Cook the pasta, drain well and toss in the butter and beaten eggs, then put in a greased ovenproof dish. Sprinkle with breadcrumbs, pour over the mussel and clam sauce, dot with butter and brown for a few minutes in a hot oven.

Variations 1. Toss the pasta in grated parmesan as well as eggs and butter.
2. Serve the pasta with a few tablespoons of tomato sauce.

BUCATINI WITH MUSSELS, CLAMS AND MUSHROOMS — **361**

1 lb. bucatini	1¼ lb. mussels
1¼ lb. small clams or	3 oz. fresh mushrooms
8 oz. cooked, shelled cockles	5 tablespoons olive oil
salt and pepper	(stock or bouillon cube)

Cook the cleaned mussels and clams in the usual way (see recipe 350), stirring frequently to distribute their liquid in the pan. Remove from their shells and strain the liquid. Wash and slice the mushrooms and fry in another pan,

LINGUINE WITH CLAMS, PRAWNS/SCAMPI AND BABY SQUID

1 lb. linguine
1 lb. prawns/scampi
½ lb. baby squid
½ onion
parsley
salt and pepper

1 lb. small clams or
8 oz. cooked, shelled cockles
3 tablespoons olive oil
½ lb. tomatoes
(eggs, flour)

Clean the clams well and cook until they open, then remove from the shells and reserve the liquid. Cook the prawns/scampi, shell them and chop the flesh. Clean the squid, removing the spine, outside skin and eyes and the ink bags. Chop the tentacles and leave the body whole. Heat the oil and brown the onion, then remove from the pan. Add the chopped prawns/scampi, season with salt and pepper and stir gently. Add the skinned, seeded and chopped tomatoes. If the sauce seems too dry add a few tablespoons of the clam liquid, strained and diluted with water. Cook until the squid are tender, then serve with the hot pasta.

Variation Use tagliatelle made in the usual way (see recipe 181) instead of linguine.

FETTUCINE WITH PRAWNS/SCAMPI, SHRIMPS AND CLAMS

1 lb. flour
½ lb. prawns/scampi
1¾ lb. small clams or
¾ lb. cooked, shelled cockles
¼ onion
salt and pepper

4 eggs
8 oz. shrimps
1 lb. tomatoes
3 tablespoons olive oil
2 cloves garlic

Make the fettucine in the usual way with the flour, eggs, a pinch of salt and a little oil. Boil the prawns/scampi and shrimps, remove the tails, then pound to obtain a rather liquid puree. Clean the clams and cook with a little oil until they open, then remove from their shells and strain the liquid from the pan. Heat the remaining oil with the chopped onion and garlic, and when they start to brown add the skinned, seeded and chopped tomatoes, the shrimp and prawn/scampi puree. Season with salt and pepper, bring to a boil, add the liquid from the clams and cook until you have a thick sauce, then add the whole prawn/scampi and shrimp tails. Stir well and serve with the hot pasta.

adding the shellfish liquid just before they are ready. Cook for another 15 minutes, add the clams and serve with the hot pasta.

Variations 1. Toss the pasta with a little butter, then add the sauce and the mushrooms.
2. Add ½ stock or bouillon cube to the sauce to give it stronger flavour.

TAGLIOLINI WITH OYSTERS **362**

1 lb. flour	4 eggs
3 dozen oysters	4 oz. butter
5 oz. bacon	salt and pepper

Make the tagliolini in the usual way with the flour, eggs, a pinch of salt and a little warm water (see recipe 181). Roll out and cut into ¼ inch strips. Cut the bacon in short pieces, remove the oysters from their shells and wrap the bacon round the oysters, then thread onto skewers, using about six on each skewer. Grill quickly so the bacon is just crisp. Cook the tagliolini, drain well and toss with the butter. Serve the pasta topped with the bacon and oysters on individual plates, and add a little salt and freshly ground pepper.

MACARONI WITH PRAWNS/SCAMPI **363**

1 lb. macaroni	72 oz. chicken stock
4 oz. butter	8 oz. prawns/scampi
3 oz. grated parmesan	parsley
4 oz. fresh mushrooms	(sugar, cinnamon)
salt and pepper	

The original version of this recipe dates to the 17th century, and includes sugar and cinnamon, but you need not use them if it does not appeal to your taste. Gently heat three ounces butter. Add the parmesan, let it melt, then add the shelled prawns/scampi. Cook for a few minutes, stirring continually. Make a puree by cooking the cleaned mushrooms with about ½ ounce butter, salt, pepper and chopped parsley, and putting the mixture through a food mill. Add to the prawns/scampi pan. Cook until it has slighly thickened, and meanwhile cook the macaroni in the chicken stock. Drain the macaroni and serve with the prawn/scampi sauce.

Variation In the original version the freshly made macaroni were added to the pan before the prawns/scampi mushroom puree; if you do this, season with sugar and cinnamon instead of salt and pepper, in the true 17th century manner.

1 lb. linguine	1 lb. mussels
1 lb. small clams or	½ lb. shrimp
½ lb. cooked, shelled cockles	½ lb. baby squid
1 lb. tomatoes	6 tablespoons olive oil
2 cloves garlic	6 oz. dry white wine
parsley	salt and pepper

The following recipes have more complicated combinations of seafood with a subtle blend of flavours. Clean the mussels and clams, cook in a pan with a little oil, and when they open remove from the shells, strain and reserve the liquid left in the pan. Wash the shrimps, remove the tails and put the rest in a pan with the mussel and clam liquid and cook over low heat so it reduces a little, then put through a food mill. Wash and clean the squid, remove the bony parts, eyes and ink bags, and cook in five tablespoons oil with the chopped garlic, adding a little of the white wine as necessary. When it has been absorbed, add the skinned, seeded and chopped tomatoes. Season with salt and pepper, add half the clam and mussel liquid. Cook over moderate heat for about 20 minutes, adding more clam and mussel liquid to make a fairly thick sauce. Add the shrimp tails, cook for another ten minutes, then serve with the hot pasta, freshly ground pepper and finely chopped parsley.

1 lb. linguine	4 oz. baby squid
2 oz. shelled shrimps	2 oz. shelled mussels
2 oz. shelled clams or cockles	2 oz. mushrooms
½ lb. tomatoes	5 oz. dry white wine
olive oil	parsley
onion	1 carrot
brandy	sage
1 hot chili pepper	(garlic)
salt	

Choose the smallest and most tender squid you can find and clean them well in the usual way (see recipe 335). The mussels, clams and shrimps should be shelled without cooking. Clean and slice the mushrooms, chop the carrot and a little piece of onion and mix with the chopped parsley and the skinned, seeded and chopped tomatoes. Heat one tablespoon oil in a pan and cook the clams and mussels for a few minutes. Heat four tablespoons oil in another pan and add the chopped hot chili pepper and the sage leaves. Add the baby squid immediately and cook over moderate heat, adding half the wine as necessary. When it has evaporated add the tomatoes and a few tablespoons warm water, and continue cooking over medium heat. Cook the mushrooms with a pinch of salt in one tablespoon oil in another pan, remove the mushrooms and add to the squid. Add another three tablespoons oil to the pan in which the mushrooms were cooked. Put in the shrimp tails, mussels and clams, mix together, moisten with the rest of the wine, let it absorb and then add one tablespoon brandy. Cook for two minutes more over high heat and pour into the pan with the squid and mushrooms. Stir well. Cook the linguine in plenty of boiling, lightly salted water and toss with half the sauce. Sprinkle with chopped parsley and serve the rest of the sauce separately.

Variation Add crushed or chopped garlic to the oil in which you cook the squid.

PASTICCIO OF SPAGHETTINI WITH SEAFOOD   **368**

1 lb. spaghettini	2½ lb. clams, mussels, shrimps
4 oz. butter	or any other small shellfish
3 tablespoons milk	1 tablespoon flour
parsley	nutmeg
breadcrumbs	salt and pepper

Melt the butter and make a bechamel with the flour, milk, salt and pepper and nutmeg and a handful of chopped parsley. Cook all the seafood, shell and add to the bechamel, then mix with the hot pasta. Grease a mould, sprinkle with breadcrumbs and fill with the pasta mixture; cover with a final tablespoon of the sauce and dot with butter. Sprinkle with breadcrumbs and brown for a few minutes in a hot oven.

TAGLIATELLE WITH FILLETS OF SOLE   **369**

1 lb. flour	4 eggs
2 large sole or 4 small ones	18 prawns/scampi
3 oz. butter	18 oz. milk
8 oz. thin cream	6 oz. white wine
salt and pepper	grated parmesan

A very ancient combination of ingredients, very popular also at the turn of the century. Make the tagliatelle in the usual way (see recipe 181) with the flour, four eggs, a pinch of salt and warm water as necessary. Roll out fairly thinly and cut into ¼ inch strips. Clean and fillet the sole, clean the prawns/scampi and cook together in the white wine with salt and pepper. Melt the butter in another pan, add two ounces flour and stir in the boiling milk to make a bechamel. Add the cream and a pinch of salt. Cook the tagliatelle, drain well and toss with the sauce, then put in a baking dish. Chop the sole, shell the prawns/scampi and put on top of the tagliatelle; cover with the remaining sauce, sprinkle with parmesan, pour over extra butter and brown for a few minutes in a hot oven.

PASTICCIO OF LASAGNE WITH SOLE AND SHRIMPS   **370**

1 lb. flour	4 eggs
6 sole	2 lb. shrimps
½ lb. butter	6 oz. grated parmesan
4 tablespoons flour	18 oz. dry white wine
2 bay leaves	1 small onion
cognac	salt and pepper

A Renaissance recipe from the famous handbook of etiquette and cooking *I Banchetti* by Cristoforo Messisbugo, chief carver at the Court of Ferrara. Cook the skinned, but unchopped onion in 30 ounces water and half the wine, with the bay leaves, a few peppercorns and a pinch of salt. Boil for ten minutes, remove from the heat, cool to lukewarm. Remove the bay leaves, onion and peppercorns, return to the heat, bring to a boil and cook the cleaned shrimps. Drain them well and reserve the cooking liquid, then remove the tails. Pound the heads and shells in a mortar, adding a few tablespoons of the strained cooking liquid. Set aside. Clean and fillet the sole. Heat four tablespoons butter and when brown add the fillets of sole, cook gently, season with salt and pepper, moisten with white wine and cook until soft. Cook the shrimp tails for two or three minutes in four tablespoons butter, season with salt and pepper and moisten with brandy. Heat until the brandy is absorbed and reserve. Melt three ounces butter in another pan, add the flour and pounded shrimps, then very gradually add a few tablespoons of the strained shrimp cooking liquid to make a fairly thin sauce. Remove from the heat and cool, stirring occasionally to prevent a skin from forming. Season with salt, add the grated cheese and stir well. Make lasagne in the usual way (see recipe 181) with one pound flour, eggs, a pinch of salt and some warm water. Roll the dough and cut into rectangles about eight by four inches. Cook three or four at a time in a large pan of lightly salted boiling water and remove gently as they cook, drying them on a cloth. Grease a baking dish, put in a layer of lasagne, then a little sauce, another layer of lasagne and half the fillets of sole. Moisten with a little of the cooking liquid, add a third layer of lasagne, the remaining fillets of sole and some shrimps, then more of the cooking liquid, a final layer of lasagne and the remaining sauce. Dot with butter and brown for about ten minutes in a hot oven. You can of course vary the quantities for this sumptuous dish.

1 lb. short pasta
1½ lb. shellfish (mussels, clams, or cockles, etc.)
1 onion
1 stick celery
1 lb. fish (brill, bass, halibut, red snapper etc.)
1 carrot
parsley
salt and pepper

Cook the fish gently for about two hours in plenty of water with the carrot, celery, onion and a pinch of salt, until the liquid reduces and takes on the flavour of the fish, then pass through a food mill. Cook the shellfish in a pan until they open, remove from the shells and strain their liquid. Put the fish puree in a pan with this liquid and cook until reduced by half. Add the shellfish and cook for a few minutes. Finally add the pasta and let it cook until still quite firm. Serve with freshly ground pepper and chopped parsley.

RIGATONI WITH SEAFOOD   **372**

1 lb. rigatoni
3 tablespoons olive oil
1 lb. tomatoes
1 onion
2 cloves garlic
basil
salt and pepper
2 lb. seafood such as squid, prawns/scampi, shrimps, cuttlefish
6 oz. dry white wine
celery
parsley
rosemary
(sage, marjoram, leeks)

A recipe from the Abruzzi and Apulia. Normally anything left in the nets after the main catch is removed goes to make up this dish. Put three parts water to one part oil in a pan—preferably a terracotta pot—and bring to a boil. Add the wine, chopped onion, celery, crushed garlic (to be discarded), parsley, basil, rosemary. Cook for 15 minutes so the sauce simmers gently. Add the chopped tomatoes and the seafood (the prawns and shrimps are washed and dried, the squid and cuttlefish cleaned and chopped). Cook for 45 minutes, drain and put through a food mill for a thick, highly flavoured stock. Return to the heat to thicken a little more, season with salt and pepper and serve with the rigatoni.

Variation Add a few sage or marjoram leaves to the sauce with the rosemary, basil and parsley; also a chopped leek as well as the onion.

1 lb. vermicelli	1 lb. fillets of any good fish
1 lb. seafood (clams, mussels, etc.)	(cod, bass, brill, John Dory, etc.)
1½ lb. tomatoes	6 salt-cured anchovy fillets
3 oz. shelled peas	3 oz. fresh button mushrooms
8 oz. olive oil	3 oz. black olives
1 tablespoon pine nuts	1 tablespoon capers
salt and pepper	1 clove garlic
breadcrumbs	parsley
½ lb. butter	1 lb. flour
2 eggs	

In spite of being a Lenten dish which was always served on Palm Sunday in Naples, this has the most lavish variety of ingredients possible. It comes from the first record of Neapolitan cooking that was ever made, compiled by the Duke di Buonvicino. The pastry crust was made in the 19th century with flour, lard, sugar and eggs like a type of pudding, but this recipe gives a rather simpler version. Rub the softened butter with the flour, then gradually add the beaten eggs and one teaspoon salt until you have a mixture resembling fine breadcrumbs. Form into a ball and wrap in a cloth or plastic film and leave to stand for about an hour in a cool place, then roll out into two sheets, one larger than the other, about ½ inch thick. Line a deep pie dish with the larger sheet so it comes up the sides, then put a piece of greaseproof/waxed paper on the bottom and weigh it down with dried peas or beans. Cut the smaller sheet of pastry into a disc and put on a greased baking sheet, bake both in a moderate oven until firm and golden (about 15 minutes), cool. Clean and fillet the fish; pound in a mortar with the seeded olives, the washed capers, the pine nuts and a handful of parsley to make a firm paste. Soften with two tablespoons oil and a few tablespoons breadcrumbs to bind well together. Form into little balls about as big as a walnut, roll in breadcrumbs and fry in plenty of really hot oil until it just starts to brown. Meanwhile prepare some tomato sauce: heat a little oil, add the pureed tomatoes and add the fish balls to this sauce. Continue cooking, add the peas (they should be very young and tender, or else you will have to parboil them first), the button mushrooms (cooked previously in a little oil) and the remaining cooked seafood. Cook until all the ingredients are soft and well blended, then add ½ tablespoon flour to thicken. Cook the pasta until still quite firm. Make another sauce: heat three tablespoons oil with the crushed garlic (to be discarded), soften the washed anchovy fillets, add some pepper and chopped parsley. Toss with the pasta, then put in the pastry case, making a layer of pasta, then fish balls and the other seafood sauce, ending with a layer of pasta. Cover with the pastry lid and bake in a moderate oven for 45 minutes. Let it stand a few minutes before serving.

1 lb. clams
½ lb. butter
2 egg yolks
olive oil
3 oz. fresh mushrooms
parsley

6 oz. flour
6 eggs
9 oz. milk
2 oz. grated parmesan
brandy
salt and pepper

Cook the mussels until they open, remove from the shells and strain their liquid. Make a bechamel with two ounces butter and eight tablespoons flour, the milk and clam liquid, salt and pepper and a little brandy. When the sauce is smooth and thick add four ounces butter and the mussels and stir well. Remove from the heat then put through a food mill or puree in a blender; add the beaten egg yolks to bind. Keep this puree warm in a bain-marie (hot water bath). Make the pancakes with four ounces flour, two ounces parmesan and six eggs beaten together to form a fairly liquid batter. Cook two tablespoons of the batter at a time in plenty of hot oil to make thin pancakes. Spread some mussel puree on each pancake, reserving two tablespoons at the end. Roll them up and arrange close together, but not overlapping, in a greased ovenproof dish. Make a sauce from two ounces butter, sliced mushrooms and the remaining mussels, salt, pepper and parsley. Spread this over the pancakes and brown for about five minutes in a hot oven.

FISH AND RICOTTA RAVIOLI **375**

1 lb. flour
6 oz. ricotta
1 lb. borage
3 eggs
sage

1 lb. cooked white fish fillets
3 oz. grated parmesan
¼ lb. butter or margarine
(clams, oil, onion, garlic, parsley)

Make a pasta dough with flour and water and a pinch of salt (see recipe 181). Roll out fairly thin and make into rectangles 2½ × 1½ inches. Make the filling: cook the borage, drain well and chop, then put in a bowl with the fish fillets (use any baked, grilled or poached fish leftovers, or prepared specially), the crumbled ricotta, grated parmesan and a pinch of salt. Mix well, then put small mounds of the filling on the dough rectangles and fold over to make ravioli, pressing the edges firmly together. Cook in boiling, salted water, drain and toss with butter which you have melted in a pan with a few sage leaves.

Variation Serve with a clam (or any seafood) sauce, made by cooking the shelled fish gently with oil, garlic, onion and parsley.

V
PASTA WITH WHITE MEAT

PASTINA IN CHICKEN SOUP 376

12 oz. pastina (or any sort of small pasta)

54 oz. chicken stock
grated parmesan

The simplest form of pasta in brodo that requires a good light chicken stock. Where chicken stock is called for you can substitute stock made from any poultry or veal bones (see Introduction). Bring to a boil, add the pastina and cook until al dente. Serve grated parmesan separately.

CHICKEN SOUP WITH BEANS AND PASTA 377

8 oz. short pasta with a hole,
e. g. tubettini or cannolicchi
54 oz. chicken stock
1 clove garlic
salt

½ lb. tomatoes
6 oz. shelled fresh or
canned white beans
1 stick celery
olive oil

Put the tomatoes through a food mill or blender, then add the puree to the pan with the stock, the celery cut in fine strips of julienne, the crushed garlic and beans. Season with salt and when the beans are almost cooked add the pasta. Cook until the pasta is just al dente, add a few tablespoons olive oil, leave to stand for a minute, then serve.

CHICKEN SOUP WITH PASTINA AND SWEET PEPPER 378

12 oz. pastina
36 oz. chicken stock
salt

1 sweet pepper
parsley

A South American recipe. Roast the pepper to remove the outer skin and cut into very fine strips. Cook the pastina, drain well and add to the hot stock with the pepper along with a good handful of chopped parsley. Chill and serve.

8 oz. small short pasta
54 oz. chicken stock
2 oz. butter
grated parmesan

8 oz. chopped vegetables (e.g. onions, turnips, celery, carrots, zucchini)
salt and pepper

Use any vegetables in season; clean and chop finely, then cook very gently in the butter with salt and pepper to taste. Boil the stock, add the vegetables, then the pasta. Cook until the pasta is al dente; serve grated parmesan separately.

MACARONI WITH WINE AND HONEY **380**

1 lb. macaroni
5 oz. honey
6 oz. white wine
cinnamon
grated parmesan

6 oz. butter
54 oz. chicken stock
1 tablespoon vinegar
ginger
(saffron, pepper, sugar)

Accounts of medieval banquets mention macaroni cooked in fat capon broth, then served with honey. This recipe makes an interesting way to serve pasta. Melt four ounces butter in a pan. Put the honey in a bowl set over hot water to make it thin, then mix with the melted butter. Add the white wine, simmer a few minutes, then add the vinegar, cinnamon and ginger. Cook the macaroni in the stock, drain and add to the butter and honey mixture. Pour over the remaining melted butter, and add a few tablespoons grated parmesan.

Variations 1. Mix the hot cooked pasta with the butter, honey, etc. in a hot serving dish without bothering to cook them first.
2. Add a pinch of saffron and pepper to the sauce.
3. Use sugar instead of honey, or both.

MACARONI WITH MUSHROOM PUREE **381**

1 lb. macaroni
6 oz. butter
3 oz. mushrooms
sugar
salt and pepper

72 oz. chicken broth
3 oz. grated parmesan
parsley
cinnamon

Another combination of sweet and savoury ingredients. Clean the mushrooms, slice them and cook in one tablespoon butter with some salt and chopped parsley, then put through a food mill or blender. Cook the macaroni in the stock, drain, add the remaining butter, grated cheese, mushroom puree and sugar and cinnamon to taste.

GRATED PASTA IN CHICKEN SOUP   **382**

---

7 oz. flour
3 eggs
grated pecorino/romano or parmesan

6 tablespoons semolina
72 oz. chicken stock
salt

Make an egg pasta dough in the usual way (see recipe 181) with the flour, semolina, eggs and a pinch of salt. Work thoroughly so it becomes fairly firm and elastic. Set aside to rest in a ball for ten minutes, then using the flat holes of a grater, grate the pasta quickly and lightly over a floured board, taking care that the pieces do not stick together. Bring the stock to a boil, add the grated pasta, and simmer for about ten minutes until the pasta is cooked. Serve with grated cheese.

CHICKEN SOUP WITH LITTLE PANCAKES   **383**

---

4 oz. flour
8 oz. milk
4 oz. scamorza cheese
lard
salt

4 eggs
54 oz. chicken stock
4 oz. grated pecorino/romano
(parsley, nutmeg, butter,
grated parmesan)

A recipe from the Abruzzi, its name in local dialect means pancakes in soup. Make a smooth, fairly thin batter with the flour, eggs, milk and a pinch of salt. Heat the lard and use two tablespoons of the batter at a time to make small pancakes. Put a little grated pecorino/romano and diced scamorza on each pancake, roll them up and put a few in each soup plate. Pour over a good chicken stock and serve very hot.

Variations 1. Add a handful of chopped parsley and a little nutmeg to the batter, or a little grated parmesan.
2. You can fry the pancakes in butter instead of lard, although it is more inclined to burn.
3. Omit the scamorza.
4. Use parmesan instead of pecorino/romano.

CHICKEN SOUP WITH QUADRUCCI, PEAS, ASPARAGUS AND EGGS

10 oz. flour
72 oz. chicken stock
2 oz. butter
salt

5 eggs
5 oz. shelled peas
3 oz. grated parmesan
cooked asparagus tips

Make the egg pasta dough in the usual way with the flour, three eggs and a pinch of salt (see recipe 181). Cut the dough as for tagliatelle, then cut the still-folded ribbons crosswise into squares called quadrucci. Cook the peas in the stock and when they are almost done add the quadrucci, and after a few seconds the asparagus tips. Cook just long enough to heat through, add the two remaining eggs, lightly beaten, and serve very hot.

CHICKEN SOUP WITH PASTA, TURNIPS AND EGGS

¾ lb. short pasta
54 oz. chicken stock
2 oz. butter

½ lb. turnips
2 eggs
3 oz. grated parmesan

Peel the turnips and dice them. Cook the turnips in the stock. When they are soft add the pasta and cook until al dente, then add the beaten eggs, butter and parmesan. Mix well and serve very hot.

CHICKEN SOUP WITH VERMICELLI, EGGS AND LEMON

¾ lb. vermicelli
2 egg yolks

72 oz. chicken stock
juice of 2 lemons

Beat the egg yolks with a few tablespoons of cool stock, together with the lemon juice in a deep serving bowl. Break the pasta into short pieces and cook in the remaining boiling stock, then pour over the ingredients in the serving bowl. Mix well and serve immediately.

CHICKEN SOUP WITH PASTA, SPINACH AND EGGS 387

¾ lb. pastina, or a long thin pasta
54 oz. chicken stock
6 tablespoons thin cream

1¾ lb. spinach
2 eggs
3 oz. grated parmesan

Wash and cook the spinach until just tender, then drain very well and chop finely. Add to the boiling stock with the cream, beaten eggs and the pasta. When the pasta is al dente add the grated parmesan and serve immediately.

COLD CONCHIGLIE OR LINGUINE WITH CHICKEN 388

¾ lb. conchiglie or linguine
olive oil
lemon juice
salt and pepper

4 oz. cooked chicken
(basil, parsley,
paprika, curry powder)

Cook the pasta, drain well and mix in a serving dish with the diced chicken, olive oil, a pinch of salt, some lemon juice and freshly ground black pepper. Serve cold.

Variations 1. Add a little chopped basil or parsley.
2. Use paprika or curry powder instead of pepper.

CHICKEN SOUP WITH PASTA 389

¾ lb. small pasta
54 oz. chicken stock
parsley
grated parmesan

4 oz. cooked chicken
(basil, pepper, paprika,
curry powder, thin cream,
sweet pepper)

Cook the pasta in the stock, add the diced chicken, a handful of chopped parsley and serve grated parmesan separately.

Variations 1. Use basil instead of parsley, or both.
2. Add a pinch of pepper, paprika or curry powder.
3. Add some thin cream to make a richer soup.
4. Add some cooked sweet pepper, chopped in small pieces.

MACCHERONCELLI WITH CAPON BREAST

1 lb. maccheroncelli
6 oz. butter
salt and pepper

1 capon breast or 1 large
chicken breast
2 large tomatoes

Heat two tablespoons of the butter and lightly brown the finely chopped chicken, then add the pureed tomatoes. Cook the maccheroncelli, drain well and toss with nearly all the remaining butter, then add the chicken and tomato sauce. Put in a greased ovenproof dish, dot with the remaining butter and brown for a few mintues in a hot oven. Serve chicken soup in bowls separately, so you can sip it while eating the pasta.

MACARONI WITH CHICKEN AND CHEESE ESCOFFIER

1 lb. macaroni
3 oz. ricotta
butter

4 oz. cooked chicken
3 oz. grated gruyere

One of the great Escoffier's recipes simplified and adapted for pasta. Shred the chicken, mash the ricotta and mix together with the gruyere. Cook the pasta, drain and toss with a little butter, and then the chicken and cheese mixture. Put in a greased ovenproof dish, dot with butter and brown for a few minutes in a hot oven.

TAGLIATELLE WITH CHICKEN AND MUSHROOMS ELSINORE

19 oz. flour
6 tablespoons butter
4 oz. cooked chicken
parsley
salt and pepper

5 eggs
18 oz. milk
3 oz. mushrooms
3 oz. grated parmesan
(thin cream)

A recipe from Denmark, if not from Hamlet's castle. Make the tagliatelle in the usual way with the flour, eggs, a pinch of salt and water as necessary (see recipe 181). Make a thin bechamel sauce with five tablespoons butter and four tablespoons flour and the milk. Use the remaining butter to cook the shredded chicken and finely sliced mushrooms, then season with salt and pepper and a handful of chopped parsley. Cook the pasta, drain well and mix with the bechamel sauce, then the mushroom and chicken mixture. Serve grated parmesan separately.

Variations 1. Dilute the bechamel with cream to make a more liquid sauce.
2. Mix the pasta with the chicken and mushrooms, half the bechamel and a few tablespoons grated parmesan; put in a greased ovenproof dish, cover with the remaining bechamel and sprinkle with grated parmesan. Brown in a hot oven.

TAGLIATELLE WITH ROAST CHICKEN　　**393**

1 lb. flour	5 eggs
2½ lb. chicken (cleaned)	6 oz. butter
3 oz. grated parmesan	white wine
sage	truffle
heavy cream	(brandy)
salt and pepper	

Make the pasta dough in the usual way with the flour, eggs and a pinch of salt (see recipe 181) and cut into tagliatelle. Melt four tablespoons butter and brown the chicken all over, then sprinkle with some salt and pepper. Add a little sage and moisten with some fairly good white wine, using about ten ounces and then add water as necessary. Cover the casserole and cook in a moderate oven or over medium heat about 40 minutes. When cooked, remove the flesh and chop into small pieces. Return the casserole to the heat and boil to reduce the juices, then add one or two tablespoons cream, boil again and add the diced chicken. Cook the pasta, drain well and toss with the remaining butter, half the grated parmesan and the chicken mixture. Mix well, cover with slices of truffle and serve immediately.

Variation Use a little brandy instead of white wine.

TAGLIATELLE WITH CHICKEN,　　**394**
APPLE AND BANANA

1 lb. flour	5 eggs
4 tablespoons butter	2 onions
1 large apple	1 banana
4 oz. cooked chicken	chicken stock
thick cream	curry powder
salt and pepper	(parmesan, truffle)

This is a wonderful blend of flavours, however unusual. Make the tagliatelle in the normal way with the flour, eggs, a pinch of salt and a little water as necessary (see recipe 181). Make the sauce: heat the butter, add the chopped onion, the grated apple and the sliced banana, then the chopped chicken. Cook for a few minutes, season with salt and pepper and a pinch of curry powder, then add two tablespoons cream. Cook a little longer; if it seems too dry add a few tablespoons stock. When the sauce is nice and thick put it through a food mill or blender. Return to the heat, add more cream if necessary for the desired consistency, then mix with the hot pasta.

Variations   1. Grate a little truffle over the finished dish.
           2. When you have mixed the pasta with the sauce put it in a greased ovenproof dish, sprinkle with grated parmesan and brown for a few minutes in a hot oven.

CAPPELLETTI IN CHICKEN SOUP   **395**

10 oz. flour	4 eggs
1 egg yolk	1 chicken breast
1 teaspoon butter	8 oz. ricotta
5 oz. grated parmesan	½ teaspoon grated lemon peel
nutmeg	olive oil
72 oz. chicken stock	salt and pepper

Make an egg pasta dough in the usual way with the flour, three eggs, a pinch of salt and a drop of oil (see recipe 181). Roll the dough out very thinly and cut into circles two inches in diameter. Brown the chicken in one tablespoon butter and some salt and pepper, then chop and mix in a bowl with the sieved ricotta, one whole egg and one egg yolk, a good tablespoon grated parmesan, the lemon peel, salt, pepper and grated nutmeg. Divide this filling between the circles of pasta, fold them over and press the edges well together, then draw the two ends into a crescent shape to make the cappelletti, or "little hats" (they are also said to resemble the navel of Venus). This is the simplest form of cappelletti, from Modena and Reggiano. You can make them up to 12 hours in advance and leave in the refrigerator, covered with a dry cloth. Cook them in the stock; freshly made cappelletti cook surprisingly quickly so test them after five minutes cooking. Dry ones take longer, from 15-20 minutes. Serve in the stock with grated parmesan, or serve grated parmesan separately.

14 oz. flour	4 eggs
4 oz. cooked chicken	6 oz. ricotta or other cream cheese
2 egg yolks	milk
salt and pepper	nutmeg
54 oz. chicken stock	(cinnamon, butter)
parmesan	

Make an egg pasta dough with the flour, eggs, salt and water as necessary (see recipe 181). Make the filling: chop or mince the chicken finely and mix with the sieved cheese, beaten egg yolks, nutmeg, salt and pepper and enough milk to make a smooth, soft paste. Divide this filling into mounds on one sheet of dough and cover with the second sheet to make ravioli (see recipe 251). Cook in the stock and serve as soup. Serve grated parmesan separately.

Variations 1. Add ¼ teaspoon cinnamon to the filling.
2. Drain the ravioli and serve with melted butter and grated parmesan.

TORTELLI WITH CHICKEN AND TRUFFLE FILLING **397**

1 lb. flour	4 eggs
4 oz. cooked chicken	3 oz. truffle
3 slices stale white bread (without the crust)	3 oz. butter
	salt and pepper
nutmeg	chicken stock
grated parmesan	

Make the pasta dough in the usual way with the flour, eggs, a pinch of salt and a little water (see recipe 181). Make the filling: chop the chicken and truffle. Soak the bread in a little stock, then squeeze well and crumble. Mix with the chicken and truffle, half the butter, salt, pepper and nutmeg to make a smooth paste. If the mixture seems too dry add a little stock, if too moist add some grated parmesan. Divide this filling in mounds on the dough to make tortellini (see recipe 251). Cook in stock or boiling salted water, then either drain and serve with grated parmesan and melted butter, or cook and serve in the stock, and serve grated parmesan separately.

CANNELLONI WITH CHICKEN, CHEESE AND MUSHROOM FILLING 398

1 lb. flour
½ lb. cooked chicken
6 oz. butter
18 oz. milk
3 oz. grated parmesan
nutmeg

4 eggs
¼ lb. mushrooms
3 egg yolks
onion
salt and pepper

Make the egg pasta dough with the flour, eggs, salt and water as necessary (see recipe 181). Roll out the dough and cut into six-inch squares, then boil them very gently for about 20 seconds and remove from the water with a slotted spoon. Make the filling: lightly brown the chicken in four tablespoons butter, add the chopped mushrooms and a little chopped onion. Prepare a thin bechamel with two ounces flour and four tablespoons butter and the milk. Put the mushroom and chicken mixture in a bowl and mix with two tablespoons of bechamel, the beaten egg yolks, two tablespoons grated parmesan, pepper and nutmeg for a smooth, soft paste. Put mounds of this filling on each square of pasta, roll them up and place in a greased ovenproof dish, fairly close together but not overlapping. Pour over the remaining bechamel, sprinkle with parmesan and dot with butter, then brown in a hot oven.

MACARONI WITH CHICKEN 399

1 lb. macaroni
6 oz. butter
6 oz. white wine
3 oz. grated parmesan
salt and pepper

2½ lb. chicken (cleaned)
1 tablespoon flour
¼ lb. tomatoes
chicken stock
(celery, carrot, leek)

Cut the chicken into serving pieces. Heat four tablespoons butter, add the chicken pieces and brown on all sides, then add the flour and a few tablespoons chicken stock. Stir well until the flour is dissolved, then add the wine. Cook until it evaporates a little, season with salt and pepper and add the pureed tomatoes. Cook gently for about one hour until the chicken is tender and the sauce well thickened. Cook the pasta, drain well, toss with the remaining butter and parmesan, then the sauce from the pan where the chicken was cooked. Serve with a piece of chicken on each helping of pasta.

Variations 1. Dilute the sauce with a little dry white wine instead of stock, or add a little wine and let it reduce before adding the stock.
2. Add a little rosemary to the oil when cooking the onion.
3. Add a few tablespoons of fresh or frozen peas and cook with the sauce.

PASTICCIO OF MACARONI WITH CHICKEN LIVERS 405

1 lb. macaroni	½ lb. chicken livers
5 tablespons olive oil	1 onion
1 stick celery	1 carrot
1 leek	¾ lb. tomatoes
6 oz. butter	salt and pepper
¼ lb. grated parmesan	

Heat the oil and brown the chopped onion, then add the chopped celery, carrot, and leek and cook until soft, then add the pureed tomatoes. Season with salt and pepper, then add the cleaned, chopped chicken livers and cook for a few minutes. Cook the macaroni, drain well and toss with most of the butter and the parmesan. Grease an ovenproof dish and put in a layer of macaroni, cover with half the chicken liver mixture and some grated parmesan. Continue in this way, ending with a layer of macaroni. Sprinkle with grated parmesan, dot with butter and brown in a hot oven.

RIGATONI WITH CHICKEN LIVERS 406

1 lb. rigatoni	4 oz. chicken livers
5 oz. mushrooms	2½ oz. butter
6 oz. white wine	3 oz. grated parmesan
parsley	salt and pepper

Clean the mushrooms and chicken livers and chop finely. Cook them for one minute in the hot butter. Season with salt and pepper, add the wine and cook until it reduces, then remove from the heat. Add a handful of chopped parsley and mix with the hot pasta. Serve grated parmesan separately.

14 oz. flour	4 eggs
½ lb. ricotta	¼ lb. chicken livers
1 oz. dried mushrooms	1¼ lb. spinach
2 oz. butter	1 large tomato
chicken stock	nutmeg
grated parmesan	salt and pepper

Make and cook the tagliatelle in the usual way with the flour, eggs, a pinch of salt and a little water (see recipe 181). Soak the mushrooms in warm water for ten minutes, then chop them roughly. Clean and chop the chicken livers. Cook the spinach, drain very well and chop finely. Sieve the ricotta and mix with the spinach and a pinch of nutmeg, then work together until you have a smooth paste. Heat the butter and cook the mushrooms, then lightly brown the chicken livers. Add the pureed tomatoes and a few tablespoons stock. Season with salt and pepper and cook over moderate heat for a few minutes, then raise the heat, add the ricotta and spinach mixture, stir well and serve with the hot pasta.

TORTELLINI WITH CHICKEN LIVERS
AND MUSHROOM FILLING **408**

10 oz. flour	3 eggs
¼ lb. chicken livers	3 oz. mushrooms
3 oz. cooked chicken	6 oz. butter
3 oz. grated parmesan	72 oz. chicken stock
nutmeg	sage
parsley	(cinnamon)
salt and pepper	

This was a favorite dish of the famous Farnese pope, Paul III. Make the pasta dough in the usual way with the flour, eggs, a pinch of salt and a little water (see recipe 181), and cut into small circles about two inches in diameter. Make the filling: cook the chopped chicken livers and mushrooms in half the butter, season with salt and pepper and a handful of chopped parsley. Finely chop the chicken and mix with the chicken livers and mushrooms together with a pinch of nutmeg. Divide this filling between the circles of pasta, fold them over and press the edges together to make tortellini, then cook in the stock. Drain and serve with the remaining butter heated with a few sage leaves, and the grated parmesan.

1 lb. flour	4 eggs
½ lb. chicken giblets	¾ lb. tomatoes
2 oz. butter	4 tablespoons olive oil
3 oz. grated parmesan	parsley
salt and pepper	

Make the tagliatelle in the usual way with the flour, eggs, a pinch of salt and a little water (see recipe 181). Clean the giblets and chop finely, then cook in the butter with salt and pepper and a little chopped parsley. Heat the oil in another pan, add the pureed tomatoes, season with salt and pepper and add the giblets. Cook for a few minutes until well blended, then serve with the hot pasta.

Variation Put the tagliatelle and the sauce in a greased ovenproof dish, sprinkle with grated parmesan, dot with butter and brown in a hot oven.

PASTICCIO OF MACARONI WITH CHICKEN GIBLETS **410**

1 lb. macaroni	½ lb. chicken giblets
36 oz. chicken stock	2 oz. flour
5 oz. butter	18 oz. milk
2 eggs	3 oz. grated parmesan
breadcrumbs	salt and pepper

Another old Neapolitan recipe. Clean the giblets, chop very finely and cook in the stock. Make a bechamel with two ounces butter, the flour and milk, and season with salt and pepper. When the sauce is smooth add two beaten eggs. Cook the pasta, drain well and toss with three ounces butter. Grease an ovenproof dish with high sides and sprinkle with the breadcrumbs. Put in a layer of macaroni, then half the giblet mixture, half the bechamel and a little grated parmesan. Make another layer of macaroni, then the remaining giblets, bechamel and parmesan. Sprinkle the final layer of macaroni with parmesan, put in a bain-marie (hot-water bath) over moderate heat and cook for ten minutes.

1 lb. bigoli	1 small pigeon
4 tablespoons olive oil	½ oz. butter
2 medium onions	1 lb. peeled tomatoes
chicken stock	3 oz. grated parmesan
salt and pepper	(milk)

Clean the pigeon. Heat the oil and butter, brown the chopped onion and then the pigeon. Add salt and pepper and the crushed tomatoes. Simmer over low heat, adding a few tablespoons stock if it seems too dry. When the pigeon is tender remove from the pan, then either cut it in serving pieces and return these to the sauce, or remove the flesh and chop or put through a food mill, then return to the sauce. Cook the pasta, drain well and mix with the pigeon. Serve grated parmesan separately.

Variation Cook the pigeon in milk instead of stock to give it a lovely delicate flavour.

¾ lb. macaroni	2 pigeons
14 oz. flour	10 oz. butter
6 oz. sugar	1 egg yolk
1 onion	1 oz. dried mushrooms
2 oz. grated parmesan	nutmeg
lemon juice	bay leaf
salt and pepper	(white wine, brandy, stock, flour)

Another ancient recipe using a sweet pie crust. Put the flour in a mound on a pastry board and make a well in the middle, then add the softened butter, sugar, egg yolk, a pinch of salt and a little grated lemon peel. Mix quickly and thoroughly to make a smooth dough (it may get too dry if you take your time). Gather into a ball, set aside to rest, then roll into two sheets, one larger one for the bottom crust and one smaller one for the top crust. Make the filling: lightly brown the finely chopped onion in butter and add the pigeons cut into serving pieces. Brown all over, then add salt and pepper and a pinch of nutmeg. Soak the mushrooms in warm water for ten minutes, chop roughly and add to the pigeons with the soaking liquid and a bay leaf. Cook over low heat until the pigeons are tender, about 1-1½ hours depending on the age of the birds. Cook the macaroni, drain well and add to the pigeons together with the grated cheese, mix well and cook for a few more minutes over moderate heat. Grease a pie dish and line with the larger sheet of dough, fill with the pigeon and

1 lb. pasta	3 dozen snails
18 oz. white wine	¾ lb. tomatoes
6 tablespoons olive oil	1 onion
salt and pepper	(garlic, celery, nutmeg,
parsley	hot chili pepper)

It is easiest to use tinned/canned snails as they are already cleaned. Follow the instructions for cooking them. Heat the oil and brown the chopped onion, add the pureed tomatoes, salt and pepper and a handful of chopped parsley. Add the cooked snails and the white wine and cook until the wine evaporates. Add a few tablespoons of hot water if the sauce seems too dry, and cook until it is the desired consistency. Serve with the hot pasta.

Variations 1. Use garlic instead of onion.
2. Add chopped celery, and finely chopped chili pepper.

MACARONI OR TROCCOLI WITH LAMB RAGU **418**

1 lb. flour	4 eggs
2¾ lb. boned lamb (shoulder or leg)	6 tablespoons olive oil
¾ lb. tomatoes	white wine
2 cloves garlic	grated pecorino/romano
bay leaf	(grated parmesan, onion, hot chili
salt and pepper	pepper, celery, sweet peppers)

A classic combination of pasta and lamb that has a very ancient origin, although the tomato is a more recent addition. Make the pasta dough in the usual way with the flour, eggs, a pinch of salt and a little water (see recipe 181). Knead the dough thoroughly for a least 20 minutes, then set aside to rest for another 20 minutes. Roll out to a thickness of about ⅛ inch. In the Abruzzi and some parts of Apulia the dough is then cut into small rectangles, the same size as a little instrument shaped like a guitar which is used to cut the pasta into macaroni. It consists of steel wires set about ⅛ inch apart on a wood board. You roll the sheet of pasta over the wires and it is cut into long square strands. In Apulia another method uses a ribbed roller called a torculo from the Latin torculum. This is rolled over the pasta dough and cuts it into strips about the same size as maccheroni alla chitarra, but they are not square. Make the lamb ragu: heat the oil and brown the crushed garlic and two bay leaves. Add the diced lamb and sprinkle with pepper and salt. Brown all over then add six tablespoons wine and cook until the wine has reduced a little. Add the peeled, chopped tomatoes and continue cooking over moderate heat for about two hours, or until the meat is very tender. Check to see if there is enough liquid in the pan and add a few tablespoons warm water or stock if it seems too dry. Cook the pasta in plenty of boiling water and mix with the lamb and as much juice from the pan as is necessary to make a good sauce. Serve grated pecorino/romano separately.

Variations 1. Add two sliced sweet peppers to the oil with the tomatoes.
2. Add some finely chopped onion and celery and grated parmesan to the meat and cook until tender.
3. Fry a piece of hot chili pepper in the oil and then discard it.

RAVIOLI WITH LAMB'S BRAIN FILLING AND WALNUTS   **419**

1 lb. flour	6 eggs
2 lb. spinach	½ lb. ricotta
½ lb. lamb's brain	½ oz. butter
6 tablespoons olive oil	¾ lb. walnut kernels
3 oz. pine nuts	3 oz. grated parmesan
1 clove garlic	salt and pepper
nutmeg	(Swiss chard, borage, sweetbreads)

Make the dough in the usual way with the flour, four eggs, a pinch of salt and a little oil (see recipe 181) and cut into rectangles, or roll into two sheets as for ravioli (see recipe 251). Make the filling: cook the spinach, drain very well and put through a food mill or blender. Blanch the brain in boiling water, cool, remove the outer membrane and chop into small pieces, and cook gently for a few minutes in butter, then put through a food mill or blender. Mash the ricotta and mix with the spinach and brain, then add the beaten eggs, a pinch of nutmeg and some salt and pepper. Divide this filling between the ravioli or in mounds on the sheets of pasta. Fold over the ravioli or cover with the second sheet of dough to make the ravioli in the usual way, then cook in plenty of boiling salted water. Make the sauce: pound the walnuts, pine nuts, one clove garlic and gradually add some olive oil to obtain a smooth puree. Heat the puree in a bowl set in a bain-marie of hot water. Mix with the hot ravioli and serve grated parmesan separately.

Variations 1. Use Swiss chard and borage instead of spinach, or a mixture of all three.
2. Use half sweetbreads and half brain (1 lamb's brain weighs about four ounces).

220

1 lb. macaroni	2 lb. mutton or lamb (shoulder or leg)
6 oz. dry white wine	2 salt-cured anchovy fillets
4 oz. butter	garlic
rosemary	3 oz. grated parmesan
salt and pepper	(nutmeg)

Make incisions in the mutton and put in pieces of garlic and rosemary, or pound the garlic and rosemary together and stick the mixture in the incisions. Pour over melted butter, season with salt and pepper and cook in a greased ovenproof dish or a baking dish in a moderate oven for 1½ hours with a few tablespoons water or stock if it seems to dry. When the meat is cooked transfer the juices to a saucepan, add the white wine and reduce a little, then cook the washed anchovy fillets until soft. Cook the pasta, toss with the remaining butter and grated parmesan, add the anchovy sauce and serve.

Variations 1. In the original recipe a pinch of nutmeg is included in the sauce.
2. In the Middle East the pasta is mixed with the mutton gravy and the meat is cut up into individual slices and served on top.

1 lb. macaroni	2 lb. boned mutton or lamb
6 oz. butter	1 onion
2 cloves garlic	2 tablespoons flour
36 oz. stock	½ lb. tomatoes
basil	3 oz. grated parmesan
parsley	marjoram
salt and pepper	

Remove any fat or tough sinews from the meat and cut into medium cubes. Brown it in four tablespoons butter with the chopped onion and garlic. Season with salt and pepper and add the flour and enough stock to cover. Add the herbs and the peeled, seeded and chopped tomatoes and cook until the meat is tender and the stock has reduced. Cook the pasta, drain well and mix with the meat and its gravy. Serve grated parmesan separately.

Variation Put a layer of the pasta mixed with the meat and gravy in a greased ovenproof dish, pour over more gravy and sprinkle with grated parmesan and continue in this way until the ingredients are used. Sprinkle with parmesan, dot with butter and brown in a hot oven.

MACARONI WITH CURRIED MUTTON OR LAMB

1 lb. macaroni	2¼ lb. boned mutton or lamb
2 onions	6 oz. butter
6 oz. white wine	stock
salt	(aubergines/eggplant, tomatoes)
2 tablespoons curry powder	

Remove any fat from the meat and dice. Brown in four ounces butter with the finely sliced onion. Moisten with the wine and let it reduce a little, then cook until the meat is tender, adding more water or stock to the pan if it seems too dry. Add the curry powder: you can vary the quantity, two tablespoons will make a fairly hot sauce. Mix with the hot pasta and top with the cooked meat, or serve the meat separately.

Variations 1. Add pureed tomatoes to the sauce.
2. Add a little diced aubergine/eggplant to the sauce.

TAGLIOLINI WITH ROAST VEAL GRAVY

1 lb. flour	3 eggs
4 oz. grated parmesan	2 lb. boned roast of veal
1½ oz. butter	1½ oz. strutto or lard
¾ lb. tomatoes	stock
garlic	rosemary
salt and pepper	(pancetta, mushrooms)

Make the pasta dough in the usual way with the flour, eggs, a pinch of salt and a little warm water if necessary (see recipe 181). Roll out very thin and cut into strips ⅟₁₆ inch wide. Make incisions in the veal and stick in small pieces of garlic and rosemary. Heat the butter and add the chopped strutto or lard, then brown the veal on all sides. Season with salt and pepper and add the pureed tomatoes. Cook gently until tender (1½-2 hours), adding a little stock if it seems too dry. Mix the meat gravy with the hot pasta and serve grated parmesan separately. Serve the veal as a separate dish.

Variations 1. Use pancetta instead of strutto or lard.
2. Add a few sliced mushrooms to the gravy.

1 lb. conchiglie	1 lb. broccoli spears
6 tablespoons thick cream	1 clove garlic
5 tablespoons olive oil	hot chili pepper
1 tablespoon roast veal gravy	salt

Heat the oil and lightly brown the crushed garlic and chopped chili pepper. Discard garlic and pepper and add the chopped broccoli to the oil. Cook a little so it absorbs the flavour, then add the cream. Cook the pasta, drain well and add to the broccoli, then mix in the veal gravy (see previous recipe).

TAGLIOLINI WITH VEAL GRAVY
AND LEMON JUICE

425

1 lb. flour	5 eggs
4 oz. stock	juice of 1 lemon
roast veal gravy	(must—see variation)
salt and pepper	

Originally a Renaissance recipe, or even older, but now part of Jewish cooking, which is always a mixture of many traditions. Make the tagliolini in the usual way with the flour, four eggs, a pinch of salt and water as necessary (see recipe 181). The veal gravy is made as in recipe 422, using a piece of veal roast or veal braised in oil, butter, herbs and a little white wine. To prepare sauce: beat one egg with the stock and lemon juice and let it cook in a bain-marie (hot-water bath) over low heat until thick. Cook the tagliolini, drain well and toss with the veal gravy and some freshly ground black pepper, and cool. Add the sauce and serve cold.

Variation   According to the original recipe agresto or must can be made as an alternative sauce for the tagliolini. This was made by pounding tart grapes and then boiling until the liquid had reduced. The agresto was then bottled and a little oil poured in to preserve it for future use.

1 lb. spaghetti	½ lb. sliced mushrooms
1 lb. peeled tomatoes	4 tablespoons olive oil
2 cloves garlic	2 salt-cured anchovy fillets
6 oz. roast veal gravy	oregano
parsley	(worcestershire sauce)
salt and pepper	

Heat the oil and brown the crushed cloves of garlic, then remove from the oil. Add the washed, chopped anchovy fillets and cook quickly until they soften (you can use more anchovy for a stronger-flavoured sauce). Add the chopped tomatoes and finely sliced mushrooms. Add the veal gravy if you have some available (it is not worth preparing it especially for this recipe). Cook a little longer until the sauce thickens, then add a handful of chopped parsley. Mix with the hot pasta and serve immediately.

Variation Worcestershire sauce gives an interesting flavour if you have no veal gravy available.

GNOCCHI WITH GORGONZOLA CHEESE   **427**

7 oz. flour	1¾ lb. potatoes
2 eggs	2 oz. butter
2 oz. gorgonzola cheese	1 tomato
2 tablespoons roast veal gravy	3 oz. grated parmesan
salt	

Make the gnocchi: cook the potatoes and put through a food mill or blender. Mix with the flour, beaten eggs and a pinch of salt to produce a fairly firm dough. Make this into gnocchi (see recipe 122). Prepare the sauce: melt the butter and add the gorgonzola, then mix well. Add the pureed tomato and then the meat gravy. Cook the gnocchi in plenty of lightly salted boiling water and remove as they float to the surface with a slotted spoon. Pour over the sauce and serve immediately.

1 lb. 3 oz. flour	5 eggs
½ lb. lean veal	½ lb. chicken livers
2 medium slices streaky unsmoked	3 oz. butter
bacon, salt pork, or	½ onion
2 oz. pancetta	1 small carrot
1 stick celery	¾ lb. tomatoes
6 oz. milk	18 oz. chicken stock
6 tablespoons marsala	parsley
nutmeg	cinnamon
5 oz. grated parmesan	salt and pepper

Garganelli are descended from home-made macaroni. They are a speciality of Romagna and are served with another traditional and ancient sauce. Make the pasta dough with the flour, eggs, a pinch of salt and three ounces grated parmesan and a pinch of nutmeg. Knead the dough until smooth and firm, then roll out not too thin and cut into 1½ inch squares. Use a comb and a pencil, unless you have the special comb and dowel used in Romagna. Lay a pasta square on the comb with a corner pointing towards you and curl this corner round the pencil, then with a gentle downward pressure push the pencil away from you and off the comb. You should have a roll of pasta with a lightly ridged surface. Leave the pasta to rest and make the ragu: melt three tablespoons butter and lightly brown the bacon/salt pork or pancetta, then the chopped onion, celery, carrot and parsley, and finally the chopped chicken liver and the chopped veal. Season with salt and pepper and a little marsala. Cook until it reduces, add the pureed tomatoes and reduce a little more. Make a bechamel with one tablespoon butter and one tablespoon flour, the milk and a pinch each of salt and nutmeg. Stir the bechamel into the ragu, add a pinch of cinnamon and cook until the meat is tender and the sauce thick and well blended. Add more stock if it seems too dry. Cook the garganelli in plenty of boiling salted water, drain and toss with the ragu. Serve grated parmesan separately.

Variations 1. The ragu can be simplified by omitting the bechamel.
2. Omit the cinnamon and nutmeg.

1 lb. flour
1 lb. spinach
½ lb. chicken livers
3 oz. butter
½ onion
1 small carrot
¾ lb. tomatoes
18 oz. chicken stock
parsley
cinnamon
5 oz. grated parmesan

4 eggs
½ lb. lean veal
2 medium slices unsmoked
streaky bacon/salt pork or
2 oz. pancetta
1 stick celery
6 oz. milk
6 tablespoons marsala
nutmeg
salt and pepper

Make as in the previous recipe, except for the addition of the spinach: Cook the spinach, drain very thoroughly, chop and pour through a food mill or blender, then add to the pasta dough. Make garganelli and the ragu as in the previous recipe.

GASSE WITH ROAST VEAL GRAVY **430**

1 lb. flour
1 onion
4 tablespoons olive oil
3 oz. grated parmesan
salt and pepper

2 lb. roast of veal
2 cloves garlic
3 tablespoons butter
rosemary
(white wine)

Gasse are a Ligurian pasta made by kneading flour and water dough with a pinch of salt. Roll out when smooth and elastic and cut into six-inch strips, then bend the strips into a gasse or bow. Leave to rest for a few hours, or better 12 hours. Prepare the veal in the usual way (see recipe 422) with the garlic and rosemary. Brown in the oil and butter with the onion, season with salt and pepper and cook over moderate heat for 1½-2 hours until the meat is tender. Cook the gasse in lightly salted boiling water, drain well and mix with the veal gravy from the pan. Serve the veal as a separate dish.

Variation Add some white wine to the veal while it is cooking.

SPAGHETTI WITH PUREED VEAL

1 lb. spaghetti	¾ lb. minced or ground veal
4 oz. olive oil	1 onion
¾ lb. tomatoes	2 bay leaves
parsley	celery
4 oz. grated parmesan	salt and pepper

Heat the oil and brown the chopped onion, then the veal. Add the chopped tomatoes, bay leaves, a little parsley and the chopped celery. Season with salt and pepper and cook over low heat until the meat is tender, then put through a food mill or blender. Return the puree to the heat, add a few tablespoons warm water or stock for the desired consistency and mix with the hot pasta. Serve grated parmesan separately.

PASTICCIO OF TAGLIATELLE WITH VEAL AND MUSHROOM RAGU

1 lb. flour	4 eggs
¾ lb. lean veal	4 oz. mushrooms
4 tablespoons olive oil	3 oz. butter
6 oz. white wine	1 onion
parsley	5 oz. grated parmesan
salt and pepper	(hard-boiled eggs)

Make the tagliatelle in the usual way with the flour, eggs, a pinch of salt and warm water as necessary (see recipe 181). Heat the oil and four tablespoons butter and brown the chopped onion. Add the chopped veal and finely sliced mushrooms. Season with salt and pepper and continue cooking until the meat is tender (about 1½ hours), adding wine if it seems too dry. Finally add a handful of chopped parsley. Cook the pasta, drain well and toss with the meat and its gravy and most of the parmesan, then put in a greased ovenproof dish. Sprinkle with the remaining parmesan, dot with butter and brown in a hot oven.

Variation   Cook the mushrooms separately in butter and season with salt and pepper. Chop two hard-boiled eggs, put a layer of tagliatelle and meat in the dish, then a layer of mushroom and egg; cover with the remaining tagliatelle, sprinkle with parmesan, dot with butter and brown in a hot oven.

BUCATINI WITH VEAL AND SCAMORZA CHEESE **433**

1 lb. bucatini
½ lb. scamorza cheese
4 tablespoons green olives
2 oz. butter
oregano

½ lb. cooked veal
¾ lb. tomatoes
2 tablespoons olive oil
basil
salt and pepper

A method of using up veal leftovers. Heat the oil, add the seeded olives, pureed tomatoes, a pinch of salt and a little basil. Dice the veal and the scamorza. Cook the pasta, drain well and toss with the sauce and some of the veal and scamorza. Put in a greased ovenproof dish and cover with the remaining veal and scamorza, sprinkle with oregano and dot with butter. Brown for a few minutes in a hot oven.

PASTA WITH VEAL BALLS **434**

1 lb. pasta
1 egg
4 oz. butter
nutmeg
salt and pepper

½ lb. minced or ground veal
5 oz. grated parmesan
6 tablespoons thick cream
parsley

Mix the veal with the beaten egg, four tablespoons grated parmesan to make a good paste, and form into little meatballs. Heat one tablespoon butter and brown the meatballs with salt and pepper and a handful of chopped parsley. Melt the remaining butter, add the cream and the hot pasta, then gently stir in the meatballs and juice from the pan. Serve with freshly ground black pepper.

BUCATINI WITH VEAL ESCALOPES **435**

1 lb. bucatini
6 oz. butter
6 tablespoons thick cream
salt and pepper

¾ lb. lean veal or 6 veal escalopes
2 onions
3 oz. grated parmesan

In Oriental cookery pasta is often used as a base for serving cooked meat. Here is one example: heat two tablespoons butter and brown the finely sliced onion, then the veal escalopes. Brown gently and add the cream as the liquid reduces. Season with salt and pepper. Cook the pasta, toss with the remaining butter and grated parmesan and serve in a mound topped with the veal escalopes and the juice from the pan.

14 oz. flour
5 eggs
2 lb. spinach
3 oz. butter
½ onion
3 oz. grated parmesan

½ lb. minced or ground veal
4 tablespoons olive oil
nutmeg
salt and pepper
(chicken, raisins, borage,
salt-cured anchovy fillets, Swiss chard)

Chopped veal and spinach are commonly used to stuff various pastas. You need to make quite a firm dough, using only three eggs to 14 ounces flour, plus a pinch of salt and warm water as necessary (see recipe 181). Roll out fairly thinly into two sheets, or just one sheet and cut rectangles from it (see recipe 251). Make the filling: cook the spinach, drain very well, chop finely and cook very gently in the oil with the chopped onion. Add the finely minced veal, two beaten eggs, salt, pepper and nutmeg. Divide mounds of this filling between one sheet of dough or the rectangles and either cover with the second sheet or just fold over to make true agnolotti or ravioli. Cook in plenty of boiling, salted water, drain well and serve with melted butter and grated parmesan.

Variations   1.   Use minced chicken instead of veal, or a mixture of the two.
2.   Add a handful of raisins to the spinach when it is cooking in the oil.
3.   Add one or two anchovy fillets which you have washed well and chopped finely to the spinach.
4.   Use Swiss chard or borage instead of spinach.

PANCAKES WITH VEAL
AND CHICKEN FILLING

437

3 oz. flour
2 eggs
½ lb. cooked veal
3 large tomatoes
1 onion
6 tablespoons olive oil
salt and pepper

6 tablespoons milk
1 lb. mozzarella
½ lb. cooked chicken
3 oz. butter
basil
2 oz. grated parmesan

Make a batter with the egg, milk and flour, adding more milk if it seems too thick. Set aside for one hour, then use two tablespoons batter for each pancake, and fry them in a little oil. Finely chop the veal and chicken and combine with half the finely chopped onion and two ounces softened butter to make a good paste. Place a little of this filling on each pancake and roll them up like cannelloni. Generously butter an ovenproof dish and arrange the pancakes in a closely-packed single layer. Cover with slices of mozzarella and a tomato sauce made in the usual way (see recipe 15) with four tablespoons oil, the pureed tomatoes, basil and seasoning. Sprinkle with parmesan, dot with butter, and brown in a hot oven.

SPAGHETTINI WITH VEAL, OLIVES AND PICKLED VEGETABLES **438**

1 lb. spaghettini	¼ lb. cooked veal and chicken
2 tablespoons olive oil	½ oz. butter
6 stuffed green olives	3 oz. mixed pickled vegetables
6 oz. white wine	1 chicken stock cube or
2 large, ripe tomatoes	1 teaspoon chicken stock extract
1 salt-cured anchovy fillet	parsley
3 oz. grated parmesan	salt and pepper

Chop the veal and chicken into very fine strips or julienne, then cook in the oil and butter with a pinch each of salt and pepper. Add the chopped olives and pickled vegetables, stir well, add the peeled, chopped tomatoes and moisten with white wine. Stir to blend, then add the chicken stock cube diluted with a little juice from the pan and the washed, chopped anchovy fillets. When all the ingredients are well blended, add a handful of chopped parsley and mix with the hot pasta. Serve grated parmesan separately.

PASTA WITH LIVER **439**

1 lb. pasta	½ lb. calf's or lamb's liver
2 oz. butter	4 tablespoons olive oil
1 onion	2 bay leaves
6 oz. white wine	parsley
3 oz. grated parmesan	salt and pepper

Cut the liver into thin strips. Heat the butter and oil and cook the onion with the bay leaves. When it is transparent remove from the heat, add the liver and then return to the heat (this prevents the liver from toughening in contact with the heat). Season with salt and pepper and add a handful of chopped parsley. Cook until the liver is nearly done, remove the bay leaves, add plenty of white wine and cook until the wine reduces. Serve with the hot pasta and serve grated parmesan separately.

1 lb. pasta	½ lb. calf's or lamb's liver
2 oz. butter	36 oz. stock
2 tablespoons vinegar	candied orange and lemon peel
fennel seeds	honey
cinnamon	cloves
nutmeg	salt and pepper

An ancient recipe with the usual sweet and savoury mixture. Cut the liver into thin strips, cook in the butter with a pinch of salt and pepper. Pound in a mortar, with the candied peel, as much of the various spices as you want, and the fennel seeds. Add honey, salt and pepper and thin as necessary with the vinegar. Add the stock and cook until it has reduced enough to make a good thick sauce, then serve with the hot pasta.

LIVER GNOCCHI **441**

7 oz. flour	¾ lb. calf's or lamb's liver
14 oz. or 10 slices stale white bread	4 tablespoons butter
3 eggs	chives
1 clove garlic	nutmeg
marjoram	36 oz. stock
parsley	pepper
milk	

Soak the bread in milk, then squeeze it dry. Chop the liver and pound together with the softened butter and the bread. Add the flour, beaten eggs, chopped garlic, chives and marjoram, a pinch of nutmeg and some salt and pepper. Make into very small cylindrical gnocchi and cook them in the boiling stock. Serve as soup with chopped parsley. If the gnocchi mixture seems too soft add extra breadcrumbs and flour as required.

1 lb. bucatini
2 oz. butter
1 clove garlic
6 tablespoons marsala
3 oz. grated parmesan
salt and pepper
parsley

1 calf's kidney of about ¾ lb.
(or the equivalent in lamb's kidneys)
olive oil
coarse salt
(hot chili pepper, mustard,
heavy cream)

Heat the oil and butter with the chopped garlic, add the cleaned, chopped kidney (add all the juice as well). Cook for a few minutes, add the marsala and let it reduce a little, then season with salt and pepper and a handful of chopped parsley. Mix with the bucatini and serve grated parmesan separately.

Variations 1. Cook a little hot chili pepper in the oil.
2. Add mustard or cream to the pan, or both.

1 lb. flour
¾ lb. calf's or lamb's brain
½ onion
salt and pepper

4 eggs
3 tablespoons olive oil
54 oz. stock
3 oz. grated parmesan

A traditional Roman dish. Make a pasta dough with the flour, three eggs, a pinch of salt and water as necessary (see recipe 181), and cut it into 1½ inch squares. Blanch the brain in boiling water, remove the outer membrane and chop. Heat the oil with the chopped onion, add the brain, season with salt and pepper and cook very gently for about 20 minutes. Cool, add a beaten egg and mix well with a wooden spatula or fork. Divide this filling between the squares of pasta and fold over diagonally to make little triangles, pressing the edges well together. Cook in stock and serve as soup with grated parmesan, or drain and serve with butter and parmesan.

CANNELLONI WITH BRAIN, RICOTTA AND SPINACH

1 lb. flour
3 egg yolks
½ lb. ricotta
nutmeg
4 oz. butter
4 oz. grated parmesan

4 eggs
¼ lb. calf's or lamb's brain
1¼ lb. spinach
salt and pepper
(cream)

Blanch the brain in boilng water, remove the outer membrane, chop and put through a food mill or blender. Sieve the ricotta. Cook the spinach, squeeze out all the liquid and put through a food mill. Mix the spinach, brain puree and ricotta with the beaten egg yolks, four tablespooons grated parmesan, nutmeg, salt and pepper. Work together with a wooden spatula to obtain a smooth firm paste. Make the pasta dough with the flour, eggs, a pinch of salt and a little water (see recipe 181). Cut into four-inch squares. Divide the filling between the squares, then roll up to make cannelloni. Put them in one layer in a greased ovenproof dish so they are not overlapping, then pour over the melted butter. Sprinkle with plenty of grated parmesan and brown in a hot oven. You can also save some melted butter and serve it separately, together with the grated parmesan.

Variation Add a few tablespoons cream to the filling mixture.

QUADRUCCI IN SWEETBREAD SOUP

¾ lb. flour
3 eggs
¾ lb. calf's or lamb's sweetbread
72 oz. stock
1 onion

1 carrot
1 stick celery
3 oz. grated parmesan
salt and pepper

Make the pasta dough with the flour, eggs, a pinch of salt and a little water as necessary (see recipe 181), roll out and cut into small squares (see recipe 384). Clean the sweetbreads under cold running water for ½ hour, blanch in boiling water, drain and dry with a cloth. Divide into two lobes, removing the fat and tissues, then wrap in a cloth and keep under a weighted plate for a couple of hours. Boil them in half the stock, drain and chop finely, then return to the stock and add the other half of the stock, the chopped onion, celery and carrot, salt and pepper. Add the quadrucci and serve when they are al dente. Serve grated parmesan separately.

1 lb. spaghetti	2 oz. olive oil
4 oz. cooked chicken	½ lb. tomatoes
1 oz. cooked ham	flour
4 oz. calf's or lamb's sweetbreads	lemon juice
4 oz. mushrooms	parsley
2 oz. butter	salt and pepper

Clean the sweetbreads under cold running water, blanch in boiling water, remove the outer membrane and chop roughly. Chop the chicken. Soak the mushrooms with a little lemon juice, then plunge for a minute in boiling water and slice finely. Cut the ham in fine strips or julienne. Heat one ounce oil and the butter and cook the sweetbreads, chicken, mushrooms and ham. Add the pureed tomatoes, season with salt and pepper and a handful of chopped parsley. Serve with the hot pasta and the rest of the fresh oil.

MACCHERONCINI WITH SWEETBREADS **447**

1 lb. maccheroncini	flour
¾ lb. calf's or lamb's sweetbreads	3 oz. grated parmesan
6 oz. butter	salt and pepper
marsala	

Wash the sweetbreads under running cold water, then blanch and remove the outer membrane. Separate the lobes, wrap in a cloth and leave under a weighted plate for a few hours. Slice the sweetbreads, flour lightly and fry gently in two ounces butter. After a few minutes add a little marsala, then season with salt and pepper. Cook for about 30 minutes, then serve with the hot pasta, the grated parmesan and the remaining butter, which can be melted. Top with the cooked sweetbreads.

1 lb. flour
4 eggs
¼ lb. cooked chicken
¼ lb. cooked chicken giblets
¼ lb. calf's or lamb's sweetbreads
2 oz. mushrooms
½ lb. butter
18 oz. milk
1 onion
6 oz. marsala
parsley
salt and pepper
3 oz. grated parmesan
stock

Use 14 ounces flour to make the pasta dough in the usual way with the eggs, a pinch of salt and a little warm water as necessary (see recipe 181). Roll out and cut into strips two inches wide and four to six inches long. Clean and blanch the sweetbreads, remove the outer membrane and divide the lobes. Dice finely and cook for about 20 minutes in one tablespoon butter with some salt and pepper. Finely slice the mushrooms and cook in butter with salt and pepper and some chopped parsley. Make a bechamel sauce with two ounces butter and two ounces flour, a little chopped onion and the milk, season with salt and pepper. Heat the remaining butter with the rest of the chopped onion and when it is transparent add the mushrooms, cook for a minute then add a few tablespoons stock and the chicken cut in strips or julienne. Let the sauce reduce a little, then add the chopped giblets. Mix in the marsala, let it reduce, add more stock if necessary to cover and cook uncovered for about 30 minutes until everything is well blended. Season with salt and pepper, add the sweetbreads and then the bechamel. Cook for a few minutes longer, then mix with the hot lasagne. Serve grated parmesan separately.

RUSSIAN SALAD WITH FARFALLINE, TONGUE AND LOBSTER **449**

½ lb. farfalline
2 oz. carrots
2 oz. turnips
2 oz. green beans
2 oz. shelled peas
2 oz. mushrooms
2 oz. potatoes
2 gherkins
1 tablespoon capers
2 oz. cooked tongue
2 small anchovy fillets
2 oz. lobster
18 oz. olive oil
3 egg yolks
lemon juice
salt and pepper
2 oz. beetroot/beets

A traditional Russian salad with pasta added. You can vary the quantities according to taste, but the dish is better if you make it in larger quantities, for at least 12 people. Make a mayonnaise with the two egg yolks, olive oil and lemon juice. Cook and dice the vegetables, except the mushrooms. The mushrooms should be cooked separately in a little oil with capers, pepper and salt. Boil the beetroot/beets and cook the pasta. Drain, and mix all the vegetables (except beetroot/beet), meat, seafood and pasta together. Cool. Slice the beetroot/beets. Arrange the salad in a mound, pour over the mayonnaise and top with slices of beetroot/beet.

PASTINA AND TONGUE IN CHICKEN SOUP **450**

¾ lb. pastina	72 oz. chicken stock
¼ lb. cooked tongue	1 onion
¼ lb. cooked chicken or veal	3 oz. grated parmesan

Heat the stock, add a whole split onion and the diced tongue and chicken or veal, then the pastina. Cook until the pastina is al dente. Serve grated parmesan separately.

PASTICCIO OF MACARONI WITH TONGUE AND TRUFFLE **451**

1 lb. macaroni	26 oz. milk
½ lb. cooked tongue	6 oz. thick cream
¼ lb. truffle	3 oz. grated parmesan
3 oz. flour	salt and pepper
6 oz. butter	

Finely slice the tongue and the truffle. Grease an ovenproof dish and line with these slices. Make a bechamel with the flour, five tablespoons butter and the milk, then stir in the cream when you have a good smooth sauce. Cook the pasta, drain well and mix with the remaining butter, the parmesan and bechamel. Put the pasta in a greased ovenproof dish, sprinkle with parmesan, dot with butter and brown in a hot oven.

1 lb. macaroni	6 oz. white wine
1 freshly cooked calf's tongue	3 oz. grated parmesan
2 onions	cloves
3 oz. butter	salt and pepper
celery	(tomatoes, olive oil)
carrot	

Plunge the tongue in boiling water to remove the outer skin, or else remove it at the end when it is cooked. Heat the butter with plenty of chopped onion, celery and carrot, and when they start to brown, add the tongue with salt, pepper and cloves. When the sauce dries, add the wine, then cover with stock and continue cooking over a low heat for two or three hours until the tongue is ready. You should have a thick sauce to serve with the hot pasta. The tongue can be served as a separate dish or cut in slices and served on top of the pasta.

Variation   Make a tomato sauce with pureed tomatoes, oil, salt and pepper. Mix the pasta with the sauce from the tongue, top with sliced tongue and cover this with the tomato sauce. Sprinkle with grated parmesan.

1 lb. macaroni	1 onion
6 oz. chicken livers	1 carrot
¼ lb. lean veal	1 stick celery
¼ lb. mushrooms	parsley
8 large tomatoes	¾ lb. flour
½ lb. butter	2 egg yolks
5 tablespoons olive oil	3 oz. grated parmesan
6 oz. marsala	salt and pepper
6 oz. roast veal gravy (see recipe 422)	(sugna, sugar)

This outstanding dish belongs to the wonderful cooking tradition of Amatrice in upper Latium. Make the pastry in the usual way with the flour, eggs, softened butter and a pinch of salt (see recipe 247). Form into a ball and set aside to rest for ½ hour. Heat the oil, add the chopped onion, celery and carrot and let them cook a little, then add the peeled, seeded, chopped tomatoes and the veal gravy. Cook over low heat and season with salt and pepper until the sauce is thick and well blended, then put through a food mill or blender. Heat two ounces butter and gently fry the chopped chicken livers and the chopped veal. Season with salt and pepper then add the marsala and a handful of chopped parsley. Cook the pasta, drain well and mix with the pureed vegetables. Roll out the pastry into one large circle to line the pie dish and a smaller one for the top crust. Fill the pie with two layers of pasta and the liver and mushroom mixture, sprinkle with grated parmesan and end with a layer of pasta. Cover with the top crust, press the edges well together and cook in a moderate oven for about 40 minutes or until the pastry is firm and golden.

MACARONI, PIGEON, SWEETBREAD AND GIBLET PIE MESSISBUGO

454

1 lb. macaroni	1 pigeon
9 oz. flour	6 tablespoons marsala
½ lb. butter	stock
6 oz. sugar	8 oz. milk
4 egg yolks	4 oz. grated parmesan
¼ lb. chicken giblets	salt
¼ lb. calf's or lamb's sweetbreads	

Clean and chop the giblets, wash and blanch the sweetbreads and remove the outer membrane and tissue. Bone and chop the pigeon and brown lightly in two tablespoons butter, then add the marsala and let it reduce a little. Add enough stock to cover and cook for about 40 minutes until the pigeon is tender, adding more liquid if necessary. Beat two egg yolks with one tablespoon flour, two ounces sugar and a little more marsala. Cook gently, add the milk and let it reduce so you have a smooth sauce. Make the pastry in the usual way with the flour, sugar, two egg yolks (see recipe 247). Roll out into two sheets and line a greased pie dish with the large one, reserving the smaller for the top crust. Cook the pasta, drain well and toss with the cream, then the pigeon, sweetbreads and giblets, then the grated parmesan. Put in the pastry case, cover with the top crust and press the edges well together. Brush the surface with melted butter and bake in a moderate oven for 40 minutes or until the pastry is firm and golden. This is another recipe from the book of etiquette and cooking by the famous Messisbugo, carver at the Court of Ferrara in the 16th century.

VI
PASTA WITH RED MEAT

MACCHERONCINI IN BEEF AND TOMATO SOUP

1 lb. maccheroncini
¾ lb. tomatoes
1 onion
stick celery

1 oz. butter
36 oz. beef stock
3 oz. grated parmesan
salt and pepper

Heat the butter and add the chopped onion and celery and pureed tomato. Cook until well thickened, season with salt and pepper and dilute with the stock to make a very thin sauce. This is neither a sauce nor a soup in the accepted sense, but half way between the two. Mix with the hot pasta and serve grated parmesan separately.

THICK TOMATO SOUP WITH PASTA

1 lb. pasta
12 large ripe tomatoes
18 oz. beef stock
2 small onions
2 oz. butter
2 oz. flour
basil

parsley
marjoram
cloves
bay leaf
salt and pepper
grated gruyere
(grated parmesan)

Melt the butter, stir in the flour and then slowly add the hot stock, stirring all the time. Let it reduce and cook over very low heat. When it is smooth add the chopped onion, the chopped and seeded tomatoes, the chopped basil and parsley, a little marjoram, and two cloves. Season with salt and pepper and cook until well blended and the vegetables are soft, then put through a food mill. Return to the pan and add more stock if necessary to make a very liquid sauce. Cook the pasta, drain well and mix with the sauce and grated gruyere. It should be a very thick soup.

Variation Use grated parmesan instead of gruyere.

PASTA AND BEAN SOUP VENETO ## 457

¾ lb. flour
¾ lb. dried white beans
5 tablespoons olive oil
1 onion

18 oz. beef stock
¾ lb. tomatoes
2 tablespoons roast meat gravy
salt

A classic recipe from the Veneto. Make the pasta dough in the usual way with the flour, a pinch of salt and a little warm water as necessary to make tagliatelle (see recipe 181), or if you cut them a little finer, tagliolini. Soak the dried beans in warm water for 12 hours. Heat the oil and lightly brown the onion, then add the drained beans and enough beef stock to cover. Cook for about an hour until the liquid has slightly reduced, then add the peeled, chopped tomatoes. Cook for about three hours over low heat. The beans will soften and absorb all the flavour from the stock; then remove some of the beans and put through a food mill and return the puree to the pan to thicken the soup, together with the meat gravy. Finally, add the tagliatelle and when they are al dente serve altogether as a soup. An old trick gives this delicious soup an even better flavour: cook the beans in a pan which held a meat roast and still has the hardened juices on the inside.

CHESTNUT AND DITALINI SOUP ## 458

¾ lb. ditalini
¾ lb. peeled chestnuts
6 oz. butter
½ onion

1 stick celery
18 oz. beef stock
salt and pepper

Boil the peeled chestnuts. Heat half the butter and cook the chopped onion and celery, then add the chestnuts when they are soft. Cook for a few minutes together, then put through a food mill or blender. Return the puree to the pan, stir in the broth and season with salt and pepper. Cook the pasta, drain well and add to the chestnut soup with a large piece of butter. Stir well and serve very hot.

PASTA WITH MEAT BROTH AND EGG

1 lb. small pasta	4 egg yolks
2 oz. butter	salt and pepper
6 oz. beef stock	(grated parmesan)

Melt the butter, add the stock and cook until it has thickened and reduced a little. Remove from the heat and add the egg yolks; mix well with a pinch of salt and pepper. Add the hot pasta, stir well and serve.

Variation Serve grated parmesan separately.

MALFATTINI IN BEEF BROTH

14 oz. flour	nutmeg
4 eggs	(grated parmesan)
72 oz. beef stock	

Beat the eggs with a pinch of nutmeg and gradually add the flour to make a firm dough. Knead well until smooth, then shape into a long loaf and cut into slices about ⅓-inch thick. This helps to dry the pasta without it becoming too hard. Using a rocker or knife chop the pasta into little pieces like rice grains. Leave to dry (even the smallest crumbs can be used), then cook in the boiling stock and serve as a soup with grated parmesan.

TRIDARINI IN BEEF BROTH

6 oz. flour	54 oz. beef stock
5 oz. breadcrumbs	nutmeg
½ lb. grated parmesan	salt and pepper
3 eggs	

Tridarini are similar to the malfattini of the previous recipe, but the pasta dough is richer. Many such variations come from the region of Padua. Put the flour in a mound on a pastry board and mix with the breadcrumbs, five ounces grated parmesan and a pinch of nutmeg. Make a well in the centre and add the eggs. Gradually work these into the flour with a little warm water, salt and pepper to make a dough firm enough to be grated. Using the flat holes of the grater grate over the floured pastry board so they do not get stuck together, then cook in the stock and serve as a soup with the grated parmesan.

½ lb. fresh breadcrumbs   54 oz. beef stock
½ lb. grated parmesan   nutmeg
3 eggs   salt

Another grated pasta, but without any flour. Work together four ounces of the grated parmesan, the breadcrumbs, beaten eggs, a pinch each of salt and nutmeg and as much warm water as necessary to make a dough firm enough to grate. Grate on the flat holes of the grater over a large floured board or tray. Cook and serve the pasta in the stock. Serve the remaining parmesan separately.

1 lb. flour   3 oz. grated parmesan
3 eggs   salt
54 oz. beef stock

A Jewish version of grated pasta, influenced by other Paduan recipes for the same type of thing. Beat the eggs adding two tablespoons cold water. Gradually add the flour (use more or less as you need) to make a firmer dough than for tagliatelle or lasagne. Form into two or three large balls and set aside to dry, then grate on the flat holes of the grater over a floured board or tray. Cook in the stock and serve as soup. Serve grated parmesan separately.

7 oz. breadcrumbs   54 oz. beef stock
½ lb. grated parmesan   nutmeg
3 eggs   salt
1 oz. beef marrow   (grated lemon peel, lean beef)

Another pasta recipe without any flour, except indirectly in the breadcrumbs. This speciality of Romagna is one of the most famous of Italian pastas. The technique consists of combining the ingredients in just the right quantities to obtain a soft, delicate dough which is still firm enough to cook without disintegrating. The ingredients vary from one village to the next so you can adapt the recipe according to your own experience. Make a dough in the usual way with five ounces grated parmesan, the breadcrumbs, eggs, beef marrow and a pinch of salt and nutmeg. Knead as lightly as possible to obtain a firm, soft dough with a slightly granular consistency, adding more parmesan and breadcrumbs if it seems too sticky. Use a special passatelli instrument or a colander or potato ricer with very large holes (about ¼ inch in diameter) and put the dough through this so the passatelli drop directly into the boiling stock. This prevents them from sticking together. Cook for a few seconds and serve in the soup with grated parmesan.

Variations 1. Omit the beef marrow if desired, but this is part of the authentic flavour of the dish.
2. Add a little finely grated lemon peel to the dough.
3. Pound a little cooked beef, then put through a food mill and add to the dough, reducing the amount of breadcrumbs accordingly.

PASSATELLI IN SOUP—II   **465**

7 oz. flour	54 oz. beef stock
7 oz. grated parmesan	milk
2 eggs	salt
1 lb. spinach	

A very different sort of passatelli from those made in Romagna. Cook the spinach, drain very well and chop finely or put through a food mill. Make a dough with four ounces grated parmesan, the beaten eggs, a pinch of salt and the spinach puree. Add warm milk as necessary to make a very soft dough, then make into passatelli as in the previous recipe, dropping them directly into the hot stock. Serve as soup and serve grated parmesan separately.

UMBRIAN PASSATELLI IN SOUP   **466**

1 lb. flour	nutmeg
4 eggs	3 oz. grated parmesan
4 tablespoons olive oil	salt
54 oz. beef stock	

A step further removed from traditional passatelli. Make a dough with the flour, eggs, a pinch of salt and nutmeg, and gradually add the olive oil—the amount given here is the maximum you should need—to make a soft, granular dough. Put through a passatelli machine or colander to make little cylinders about one to two inches long. Gently make little indentations in these like the beads on a rosary. Set aside to dry on a floured board. Cook for one minute in boiling stock. Serve as soup with grated parmesan.

ITALIAN CHOUX PASTE IN SOUP **467**

4 oz. butter
2½ oz. flour
3 eggs
54 oz. beef stock

3 oz. grated parmesan
olive oil
salt

Heat the butter with a pinch of salt and when it is boiling remove from the heat and stir in the flour. Beat until you have a smooth paste, then return to the heat and let it cook for five minutes (stirring occasionally). Remove from the heat, add the eggs one by one, beating thoroughly for a smooth, fairly soft dough. Oil a baking sheet and use a pastry bag (or put spoonfuls of dough) with a ½-inch nozzle and pipe tiny balls of dough as for cream puffs. Cook for about 15 minutes in a hot oven or until they are golden brown. Cool, put in a very hot serving bowl and pour over the hot stock. Serve immediately with grated parmesan served separately.

PASTA STRANDS IN SOUP **468**

1 lb. flour
3 eggs
4 tablespoons olive oil

54 oz. beef stock
3 oz. grated parmesan
salt

A traditional Jewish dish served at the feast of Yom Kippur. Make a dough with the flour, eggs and a pinch of salt and knead thoroughly to obtain a firm dough. Make into a ball and keep covered while you break off small pieces and roll them into small sheets of dough of medium thickness. Heat the oil and remove from the heat before it boils. Pour the oil over the pieces of pasta. Divide them into strips about one to two inches long. Grease your fingertips and pull these strips out as long as they will go, at the same time rolling them between thumb and forefinger. Cook in hot stock and serve as soup with grated parmesan served separately.

ANELLINI IN BEETROOT/BEET SOUP **469**

¾ lb. anellini or any small pasta
54 oz. beef stock
1 large beetroot/beet
3 egg yolks

5 oz. grated parmesan
nutmeg
salt and pepper

Bring the stock to a boil and add the grated beetroot/beet or the beetroot juice. Strain, season with salt and pepper and nutmeg. Return to a boil and add the pasta. Cook until al dente, remove from the heat and stir in the egg yolk and half the parmesan. Mix well. Serve the remaining parmesan separately.

11 oz. semolina

3 oz. butter

6 eggs

54 oz. beef stock

nutmeg

3 oz. grated parmesan

salt and pepper

Soften the butter in a bowl and beat with a wooden spoon until light and creamy. Add one egg yolk and continue beating, gradually adding the remaining yolks. When you have a smooth, almost foamy mixture gradually beat in the semolina. Whisk the egg whites until stiff then fold into the semolina mixture with a pinch each of nutmeg, salt and pepper. You should have a smooth, soft dough. Form into little balls and cook and serve in the boiling stock. Serve grated parmesan separately.

CAPPELLETTI WITH CHEESE FILLING IN SOUP **471**

1 lb. flour

5 eggs

½ lb. ricotta

¼ lb. cream cheese

54 oz. beef stock

2 oz. grated parmesan

nutmeg

salt

Make a dough with the flour, eggs, a pinch of salt and warm water as necessary (see recipe 181). Make the filling: sieve the ricotta and work it with the crumbled cheese, grated parmesan, nutmeg and salt. Make the cappelletti with this filling, folding the dough as in recipe 395. Cook and serve in a good meat stock. Serve grated parmesan separately.

SMALL RAVIOLI WITH CHEESE FILLING IN SOUP **472**

11 oz. flour

6 eggs

6 oz. cream cheese

½ lb. grated parmesan

54 oz. beef and chicken stock

salt and pepper

Another delicious dish from Romagna, the home of so much good cooking. Make a dough with the flour, three eggs, a pinch of salt and warm water as necessary (see recipe 181). Crumble the cream cheese and mix with five ounces grated parmesan, three eggs and salt and pepper. Put mounds of this filling on one sheet of pasta and cover with the other to make a very small ravioli (see recipe 251). Cook in the stock and serve as soup. Serve grated parmesan separately.

10 oz. or 8 slices stale white bread	nutmeg
½ lb. calf's or lamb's liver	cloves
¼ lb. beef suet	1 clove garlic
6 tablespoons flour	marjoram
1 egg	milk
1 onion	lemon peel
54 oz. beef stock	salt
parsley	(butter)

A variation on other dumplings, this recipe from Ticino only contains a small quantity of flour, the rest is in the bread. Dice the stale bread very small. Chop the liver, onion and a good bunch of parsley and mix with a finely minced clove of garlic, one clove, a pinch each of salt, marjoram and nutmeg, a little grated lemon peel and the beaten egg. Soak the mixture with enough milk to make a smooth, soft paste, then add the finely minced suet and as much flour as you need to make large round gnocchi or dumplings. Cook them in boiling salted water and remove with a slotted spoon as they come to the surface. Serve in the hot beef stock.

Variations 1. Use butter instead of beef suet.
          2. Soak the bread in milk separately, then squeeze dry and add to the liver mixture.

1 lb. spaghetti	½ lb. tomatoes
1¼ lb. vegetables: onions, carrots, courgettes/zucchini, celery, fennel, sweet peppers, mushrooms, etc.	54 oz. beef stock
	1 clove garlic
	1 bay leaf
4 oz. butter	3 oz. grated parmesan
2 tablespoons olive oil	salt and pepper
6 oz. white wine	(roast veal gravy)

A healthy and sustaining recipe. Heat two ounces butter and the oil and lightly brown the finely chopped mixed vegetables. Add the white wine and cook until it reduces a little, then add the pureed tomatoes. Reduce again and add the stock, salt and pepper, then crushed clove of garlic and crumbled bay leaf. Cook gently over low heat for a thick sauce. Cook the pasta, drain well and mix with the remaining butter and the sauce. Serve grated parmesan separately.

Variation Add a few tablespoons veal gravy to the sauce if you have any available.

RIGATONI WITH TOMATOES AND MUSHROOMS

475

1 lb. rigatoni	½ lb. tomatoes
4 oz. butter	4 oz. beef stock
4 tablespoons olive oil	parsley
1 onion	3 oz. grated parmesan
1 oz. dried mushrooms	salt and pepper

Heat two ounces butter and the oil and lightly brown the finely sliced onion, then the mushrooms (soaked in warm water then squeezed dry). Cook for two minutes, season with salt and pepper, add a handful of chopped parsley and the pureed tomatoes. Cook for a few more minutes and stir in the hot stock, then continue cooking until the mushrooms are soft. Cook the pasta, drain well and toss with the remaining butter and the parmesan. Stir in the sauce and serve immediately.

MACARONI WITH NUTS AND RAISINS

476

1 lb. macaroni	basil
2 oz. butter	hot chili pepper
4 oz. beef stock	nutmeg
¾ lb. mixed raisins and	cinnamon
nuts (walnuts, hazelnuts, almonds)	salt
olive oil	

A 15th century sauce with a delightfully delicate flavour. Pound the raisins in a mortar with the walnuts, almonds and hazelnuts. Soften this paste by gradually adding a little olive oil, then pound in a few bay leaves and a piece of hot chili pepper (or a little powdered pepper) and some nutmeg, cinnamon and a pinch of salt. Heat the butter, add the paste and enough stock to make a creamy sauce, then serve with the hot pasta.

MACARONI WITH MARSALA

477

1 lb. macaroni	1 teaspoon beef stock extract
4 oz. butter	or 1 stock/bouillon cube
1 oz. flour	salt
6 oz. marsala	3 oz. grated parmesan

Good quality stock cubes or stock extract makes a suitable substitute for the real thing, but remember to check the flavour by diluting with a little water before adding to a sauce as you may need to add less salt and spices. Heat two

RIGATONI WITH TOMATOES AND MUSHROOMS

1 lb. rigatoni
4 oz. butter
4 tablespoons olive oil
1 onion
1 oz. dried mushrooms

½ lb. tomatoes
4 oz. beef stock
parsley
3 oz. grated parmesan
salt and pepper

Heat two ounces butter and the oil and lightly brown the finely sliced onion, then the mushrooms (soaked in warm water then squeezed dry). Cook for two minutes, season with salt and pepper, add a handful of chopped parsley and the pureed tomatoes. Cook for a few more minutes and stir in the hot stock, then continue cooking until the mushrooms are soft. Cook the pasta, drain well and toss with the remaining butter and the parmesan. Stir in the sauce and serve immediately.

MACARONI WITH NUTS AND RAISINS **476**

1 lb. macaroni
2 oz. butter
4 oz. beef stock
¾ lb. mixed raisins and
nuts (walnuts, hazelnuts, almonds)
olive oil

basil
hot chili pepper
nutmeg
cinnamon
salt

A 15th century sauce with a delightfully delicate flavour. Pound the raisins in a mortar with the walnuts, almonds and hazelnuts. Soften this paste by gradually adding a little olive oil, then pound in a few bay leaves and a piece of hot chili pepper (or a little powdered pepper) and some nutmeg, cinnamon and a pinch of salt. Heat the butter, add the paste and enough stock to make a creamy sauce, then serve with the hot pasta.

MACARONI WITH MARSALA **477**

1 lb. macaroni
4 oz. butter
1 oz. flour
6 oz. marsala

1 teaspoon beef stock extract
or 1 stock/bouillon cube
salt
3 oz. grated parmesan

Good quality stock cubes or stock extract makes a suitable substitute for the real thing, but remember to check the flavour by diluting with a little water before adding to a sauce as you may need to add less salt and spices. Heat two

250

PASTA WITH CABBAGE

1 lb. pasta	1 teaspoon beef stock extract
1 large cabbage	or 1 stock/bouillon cube
½ onion	3 oz. grated parmesan
2 oz. butter	salt and pepper
2 oz. olive oil	½ lb. tomatoes

Wash the cabbage, remove the outer leaves, then chop the rest in strips and squeeze to remove as much liquid as possible. Heat the butter and oil and lightly brown the chopped onion, then add the cabbage, season with salt and pepper and stir over the heat for a few minutes. Cover the pan and cook for about one hour over moderate heat, stirring occasionally. Add the pureed tomatoes, stir well and add the beef extract diluted with very little hot water. Cook for another hour until the sauce is thick and well flavoured and mix with the hot pasta. Serve grated parmesan separately.

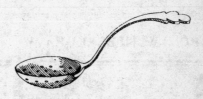

FETTUCCINE WITH CREAM

1 lb. flour	6 tablespoons white wine
5 eggs	18 oz. cream
1 onion	1 tablespoon beef stock extract
4 oz. butter	or 1 stock/bouillon cube
3 oz. grated parmesan	grated parmesan
2 oz. almonds	salt

Make the egg pasta dough in the usual way with the flour, eggs, a pinch of salt and a little warm water as necessary (see recipe 181). Roll out not too thin and cut into ¼-inch strips. Make the sauce: lightly brown the chopped onion in two ounces butter over moderate heat, add the wine and cook until it reduces. Add the cream and reduce again. Chop the blanched almonds in thin strips of julienne and toast them in a hot oven. Add to the sauce when the cream has reduced, then add the beef extract, stir well and serve with the hot pasta. Serve grated parmesan separately.

1 lb. spaghetti	1 oz. dried mushrooms
4 oz. butter	3 eggs
2 oz. flour	nutmeg
18 oz. milk	salt and pepper
1 beef stock/bouillon cube or	breadcrumbs
1 teaspoon beef stock extract	olive oil
2 oz. grated parmesan	

Heat two ounces butter in a pan and add the flour, milk, salt, pepper and nut-meg to make a bechamel. Add the stock cube, softened first in a little milk, and the grated parmesan. Chop the mushrooms, which have been soaked in warm water, and cook lightly in the rest of the butter. Break the spaghetti into short pieces and cook until al dente. Combine the spaghetti with the sauce and add two beaten eggs. Cool and form the mixture into patties or croquettes, dip in beaten egg, coat with breadcrumbs and fry in plenty of oil.

MACARONI WITH BEEF GRAVY **483**

1 lb. macaroni	1 carrot
1½-2 lb. lean stewing	3 oz. grated parmesan
beef (topside, chuck steak)	salt and pepper
6 tablespoons olive oil	(red wine, butter,
1 lb. onions	pancetta or streaky bacon,
1 stick celery	leek, beef stock)

This form of stracotto, or braised beef is often prepared just to obtain a won-derful gravy to serve with pasta. In southern Italy the meat is braised very slowly for as much as five or six hours, so all the juices come out into the liquid, but the meat is not usually fit for eating. Obviously you can make your stracotto fit you needs; use a larger or smaller piece of meat according to what is available, and whether you want to serve it as another course—in which case three hours is probably long enough to cook it. The base is always the same: heat the oil and cook the chopped onion, celery and carrot until they soften without browning, then add the meat and season with salt and pepper. Brown on all sides, then if the piece of beef is not too large, cover with hot water. Too much liquid does not give a nice thick gravy, so just cover a larger piece of meat half way up and turn it occasionally. Cover with a well fitting lid and stew very slowly until the sauce is thick and well flavoured. It is usually easier to cook a stracotto over low heat rather than in the oven. Some people also find you need to add a couple of tablespoons of flour to the vegetables when they have softened in the oil, as this blends with the liquid and gives a slightly thicker gravy. When the meat is done, strain, reserve the meat for another use, and serve the gravy with the hot pasta.

Variations 1. Use a mixture of oil and butter.
2. Add some chopped pancetta or streaky bacon to the hot oil before adding the vegetables.
3. Use a chopped leek as well as the onion.
4. When you have browned the meat add five tablespoons red wine to the pan, let it reduce then add water as necessary.
5. Use beef stock instead of water.

MACARONI WITH BEEF GRAVY AND TOMATOES   **484**

1 lb. macaroni	1 lb. tomatoes
1½-2 lb. lean stewing beef	3 oz. grated parmesan
6 tablespoons olive oil	salt and pepper
¾ lb. onions	(red wine, leeks, butter,
1 stick celery	pancetta or streaky bacon)
1 carrot	

This is a modern version of the previous recipe as tomatoes were a comparatively late arrival in Italian cooking. They alter the flavour considerably. Heat the oil, add the chopped onion, carrot and celery and brown lightly, then add the meat. Brown all over, season with salt and pepper and add the pureed tomatoes; cook for a few minutes then add enough water to cover the meat as in the previous recipe. Cover and cook until the gravy is rich and thick and serve with the hot pasta, reserving the meat for another dish. Serve grated parmesan separately. See previous recipe for possible variations.

MACARONI WITH BEEF GRAVY AND MUSHROOMS   **485**

1 lb. macaroni	1 carrot
1½-2 lb. lean stewing beef	hot chili pepper
6 tablespoons olive oil	3 oz. grated parmesan
1 oz. dried mushrooms	salt
½ lb. onions	(red wine, leeks, butter,
1 stick celery	pancetta or streaky bacon)

The strong flavour of the dried mushrooms completely alters the gravy. Soak the mushrooms in warm water for at least ten minutes, drain (reserving the water), wash and chop. Heat the oil and lightly brown the chopped onion, celery and carrot, then add a little hot chili pepper and a pinch of salt. Brown the meat on all sides, add the mushrooms and their liquid and cook for about ten minutes then add the pureed tomatoes. Let the sauce thicken then cover the meat with water (see recipe 483) and cook until you have a good gravy. Serve this with the hot pasta and serve the grated parmesan separately. See recipe 483 for variations.

MACARONI WITH BEEF GRAVY AND CHEESES 486

1 lb. macaroni	1 lb. tomatoes
1 lb. lean stewing beef (or more as desired)	2 oz. grated parmesan
	2 oz. grated gruyere
6 tablespoons olive oil	2 oz. grated fontina
½ lb. onions	salt and pepper
1 stick celery	breadcrumbs
1 small carrot	butter

Melt four tablespoons of the oil and lightly brown the onion and other vegetables, then the meat. Season with salt and pepper, add the wine, let it reduce a little, then add water as necessary and cook the meat as in recipe 483. Make a separate sauce with the remaining oil and the pureed tomatoes. Cook the macaroni, drain well and mix with the meat gravy, then the tomato sauce, then fold in the grated cheeses lightly so they do not get too lumpy. Put the macaroni in a greased ovenproof dish, sprinkle with breadcrumbs, dot with butter and brown in a hot oven. This is really a Swiss recipe.

BUCATINI WITH BEEF GRAVY AND RICOTTA 487

1 lb. bucatini	1 carrot
1 lb. lean stewing beef (or more if desired)	¾ lb. tomatoes
	6 oz. ricotta
6 tablespoons olive oil	3 oz. grated parmesan
1 lb. onions	salt and pepper
1 stick celery	

Make the meat gravy as in recipe 483. Cook the pasta, drain well, put in a hot serving bowl and toss with the parmesan, then the gravy, then add the crumbled ricotta, mixing gently so it is not reduced to a puree. Serve with freshly ground black pepper.

1 lb. spaghetti
¾ lb. thinly sliced beefsteak (rump or fillet)
1 lb. tomatoes
2 cloves garlic

1 tablespoon capers
4 tablespoons olive oil
3 oz. grated parmesan
salt and pepper
parsley

Pizzaiola means with a pizza flavour, in other words with a tomato sauce. Heat the oil with a few tablespoons butter. Add the finely sliced meat, the peeled, chopped tomatoes, chopped garlic, washed capers, a handful of chopped parsley and a little pepper. Cook for about 20 minutes and serve the sauce with the hot pasta and the meat as a separate dish, or cut the meat into smaller pieces and return to the sauce.

MACARONI WITH PIQUANT BEEF GRAVY   **489**

1 lb. macaroni
1½-2 lb. lean stewing beef (or more if desired)
salt and pepper
4 tablespoons olive oil

1 medium onion
3 oz. grated parmesan
6 anchovy fillets, salt-cured
2 oz. butter
(beef stock)

Use a regular shaped piece of beef. Make a slit down one side and stuff with the washed anchovy fillets pounded with the butter and a little pepper into a thick paste. Sew up the slit. Brown the chopped onion in the oil, then add the meat and brown on all sides. Cover with hot water and cook slowly over low heat for at least three hours (see recipe 483). Mix the gravy with the hot pasta and serve the stuffed meat as a second course.

1 lb. macaroni
½ lb. fontina cheese
2 eggs
1½-2 lb. lean stewing beef (more or less as desired)
3 oz. grated parmesan
salt and pepper

1 stick celery
1 small carrot
1 lb. tomatoes
6 oz. milk
5 tablespoons olive oil
2 oz. butter
2 medium onions

Heat the oil and lightly brown the chopped vegetables, then the meat. Add the tomato puree, salt and pepper and enough water to cover and cook as in recipe 483. Dice the fontina and soften in the boiling milk. Mix with the hot pasta, then put in a greased ovenproof dish in layers with the cheese, meat gravy and grated parmesan. Finish with a layer of pasta, pour over two beaten eggs and a little butter. Sprinkle with grated parmesan and brown in a hot oven.

GNOCCHETTI WITH BEEF GRAVY **491**

1 lb. flour
1½-2 lb. lean stewing beef (more or less as desired)
1 lb. tomatoes
3 oz. grated pecorino/romano

1 stick celery
1 carrot
6 tablespoons olive oil
¾ lb. onions

Make the meat gravy as in recipe 483. Make the gnocchi with the flour, and enough warm water to obtain a fairly firm dough, then take pieces of the dough, roll into little cylinders, then divide these into smaller pieces. Give them the characteristic gnocchi shape by pressing against a fork or the edge of a pastry board. Cook in plenty of boiling salted water and remove with a slotted spoon as they rise to the surface. Mix with the meat gravy and serve grated parmesan separately.

11 oz. flour
3 lb. potatoes
1½-2 lb. lean stewing beef (more or less as desired)
3 oz. grated parmesan
salt and pepper

1 stick celery
1 carrot
1 lb. tomatoes
6 tablespoons olive oil
¾ lb. onions

Make the gnocchi in the usual way with the potatoes, flour and a little salt (see recipe 122). Cook them in boiling salted water and mix with a meat gravy made as in recipe 483. Serve grated parmesan separately.

ORECCHIETTE OR MINUICCHI WITH BEEF GRAVY **493**

½ lb. semolina
½ lb. flour
1½-2 lb. lean stewing beef (more or less as desired)
salt and pepper
2 sticks celery

1 lb. tomatoes
3 oz. parmesan
basil
6 tablespoons olive oil
¾ lb. onions
(peas)

Make the orecchiette or minuicchi, as they are also called. The proportions vary throughout Apulia, but the semolina makes them harder and chewier than other sorts of pasta. Put the flour, semolina and salt in a mound and make a well, then add the water a few tablespoons at a time so the flour incorporates as much water as possible without becoming stiff and dry. Your final dough should be softer than an egg pasta, but not at all sticky. Knead until smooth and elastic. Take a ball of dough and roll into a cylinder about ¾ inch thick. Slice into very thin discs, then put this in your palm and press down with the thumb of your other hand to make the mushroom cap shape of orecchiette—like the tumuli or burial mounds found from Bari to Taranto. Set aside to rest at least 12 hours. Cook in plenty of boiling, salted water and serve with a beef gravy made as in recipe 483. Serve grated parmesan separately.

Variation Omit the basil and add a few peas to the sauce at the end.

1 lb. flour
2 eggs
1½-2 lb. lean stewing beef (more or less as desired)
3 oz. butter
3 oz. grated parmesan
salt and pepper

6 oz. red wine
½ lb. tomatoes
garlic
2 medium onions
1 carrot
1 stick celery
pork fat

Old traditions survive longer in the vastness of the Appennines, such as at Bobbio, and people still make their own macaroni. The local variety is an egg pasta, like garganelli from Romagna (see recipe 428). Make the dough in the usual way with the flour, eggs and a pinch of salt (see recipe 181) to obtain a smooth, firm dough. Take little pieces of dough, roll into rectangles ½ inch wide and ¾ inch long, then cut these into strips ¾ inch wide. Roll these round the special instrument, or a knitting needle will do. Remember to cover the rest of the dough while you are working. Leave your macaroni to dry for one hour. Have ready a meat gravy made in the usual way (see recipe 483) although in the Piacentino this addition is made: make small incisions in the meat and stuff with pieces of garlic and pork fat and then brown all over and cook as usual. Cook the macaroni in plenty of boiling, salted water, drain well and serve with the meat gravy. Serve grated parmesan separately.

SPAGHETTI WITH BEEF GRAVY AND CHICKEN LIVERS AU GRATIN **495**

1 lb. spaghetti
1½-2 lb. lean stewing beef (more or less as desired)
3 oz. grated parmesan
salt and pepper
1 carrot

1 stick celery
½ lb. chicken livers
½ lb. butter
¾ lb. onions
(truffle, beef stock, white wine)

Make the beef gravy as in recipe 483. Clean and chop the chicken livers and brown lightly in a little butter. Heat the remaining butter in another pan and add the hot cooked spaghetti, the meat gravy, chicken livers and some grated parmesan. Mix well and serve.

Variations 1. Add six tablespoons white wine to the beef when cooking the gravy.
2. Use beef stock instead of water to cook the meat, and to cook the spaghetti.
3. Grate a little truffle over the finished dish.

1 lb. conchiglie	6 oz. butter
1 lb. lean stewing beef (more or less as desired)	½ lb. chicken livers
¾ lb. onions	3 oz. mushrooms
1 stick celery	6 oz. red wine
1 carrot	3 oz. grated parmesan
	salt and pepper

Make the beef gravy as in recipe 483 using only ½ pound onions. Heat two tablespoons butter in another pan and cook the remaining chopped onion until soft, then add the finely sliced mushroom. Cook for a minute, add the cleaned, chopped chicken livers, and after a few minutes, the wine. Cook until the wine reduces a little then add six ounces beef gravy and mix well to make a thick sauce. Remove the livers and add the hot pasta. Cook together for a few minutes, then return the livers to the sauce and stir in the grated parmesan. Serve very hot.

1 lb. flour	¾ lb. onions
4 eggs	1 carrot
½ lb. butter	3 oz. mushrooms
1 stick celery	¼ lb. chicken livers
6 oz. madeira	nutmeg
3 oz. grated parmesan	salt and pepper
1½-2 lb. lean stewing beef	breadcrumbs
(more or less as desired)	(milk, white wine)

Make the tagliatelle in the usual way with the flour, eggs, a pinch of salt and warm water as necessary (see recipe 181). Clean and slice the mushrooms and cook in two tablespoons butter over a low heat. After a few minutes add the chicken livers and brown lightly, then add half the madeira. Cook for a few more minutes. Make the beef gravy in the usual way (see recipe 483), adding the remaining madeira to the pan when the meat has browned, then let it reduce, add water as necessary and a pinch of nutmeg and cook in the usual way. Cook the tagliatelle, drain well and toss with three ounces butter, the parmesan and meat gravy. Grease an ovenproof dish and sprinkle the inside with breadcrumbs, then put in a layer of pasta, cover with the liver and mushrooms mixture (not right to the edges) and then with the remaining pasta. Sprinkle with breadcrumbs, dot with butter and brown in a hot oven.

Variations 1. Drain the tagliatelle and toss them in a mixture of two beaten eggs, a little milk and the butter and parmesan, to give an even better flavour.

2. Use any sweet wine such as marsala or sherry.

SPAGHETTI IMPERIAL · **498**

1 lb. spaghetti	3 oz. mushrooms
1½-2 lb. lean stewing beef (more or less as desired)	4 oz. foie gras
	6 oz. butter
2 oz. black truffle	1 lb. onions
6 tablespoons madeira or marsala	1 carrot
salt and pepper	1 stick celery

Make the beef gravy in the usual way (see recipe 483) with three ounces of the butter and three quarters of the onions. Heat the remaining butter in another pan and brown the rest of the chopped onion, then add the sliced mushrooms. Cook for a few minutes then add the meat gravy. Stir over the heat until well blended, and add the wine. Cook until it reduces a little, add the diced foie gras and mix very gently, then add the crumbled truffle. Heat gently for a few more minutes then mix with the hot pasta.

LASAGNE AND CHICKEN GIBLETS PIE **499**

2 lb. flour	2 cloves garlic
4 eggs	1 small hot chili pepper
3 egg yolks	cinnamon
4 oz. lard or strutto	basil
4 tablespoons olive oil	salt
2 oz. butter	parsley
1¼ lb. tomatoes	1 clove
3 oz. mushrooms	meat stock and gravy
¼ lb. chicken livers and giblets	3 oz. grated parmesan

Make the pasta dough with one pound flour, four eggs, a pinch of salt and warm water as necessary. Roll it out and cut into quite broad strips about five inches wide and 11 inches long. Make the pastry with another one pound flour, the egg yolks and lard. Set aside to rest for one hour, then roll out into two circles, a larger one for the bottom crust and the smaller one for the top crust. Heat the oil, add the chopped garlic (or whole crushed cloves, to be discarded), the chopped pepper, a little basil, a pinch of cinnamon and the clove. Stir in the pureed tomatoes and a few tablespoons meat gravy. Cook over low heat adding beef stock if it gets too dry. Clean and slice the mushrooms and cook in about two tablespoons butter with a little chopped parsley. Chop the giblets and brown in another two tablespoons butter, then add the chopped chicken livers. Cook the pasta and mix with a little butter, grated parmesan, the meat gravy and tomato mixture. Grease a pie dish and line with the larger sheet of pastry, then half the lasagne, and pour over the mushroom, giblet and liver sauce which you have mixed at the last minute. Cover with the remaining lasagne, then the top crust. Press the pastry edges together, pour over the melted butter and cook in a moderate oven about 45 minutes or until the pastry is firm and golden. Leave to stand a few minutes before serving.

PASTINA WITH MEAT BROTH AND SWEET PEPPER — 500

¾ lb. pastina
1 large skinned sweet pepper
(tinned or canned)
½ lb. lean fillet or rump steak

54 oz. beef stock
3 oz. grated parmesan
salt and pepper

Finely chop or mince the raw beef, season with salt and pepper and mix with the finely chopped sweet pepper. Cook the pastina in the hot stock and serve with one tablespoon chopped pepper and one tablespoon chopped raw meat in each individual soup dish. Serve grated parmesan separately.

TAGLIOLINI IN BEEF BROTH WITH BOILED BEEF — 501

¾ lb. flour
3 eggs
¾ lb. boiled beef

54 oz. beef stock
salt
3 oz. grated gruyere

Make the pasta dough in the usual way with the flour, eggs, a pinch of salt and warm water as necessary and cut into very thin strips or tagliolini (see recipe 182). Cook them in the stock and when ready serve in the soup with finely chopped boiled beef and grated gruyere in each serving.

3 oz. fresh breadcrumbs	1½ oz. butter
1 lb. lean beef	4 eggs
¾ lb. spinach	54 oz. beef stock
5 oz. grated parmesan	nutmeg
1 oz. beef marrow	salt and pepper

A specialty of Urbino, they are only pasta by virtue of the breadcrumbs. Cook the spinach, drain very well, chop and mix with the beef marrow, butter and finely chopped or minced beef. Add the breadcrumbs, egg yolks and a pinch each of salt, pepper and nutmeg. Work together for a smooth, firm paste, adding more breadcrumbs or parmesan if it seems too soft. Bring the stock to a boil and make the passatelli over it in the usual way (see recipe 464). Let them cook for one minute, then serve in the soup. Serve grated parmesan separately.

MACARONI WITH MEAT GRAVY, ONIONS AND FENNEL **503**

1 lb. macaroni	1 lb. lean stewing beef (more or
4 large onions	less as desired)
4 heads of fennel	rosemary
4 tablespoons olive oil	salt and pepper
1 oz. lard or strutto	3 oz. grated parmesan

Heat the oil and lard and lightly brown the chopped onion and fennel, then the beef. Season with salt and pepper and cook in the usual way to get a good thick gravy (see recipe 483). The vegetables will disintegrate nicely, but you can sieve the gravy if desired. Serve the gravy with the hot pasta, reserving the meat for other uses. Serve grated parmesan separately.

1 lb. pasta	thyme
¾ lb. lean stewing beef	bay leaf
3 oz. butter	1 clove
½ onion	beef stock
1 stick celery	3 oz. grated parmesan
1 small carrot	salt and pepper
parsley	(flour)

This Bolognese meat sauce has become one of the best-known pasta recipes in the world. A ragu is different from the previous braised beef recipes as the meat is cut up and served in the gravy. There are many different versions of this Bolognese ragu, but here is the simplest: melt the butter and lightly brown the chopped onion, celery and carrot, then the chopped or minced meat (add any resulting juice when you chop it). Moisten with a few tablespoons stock, add a bouquet garni with the herbs, or just the loose parsley, thyme and bay leaf. Stir, add one clove and season with salt and pepper. Bring to a boil until the sauce is thick, then lower the heat, cover the pan and continue cooking at least one hour. Serve with any pasta. Serve grated parmesan separately.

Variations 1. When browning the meat add a little flour, stir immediately and then stir in the liquid.
      2. Use water instead of stock.
      3. Omit the herbs if they are not available.

1 lb. pasta	6 oz. red wine
¾ lb. lean beef	beef stock
½ onion	bay leaf
1 stick celery	nutmeg
1 small carrot	3 oz. grated parmesan
3 oz. butter	salt and pepper
¾ lb. tomatoes	(pancetta or streaky bacon)

Heat the butter and lightly brown the chopped onion, celery and carrot, then add the coarsely minced or chopped meat. Stir so it browns evenly, season with salt and pepper, a pinch of nutmeg and a bay leaf. When the meat has browned, add the wine, let it reduce a little, then add the pureed tomatoes. Bring to a boil, lower the heat and cook slowly for about an hour, checking to see if there is enough liquid. Add more stock if necessary. Serve with any type of pasta and serve grated parmesan separately.

Variations 1. Use warm water instead of stock.
2. Reduce the quantity of butter and use a little finely chopped pancetta or streaky bacon instead.

PASTA WITH BOLOGNESE RAGU—III **506**

1 lb. pasta
¾ lb. lean beef
¼ lb. butter
1 onion
¾ lb. tomatoes

6 tablespoons cream
nutmeg
3 oz. grated parmesan
salt and pepper

Heat three ounces butter and add the chopped onion. Cook until transparent, then add the meat. Brown on all sides, then remove from the pan and chop. Carefully retain the juices and return to the pan with the meat. Let the liquid evaporate so the meat is quite dry and the onion disintegrates, then add the pureed tomatoes. Add one tablespoon butter, salt and pepper and a pinch of nutmeg. When the liquid has reduced again add enough cream to make a smooth, thick sauce. Mix with the hot pasta and serve grated parmesan separately.

PASTA WITH NEAPOLITAN BEEF RAGU **507**

1 lb. pasta
4 tablespoons olive oil
2 oz. prosciutto fat or fat salt pork
¾ lb. lean beef
½ onion
1 stick celery
1 small carrot
1 clove garlic

6 oz. red wine
1 lb. tomatoes
3 oz. grated parmesan
marjoram
nutmeg
salt and pepper
(flour)

Heat the oil and the prosciutto fat. Lightly brown the chopped onion, carrot and celery. Add the roughly chopped meat, a pinch each of marjoram, nutmeg and pepper and cook for a few minutes, stirring continuously, then pour over the wine. Let it reduce, then add the pureed tomatoes. Bring to a boil, then lower the heat and cook until the sauce reduces and thickens (add a few tablespoons hot water if it seems too dry). Mix with the hot pasta and serve grated parmesan separately.

Variation Before adding the tomato puree add a little flour to the sauce and stir it in well so it does not burn.

1 lb. bucatini	1 lb. tomatoes
5 tablespoons olive oil	parsley
¾ lb. lean beef	1 teaspoon paprika
¾ lb. onions	salt
2 cloves garlic	(beef stock, grated parmesan)

A rustic version of the classic Bolognese ragu. Heat the oil and lightly brown the chopped onion and garlic, then add the peeled, chopped tomatoes and plenty of chopped parsley. Add the chopped meat, mix well, then stir in the paprika and a pinch of salt and cook until the meat is tender—about 1 hour. The sauce should be thick, but if it seems too dry add more hot water (or stock) as necessary. If desired, serve grated parmesan separately.

1 lb. spaghetti	6 oz. butter
4 tablespoons olive oil	1 tablespoon brandy
1 onion	worcestershire sauce
1 carrot	hot chili pepper
1 stick celery	6 oz. thick cream
¾ lb. lean beef	3 oz. grated parmesan
1 lb. tomatoes	salt and pepper

The smooth consistency of the cream is a nice contrast to the hotness of this sauce. Heat the oil and lightly brown the chopped onion, celery and carrot, and then the coarsely chopped meat. Add the pureed tomatoes, season with salt and pepper and continue cooking without adding any extra liquid. Make another sauce in a separate pan: heat the butter, add the brandy, let it reduce, then add coarsely ground black pepper and the chili pepper (according to taste). Mix well, sprinkle with worcestershire sauce and stir in the cream. Have the spaghetti ready at the same time and mix with the hot pepper sauce and then the ragu. Mix well and serve grated parmesan separately.

1 lb. pasta	1 stick celery
¾ lb. lean beef	1 carrot
5 tablespoons olive oil	beef stock
6 oz. shelled peas	salt and pepper
¾ lb. onions	3 oz. grated parmesan

Heat the oil and add the chopped onion, celery and carrot. Cook for a few minutes, then add the coarsely chopped meat and brown all over. Season with salt and pepper and cover with plenty of stock. Cook for a few more minutes, add the peas and cook over moderate heat until the liquid has reduced and the peas are cooked. Serve wtih the hot pasta and serve grated parmesan separately.

PASTA WITH BEEF RAGU AND SWEET PEPPER **511**

1 lb. pasta	1 stick celery
¾ lb. lean beef	1 carrot
5 tablespoons olive oil	beef stock
1 large sweet pepper	salt and pepper
¾ lb. onions	3 oz. grated parmesan

Similar to the previous recipe but the sweet pepper gives a very different flavour. Roast the pepper over an open flame until brown all over, then moisten your fingers and remove the skin immediately (or used peeled, tinned/canned peppers). Chop roughly and remove the seeds and ribs. Heat the oil and lightly brown the chopped onion, celery and carrot, then add the coarsely chopped meat. Let it brown all over, then add the chopped pepper. Season with salt and pepper, add enough stock to cover and cook until the meat is tender—about one hour. Serve with the hot pasta. Serve grated parmesan separately.

1 lb. macaroni	¾ lb. aubergines/eggplant
1 lb. lean beef	parsley
6 oz. olive oil	beef stock
¾ lb. onions	3 oz. grated parmesan
1 stick celery	salt and pepper
¾ lb. tomatoes	(pecorino/romano, sugar, cinnamon)

An ancient Sicilian recipe, slightly modified for modern use. Peel and dice the aubergine/eggplant and leave to drain for a few hours sprinkled with coarse salt. Rinse and then fry in plenty of hot oil with a handful of chopped parsley. Make the ragu: heat the oil and add the chopped onion, celery and carrot, then the coarsely chopped meat. When it browns add the peeled, seeded and chopped tomatoes, a pinch of salt and the fried aubergines/eggplant. Cook over low heat until the sauce is thick, adding a little stock if it seems too dry. Serve with the hot pasta and serve grated parmesan separately.

Variations 1. Add a little cinnamon and sugar to the sauce for a smoother flavour.
2. Use grated pecorino/romano instead of parmesan.

TAGLIATELLE WITH BEEF RAGU AND CREAM

513

1 lb. flour	1 carrot
4 eggs	6 oz. heavy cream
1 lb. lean beef	3 oz. grated parmesan
3 oz. butter	beef stock
¾ lb. onions	salt and pepper
1 stick celery	(tomatoes, truffles)

Make the tagliatelle in the usual way with the flour, eggs, a pinch of salt and warm water as necessary (see recipe 181). Heat three ounces butter and brown the chopped onion, celery and carrot, then the finely chopped or minced meat (remember to add all its juice too), salt and pepper and enough stock to make a good sauce. Cook for about one hour until the meat is done. Cook the tagliatelle, drain well and mix with the cream and parmesan, then transfer to a hot serving bowl. Top with a little butter, then pour over the ragu, mix well and serve grated parmesan separately.

Variations 1. Add pureed tomatoes to the sauce.
2. Grate a little truffle over each individual serving.

MACARONI WITH BEEF RAGU AND RICOTTA

1 lb. macaroni
¾ lb. lean beef
¼ lb. butter
¾ lb. onions
1 stick celery
1 carrot

½ lb. ricotta
beef stock
3 oz. grated parmesan
salt and pepper
nutmeg

Heat three ounces butter and lightly brown the chopped onion, celery and carrot. Add the coarsely chopped meat, salt and peper and a pinch of nutmeg. Cook over low heat for about one hour with enough stock to make a good sauce. Cook the pasta, drain well and put in a greased ovenproof dish in alternate layers with the ragu, a little crumbled ricotta and some grated parmesan. Finish with a layer of pasta, dot with butter, sprinkle with parmesan and brown in a hot oven.

MACARONI WITH RAGU AND MOZZARELLA

1 lb. macaroni
4 tablespoons olive oil
2 onions
1 small carrot

½ lb. lean beef
1½ oz. butter
3 oz. mozzarella
salt and pepper

A quick and delicious adaptation of the classic Bolognese ragu. Heat the oil and lightly brown the chopped onion and carrot. Add the coarsely chopped meat, brown on all sides and season with salt and pepper. Add one or two tablespoons warm water if it seems too dry and cook for about 45 minutes or until the meat is tender. Cook the pasta, drain well. Dice the mozzarella. Put the pasta in a hot serving bowl with the mozzarella and a large piece of butter. Stir gently to melt the cheese, add the ragu, mix well and serve.

1 lb. macaroni
¾ lb. lean beef
¼ lb. butter
4 tablespoons olive oil
2 medium onions
¼ lb. mushrooms
½ lb. mozzarella

¼ lb. grated parmesan
parsley
salt and pepper
nutmeg
meat stock
breadcrumbs

Heat two ounces butter and the oil and brown the chopped onion, then the chopped meat. Season with salt and pepper and a pinch of nutmeg, add some stock and continue cooking slowly for about one hour until the meat is tender. Heat two ounces butter in another pan and cook the cleaned, chopped mushrooms with a handful of chopped parsley. Cook the pasta and drain well. Grease an ovenproof dish and put in layers of pasta, ragu, mushroom sauce, a few slices of mozzarella and grated paremsan. Make a final layer of pasta, sprinkle with grated cheese and breadcrumbs, dot with butter and brown in a hot oven.

LASAGNE VERDI WITH RAGU   **517**

1 lb. flour
4 eggs
1¼ lb. spinach
¾ lb. lean beef
½ lb. butter
¾ lb. onions
¾ lb. tomatoes

6 oz. mozzarella
18 oz. milk
3 oz. grated parmesan
nutmeg
beef stock
salt and pepper

This classic dish combines ragu and bechamel in a deliciously succulent way. Heat three ounces butter and cook the chopped onion until transparent, then add the chopped meat. Brown on all sides, season with salt and pepper and nutmeg and then add the pureed tomatoes. Cook over low heat for about one hour, adding more stock if it seems too dry. Cook the spinach, drain very well and chop finely. Make a bechamel sauce: melt another two ounces butter and stir in two ounces flour, then gradually add the milk and a pinch each of salt and pepper and some nutmeg. Make the lasagne with the flour, eggs, the spinach puree, a pinch of salt and warm water as necessary (see recipe 191). Roll out and cut into fairly broad strips (two by five inches). Cook in plenty of boiling, salted water, drain well and mix with one tablespoon butter, then put in layers in a greased ovenproof dish with the ragu, slices of mozzarella, a few tablespoons bechamel and grated parmesan. Finish with a layer of pasta, dot with butter, sprinkle with parmesan and brown for 10–15 minutes in a hot oven.

TUBETTINI OR CONCHIGLIETTE WITH BOILED BEEF AND SWEET PEPPER

½ lb. tubettini or conchigliette
½ lb. boiled beef
1 medium sweet pepper

54 oz. beef stock
3 oz. grated parmesan

Roast the pepper over a flame, remove the skin with moistened fingers, remove the ribs and seeds and dice very finely (or use tinned/canned sweet peppers). Cook the pasta in the hot stock and when it is al dente add the diced pepper and diced boiled beef. Serve grated parmesan separately.

COLD CONCHIGLIE OR FARFALLE WITH BOILED BEEF

¾ lb. conchiglie or farfalle
¾ lb. boiled beef
oil
vinegar

capers
gherkins
parsley
salt and pepper

Cook the pasta, drain well and cool. Mix with the diced meat—you can use leftovers—and as much oil, vinegar, capers and diced gherkins as you want. Season with chopped parsley, salt and pepper and serve cold.

RIGATONI WITH BEEF

1 lb. rigatoni
¾ lb. lean beef (rump or fillet steak)
2 oz. butter
4 tablespoons olive oil
1 lb. peeled tomatoes

rosemary
bay leaf
sage
3 oz. grated parmesan
salt and pepper

The meat gives a very pleasant consistency to the pasta as it is diced rather than chopped. Heat the oil and butter until almost boiling, then add a little rosemary, three or four bay leaves, a little sage and some pepper. Leave the oil to absorb the flavour of the herbs. Dice the meat very small and brown in the oil, then add the drained tomatoes. Cook for a few minutes just until the meat is done. Mix with the hot pasta so the sauce fills the rigatoni, then serve with grated parmesan.

¾ lb. ditalini
3 oz. margarine
¼ lb. lean minced or ground beef
2 eggs
½ lb. spinach

1 clove garlic
5 oz. grated parmesan
2 oz. gruyere
breadcrumbs
salt and pepper

Make little meat balls with the meat, beaten eggs, two ounces parmesan, salt and pepper. Fry them quickly in two ounces margarine until crisp and brown on the outside but still soft inside. Remove from the fat with a slotted spoon and drain on absorbent paper. Brown the crushed clove of garlic in the margarine still left in the pan, then discard the garlic and add the cooked, well drained and chopped spinach. Cook the pasta, drain well and mix with two tablespoons margarine, the parmesan, meat balls and spinach. Put half the pasta in a greased ovenproof dish, then a layer of finely sliced gruyere. Cover with the remaining pasta, sprinkle with breadcrumbs, dot with margarine and brown for about 20 minutes in a hot oven.

MACARONI WITH TONGUE **522**

1 lb. macaroni
½ lb. cooked tongue
6 oz. sliced gruyere

3 oz. grated parmesan
¼ lb. butter
salt

Cook the pasta, drain well and toss with three ounces butter and three ounces grated parmesan. Put a layer of pasta in a greased ovenproof dish, add a layer of diced tongue and slices of gruyere, ending with a layer of pasta. Sprinkle with grated parmesan, dot with butter and brown for a few minutes in a hot oven.

TUBETTINI WITH TONGUE AND CREAM **523**

1 lb. tubettini
¼ lb. tongue
3 oz. mushrooms
3 oz. onions
2 oz. butter

2 oz. fat salt pork
6 oz. thick cream
3 oz. grated parmesan
salt and pepper

Heat the butter with the diced fat salt pork and chopped onion. Add the diced tongue and the cleaned, finely sliced mushrooms. Cook for a few minutes, season with salt and pepper then moisten with cream. Serve with the hot pasta and grated parmesan.

1 lb. mezze maniche (the largest
sort of macaroni)
½ lb. braised beef
½ lb. grated parmesan
3 oz. breadcrumbs
2 tablespoons beef gravy

1 egg
2 egg whites
72 oz. beef stock
nutmeg
salt and pepper

Braise the beef as in recipe 484 and use ½ pound of the meat and some gravy
for this recipe. Chop the meat finely and mix with four ounces grated parmesan, the breadcrumbs, one egg, salt, pepper, nutmeg and the gravy. Stuff
each piece of macaroni with this filling and seal the ends with a little beaten
egg white. Cook the macaroni in boiling stock and serve with the remaining
parmesan.

JEWISH BEEF RAVIOLI **525**

11 oz. flour
5 eggs
¾ lb. lean beef
2 lb. spinach

1 carrot
1 onion
4 tablespoons olive oil
salt and pepper

A Jewish version of ravioli using beef instead of pork. Make the pasta dough in
the usual way with the flour, eggs, a pinch of salt and a little warm water as
necessary (see recipe 181) to obtain a fairly smooth, firm dough. Make the
filling: heat the oil and cook the chopped onion, grated carrot and the spinach,
which has been cooked in its own liquid, squeezed gently and chopped finely,
then add the finely minced meat, and a pinch each of salt and pepper. Continue cooking until soft and firm, then add two beaten eggs to bind. Put mounds
of this filling on the pasta to make ravioli (see recipe 251). Cook in plenty of
boiling salted water and serve with a meat or tomato sauce.

1 lb. flour	3 oz. or 2 slices stale white bread
6 eggs	about 100 oz. beef stock
1¼ lb. lean beef	6 oz. grated parmesan
2 oz. pancetta or streaky bacon	cloves
2 oz. butter	cinnamon
½ onion	garlic
1 small carrot	salt and pepper
1 stick celery	nutmeg
1 tablespoon tomato puree	olive oil

Recipes for anolini vary from one village to another, and the shape and fillings are never the same. This version from Parma calls for very small anolini. Lard the beef with thinly sliced strips of pancetta or bacon and a few whole cloves of garlic (to be discarded when the meat is cooked). Heat the butter and two tablespoons oil, if possible in an earthenware pan, and brown the meat with the chopped celery and sliced onion and carrot. Season with salt and pepper then add the tomato puree diluted with a little stock. Cover the meat with the stock, then add a pinch of cinnamon and a few cloves. Cook as slowly as possible for at least three hours to obtain a thick, highly flavoured gravy (the pot used to be kept simmering over a wood fire for three days and the lid had a special container for red wine which gave more flavour to the meat as it evaporated). Remove the meat to use for a separate dish and strain the gravy. Brown the breadcrumbs lightly in a little oil (they should be very dry, but not hard) and mix with the gravy, then the parmesan, two beaten eggs and a pinch of nutmeg. Add more parmesan if it is too soft. Make a pasta dough in the usual way with the flour, four eggs, a pinch of salt and warm water as necessary (see recipe 181) and roll out very thinly. Make into ravioli with the filling, but cut them as crescent shapes for anolini. Leave to stand for a few hours and cook in beef stock.

Variations 1. Add four ounces of the chopped stracotto meat to the gravy to make the filling for the anolini.
2. Cook the anolini in water or broth, drain well and serve with a Bolognese beef ragu (see recipe 504).

1 lb. semolina	4 oz. grated caciocavallo cheese
4 eggs	1 oz. butter
¾ lb. braised beef and its gravy	salt

Make this dish when you have some stracotto beef leftovers (see recipe 483). Make a pasta dough with the flour, two eggs, a pinch of salt and warm water as necessary to obtain a fairly firm dough (see recipe 181). Roll it out and cut into rectangles two by three inches. Cook them in plenty of lightly salted boiling water for about 20 seconds, drain well and leave on a cloth to dry. Make the filling: chop the beef and mix with a little of the gravy (which you have reduced by boiling for a little over high heat). Put a teaspoonful of this mixture on each pasta rectangle, add a little grated cheese, then fold over to make cannelloni and put in a greased ovenproof dish. Pour a few tablespoons of the remaining gravy on each layer and sprinkle on a little cheese, then bake for 15 minutes in a hot oven. Remove from the oven and pour over two lightly beaten eggs to cover the cannelloni. Cook for another few minutes so the egg sets, then serve immediately.

LASAGNE VERDI WITH BEEF RAGU AND CHICKEN LIVERS **528**

1 lb. flour	parsley
4 eggs	thyme
1¼ lb. spinach	bay leaf
¼ lb. chicken livers	1 clove
¾ lb. lean beef	meat stock
¼ lb. butter	3 oz. grated parmesan
½ onion	salt and pepper
1 stick celery	(black truffle)
1 small carrot	

Make the dough for the lasagne with the flour, eggs, pureed spinach (cooked in its own liquid, then squeezed dry and finely chopped), and a pinch of salt (see recipe 191). Roll out the dough and cut into strips about two inches wide and five inches long. Make the ragu: melt three ounces butter, brown the chopped onion, celery and carrot and the coarsely chopped meat. Brown the meat and moisten with stock. Add a bouquet garni (parsley, thyme, bay leaf) and salt and pepper and continue cooking slowly. Clean and chop the chicken livers and brown with one tablespoon butter. Remove the meat from the ragu (it can be used for another dish) and add the chopped chicken livers, then the gravy. Cook for a few more minutes, stirring with a wooden spoon. Grease an ovenproof dish and put in a layer of lasagne, then pour over a few tablespoons ragu and liver mixture, sprinkle with grated parmesan and put a final layer of grated parmesan and melted butter. Brown for 15 minutes in a hot oven.

Variation Crumble a little truffle over the layers of pasta.

MACARONI WITH BEEF RAGU, CHICKEN LIVERS AND BREASTS **529**

1 lb. macaroni	1 small carrot
¼ lb. chicken livers	3 oz. grated parmesan
½ lb. lean beef	thyme
6 oz. butter	bay leaf
½ lb. chicken breasts	1 clove
½ onion	salt and pepper
parsley	beef stock
1 stick celery	(tongue)

Make a beef ragu in the usual way with two ounces butter, the chopped carrot, onion and celery and the chopped beef. When the beef is brown add the stock, salt and pepper and bouquet garni (thyme, parsley, bay leaf and clove). Cook slowly for about one hour. Heat two ounces butter in another pan and brown the diced chicken breast, then add the cleaned, chopped chicken livers. Season with salt and pepper and cook until the meat is tender, then add to the ragu. Mix some of this sauce with the hot pasta. Put alternate layers of macaroni, ragu and grated parmesan in a greased ovenproof dish. Sprinkle with grated parmesan, dot with butter and brown in a hot oven.

Variations 1. Cut the chicken breasts into quite broad strips and do not mix them with the ragu. Mix the pasta with the ragu and liver mixture, put in a serving bowl, cover with the chicken breasts and serve grated parmesan separately.
2. Dice a little tongue and add to the ragu when putting it on the layers of macaroni, or else add it to the chicken breasts on top.

1 lb. spaghetti
½ lb. boiled or braised beef
1 calf's kidney (about ½ lb.)
6 oz. butter
2 oz. flour

½ onion
3 oz. grated gruyere
breadcrumbs
salt and pepper
meat stock

A French recipe originally, it is a good way of using up any boiled or braised beef leftovers. Remove the outer membrane of the kidney and brown it gently in about two tablespoons butter, then cut in half and remove the tissues and slice carefully over a plate so you do not lose any of the juice. Heat four tablespoons butter and stir in the flour gradually, then add the chopped onion and the kidney. Season with salt and pepper. Dilute with meat stock for a fairly thick sauce. Grease an ovenproof dish. Cook the spaghetti, drain well and toss with two ounces butter and some of the kidney sauce. Put a layer of spaghetti in the ovenproof dish, then a few tablespoons sauce, a few tablespoons beef cut in fine strips or julienne and some grated gruyere. Finish with a layer of pasta, sprinkle with parmesan and breadcrumbs, dot with butter and brown in a hot oven.

PASTICCIO OF MACARONI CARNIVAL **531**

1 lb. macaroni
1 lb. lean beef
¼ lb. chicken giblets
1 oz. dried mushrooms
3 oz. fresh pork sausage
2 eggs
5 egg yolks
1 lb. flour
6 oz. sugar
18 oz. milk
10 oz. butter
¼ lb. lard or strutto

1 tablespoon marsala
6 oz. red wine
1 onion
1 carrot
1 stick celery
vanilla
lemon
cinnamon
vanilla sugar
salt and pepper
5 oz. grated parmesan

This is the ultimate masterpiece of Roman macaroni, an ancient recipe from the time when Carnival was a long period of feasting and merriment. It has the usual old-fashioned combination of sweet and savoury ingredients. Braise the beef: heat two ounces butter and lightly brown the chopped onion, celery and carrot. Add the meat and brown on all sides, then cover with red wine and let it reduce a little. Season with salt and pepper and cook until the meat is tender (about three hours), adding warm water if it seems too dry. Strain the gravy, cool and remove the fat from the surface. Cook the giblets and mushrooms: soak the mushrooms in warm water for at least ten minutes, then chop roughly. Melt two ounces butter and add the chopped giblets, mushrooms and sliced sausage. Make little meat balls with eight ounces of the braised beef, minced or finely chopped, some grated parmesan and one beaten egg to bind, then brown with the other ingredients in the pan. Season with salt and pepper, add the marsala, let it reduce, then cook for a few more minutes with a few tablespoons meat gravy. Make a savoury sauce: mix one ounce butter in a bowl with three egg yolks, a pinch each of salt and cinnamon, then transfer to a saucepan and bring to a boil, gradually stirring in the milk. Continue cooking, beating all the time with a whisk until the sauce thickens (do not let it return to a boil). Put it back in the bowl and cool, stirring occasionally to prevent a skin from forming. Make a sweet pastry with 14 ounces flour, the sugar, three ounces butter, three ounces lard, a large pinch of cinnamon, a small pinch of salt, two egg yolks, the grated lemon peel and about two ounces vanilla sugar. Roll out into two sheets, one larger one for the bottom crust and the smaller one for the top crust. Cook the macaroni and mix with the remaining butter and parmesan. Grease a large pie dish and line with the bottom crust of pastry, then put in half the macaroni and the sauce. Cover with the remaining macaroni and then the savoury sauce, spreading it over the pasta with a knife. Cover with the top crust, press the edges well together (do not overfill the case) and decorate the top with extra pastry. Brush with beaten egg mixed with ½ teaspoon water and bake in a hot oven for about 45 minutes until the pastry is firm and golden. Sprinkle with vanilla sugar and serve very hot.

VII
PASTA WITH PORK

¾ lb. trenette
4 oz. lardo or fat salt pork
2 oz. basil
2 oz. mixed herbs (parsley, marjoram and anything else available)
2 cloves garlic
1 oz. grated pecorino/romano and parmesan, mixed
½ lb. dried beans, soaked for 12 hours in cold water

1 medium potato
1 carrot
1 stick celery
1 leek
3 oz. grated pecorino/romano
salt
olive oil
(pine nuts, walnuts)

Make a pesto sauce by pounding the basil, garlic, other herbs and the mixture of grated pecorino/romano and parmesan together with a little oil added gradually to make a smooth fairly liquid paste. Put the chopped lardo or fat salt pork in a large pan and cook over high heat. Add the pesto sauce, mix well, then add the beans, the peeled, sliced potato and carrot and the chopped celery and leek. Cover with water, add some salt and continue cooking until the beans and potatoes are almost done. Add more boiling water if it seems too dry, then cook the pasta in the same pan. Serve grated parmesan separately.

Variation Add a few walnuts and pine nuts to the pesto (remove the walnut skins in boiling water first).

FRIED RIGATONI WITH LARDO OR FAT SALT PORK **533**

1 lb. rigatoni
3 oz. lardo or fat salt pork
2 medium onions
1 lb. tomatoes

4 oz. butter
4 oz. grated parmesan
salt and pepper

Chop the lardo or fat salt pork and fry gently in a pan. Brown the chopped onion with it together with a pinch of salt. Add the pureed tomatoes and cook for a few more minutes. Cook the pasta, drain well and mix with half the butter and the lardo mixture. Heat the remaining butter, add the pasta and lardo and fry gently for a few minutes with a little freshly ground black pepper. Serve grated parmesan separately.

PASTA WITH BROCCOLI AND LARDO OR FAT SALT PORK

534

1 lb. pasta
¾ lb. broccoli spears
3 oz. lardo or fat salt pork
1 clove garlic

1 hot chili pepper
3 oz. grated pecorino/romano
salt

Chop the lardo or fat salt pork and fry with the chopped garlic and chili pepper (then discard the pepper). Boil the broccoli spears until just tender, chop and brown gently with the lardo. Mix with the hot pasta and serve grated pecorino/romano separately.

VERMICELLI WITH LARDO OR FAT SALT PORK AND EGGS

535

1 lb. vermicelli
5 oz. lardo or fat salt pork
3 oz. butter

3 eggs
salt and pepper
3 oz. grated gruyere

Chop the lardo or fat salt pork and fry gently. Beat the eggs with the grated gruyere and a pinch each of salt and pepper. Cook the vermicelli and mix with half the butter, the lardo and beaten eggs. Heat the remaining butter and add the pasta. Make into a large pancake and fry until brown and crisp on the outside.

PASTA WITH ONIONS AND LARDO OR FAT SALT PORK

536

1 lb. pasta
3 oz. lardo or fat salt pork
¾ lb. onions
3 eggs

2 oz. butter
3 oz. grated parmesan
salt and pepper
(strutto, pancetta)

Melt the butter and lightly brown the chopped lardo. Add the chopped onions and cook over low heat with salt and pepper and a few tablespoons warm water (to prevent it drying out) until the onion is very soft. Add the beaten eggs, stir well and mix with the hot pasta. Serve grated parmesan separately.

Variation Use pancetta or strutto instead of lardo: about three ounces pancetta and four ounces butter will be necessary.

¾ lb. flour	1 onion
3 eggs	3 oz. grated pecorino/romano
10 oz. shelled peas	salt
4 oz. lardo or fat salt pork	(tomatoes, parmesan)

Make an egg pasta dough in the usual way with the flour, eggs, a pinch of salt and warm water as necessary (see recipe 181). Roll out the dough and cut in very small squares. Brown the chopped lardo or fat salt pork, add the chopped onion and let it brown also, then add enough hot water to cook the peas (they should be very young and tender). Add a little more water, bring to a rolling boil and add the pasta. When this is cooked (only a few seconds will be necessary) serve with grated pecorino/romano.

Variations 1. Use grated parmesan instead of pecorino/romano.
             2. Add two tablespoons pureed tomatoes before adding the peas.

FARFALLE WITH TONGUE, MUSHROOMS AND LARDO OR FAT SALT PORK

538

1 lb. farfalle	2 oz. lardo or fat salt pork
6 oz. cooked tongue	salt and pepper
6 oz. mushrooms	3 oz. grated parmesan
3 oz. butter	(tomatoes, stock)

Chop the lardo and brown in half the butter, then add the diced tongue and sliced mushrooms. Cook until the mushrooms are tender with salt and pepper and a little warm water if it seems too dry. Cook the pasta, drain well and mix with the remaining butter and this sauce. Serve grated parmesan separately.

Variations 1. Add a few tablespoons pureed tomatoes.
             2. Dilute with stock instead of water.

TUBETTI WITH SUGNA AND BASIL **539**

1 lb. tubetti
3 oz. sugna or lard
1 tablespoon olive oil
1 clove garlic
2 oz. basil

2 oz. grated parmesan
2 oz. grated pecorino/romano
salt and pepper
(strutto, lardo, prosciutto fat)

Another recipe from the more frugal, but still delicious Neapolitan tradition. Heat the chopped sugna with one tablespoon olive oil and the chopped garlic. Add the chopped basil, stir well, season with salt and pepper and cook over very low heat. Mix with the hot pasta and serve the two grated cheeses separately.

Variation Use strutto, or chopped lardo or prosciutto fat instead of sugna.

RIGATONI WITH RICOTTA, TOMATOES AND SUGNA **540**

1 lb. rigatoni
½ lb. ricotta
2 lbs. tomatoes
2 oz. sugna or lard
2 tablespoons olive oil

4 oz. grated parmesan
½ onion
basil
salt and pepper

Heat the sugna and oil and lightly brown the chopped onion. Add the pureed tomatoes and cook for a few minutes. Season with salt and pepper and a few leaves of basil. Soften the ricotta with a little of this sauce. Cook the pasta and mix first with the sauce, then the ricotta and a few tablespoons grated parmesan. Serve grated parmesan separately.

MACARONI WITH NEAPOLITAN RAGU **541**

1 lb. macaroni
2 lb. loin of veal (or lean beef)
3 oz. sugna or lard
4 tablespoons olive oil
2 teaspoons tomato puree
1 onion

1 carrot
1 stick celery
3 oz. grated parmesan
basil
salt and pepper
(strutto, fresh tomatoes)

This recipe follows a time-honoured method of making ragu. Try to use an earthenware cooking pot: they used to be kept simmering over open fires outside every home in Naples and the thick meat gravy that could be made in this way was one of the most delicious accompaniments ever for pasta. Heat the sugna and brown the chopped onion, carrot and celery. Tie up the meat so it does not disintegrate, brown over moderate heat and cook for as long as possible (see recipe 483). Add the tomato puree halfway through with salt, pepper and a little oil. You can also add fresh basil to the cooking pot, or directly on the individual helpings. Cook the pasta, drain well and mix with the meat gravy. You can chop some of the meat and return it to the gravy, or serve it as a separate dish.

Variations 1. Use strutto instead of sugna.
  2. Use fresh pureed tomatoes instead of tomato puree.

BUCATINI WITH BACON AND TOMATOES **542**

1 lb. bucatini	6 small tomatoes
4 oz. guanciale, pancetta or	1 piece hot chili pepper
unsmoked streaky bacon	3 oz. grated pecorino/romano
1 tablespoon olive oil	salt
1 small onion	(strutto, tomato puree)

One of the most famous of Italian recipes. Guanciale is hard to obtain out of Italy, so pancetta makes a reasonable substitute although it has not the same sweetness and delicacy as guanciale. Unsmoked, streaky bacon can be used, but again it lacks the spiciness and interest of Italian bacon. Any form of pasta goes well with this sauce, especially penne. It is best to use a heavy-bottomed or cast-iron frying pan to make the sauce. Put the oil in the pan with the chopped bacon and brown very lightly over high heat. Remove the bacon, drain well and keep warm, then add the chopped onion and hot chili pepper. Cook until the onion begins to brown, then add the peeled, seeded tomatoes. Season with salt and cook for a little over medium heat. Remove the chili pepper and add the cooked bacon. Stir gently and mix with the hot pasta and some grated pecorino/romano. Serve more grated pecorino/romano separately.

Variations 1. The original version of this recipe was a shepherd's dish and contained no tomato as they did not exist in Italy at such an early date. If you want to omit the tomatoes it is still interesting to add tomato puree diluted with a little warm water instead.
  2. Use strutto instead of olive oil for frying.

1 lb. penne
1½ lb. tomatoes
4 oz. guanciale, pancetta or
unsmoked streaky bacon
½ oz. strutto or lard

1 onion
2 cloves garlic
salt
hot powdered chili pepper
3 oz. grated pecorino/romano

This contains more tomato and more hot pepper than the previous recipe, so the stronger flavoured pancetta is an acceptable substitute for guanciale. Heat the strutto or lard in a big pan and lightly brown the chopped onion and garlic. Cut the bacon in fine strips and fry a little, then add the pureed tomatoes. Season with salt and plenty of powdered hot chili pepper. Cook for a few minutes over high heat until the right consistency, then mix with the hot pasta and a few tablespoons grated pecorino/romano. Serve the remaining grated pecorino/romano separately.

¾ lb. cannolicchi
¾ lb. shelled broad beans
or lima beans
1 large tomato
72 oz. beef stock
3 oz. grated pecorino/romano
salt and pepper

parsley
1 clove garlic
4 oz. guanciale, pancetta or
unsmoked streaky bacon
1 stick celery
1 small onion

Chop the bacon, onion, celery, garlic and parsley and brown in a little oil or in the bacon fat. Add the pureed tomatoes and a pinch each of salt and pepper, then cook for about ten minutes over moderate heat. Stir in the beans and cook for a minute, then add the stock. Cook until the beans are almost tender, bring to a rolling boil and add the pasta. When it is al dente put in a hot serving bowl with the grated cheese, then leave to stand for a few minutes before serving.

1 lb. bucatini
4 oz. guanciale or pancetta
or unsmoked streaky bacon
2 oz. butter
1 tablespoon olive oil

5 eggs
2 tablespoons thick cream
3 oz. grated pecorino/romano
salt and pepper
(parmesan)

Prepare the sauce quickly while the pasta is cooking so nothing has to stand and wait. Brown the chopped bacon in the oil. Beat the eggs, add the cream, two ounces grated pecorino/romano, a pinch of salt and some freshly ground black pepper. Heat the butter in a deep saucepan until golden, then add the beaten eggs and cook until they start to thicken (like scrambled eggs). Quickly add the bacon and the hot pasta. Stir lightly and serve immediately.

Variation Use half pecorino/romano and half parmesan, or just parmesan.

SPAGHETTI WITH BACON AND TUNNY/TUNA FISH **546**

1 lb. spaghetti
2 oz. guanciale, pancetta
or unsmoked streaky bacon
2 oz. tunny/tuna fish
½ lb. mushrooms

2 cloves garlic
4 tablespoons olive oil
9 oz. meat gravy
3 oz. grated parmesan
salt and pepper

Heat the oil and lightly brown the chopped garlic (or whole crushed cloves, to be discarded after they are brown); add the diced bacon and the cleaned, sliced mushrooms. Season with salt and pepper and cook for a few minutes, then mix in the crumbled fish and continue cooking until the sauce is well blended. Put the hot pasta in a serving bowl, toss with this sauce and cover with hot meat gravy (made as in recipe 483). Mix gently and serve. Serve grated parmesan separately.

VERMICELLI AND BACON AU GRATIN

1 lb. vermicelli
4 oz. guanciale, pancetta or
unsmoked streaky bacon
3 oz. strutto or lard
5 tablespoons olive oil

1½ medium onions
2 oz. raisins
2 oz. pine nuts
4 hard-boiled eggs
salt and pepper

Heat four tablespoons oil and two ounces strutto or lard and lightly brown the chopped onion. Add the bacon cut in thin strips. Cook for a minute and add the chopped eggs, raisins and pine nuts. Season with salt and cook for a little longer. Mix part of the sauce with plenty of liquid and the hot pasta. Put half of this in an ovenproof dish greased with lard, pour over the remaining sauce, cover with the remaining pasta and a little oil and brown in a hot oven.

PASTA AND PEAS WITH BACON

1 lb. short pasta
1¼ lb. shelled peas
¾ lb. onions
4 oz. pancetta or
unsmoked streaky bacon
2 tablespoons olive oil

1 oz. strutto or lard
parsley
3 oz. grated parmesna
salt and pepper
parsley
(tomatoes or tomato puree)

Heat the oil and the lard and lightly brown the chopped onion—or use tiny spring onions and leave them whole. Add the diced bacon, brown lightly and add the peas. Cook over low heat with salt and pepper. When they are just tender add the hot pasta, stir gently and serve—it should be thick enough for a spoon to stand up in it. Sprinkle with a handful of chopped parsley and serve grated parmesan separately.

Variation Since this is a Neapolitan recipe you can add a few tablespoons
pureed tomatoes or tomato puree to the pan.

BUCATINI WITH BACON AND TOMATOES

1 lb. bucatini
1¼ lb. tomatoes
½ lb. pancetta or unsmoked
streaky bacon
salt and pepper

2 onions
marjoram
4 tablespoons olive oil
3 oz. grated pecorino/romano

A dish from the Spoleto region with a distinctive flavour due to the fresh marjoram used in the sauce. Lightly brown the chopped onion and the diced bacon. Add the peeled, seeded chopped tomatoes, season with salt and pepper and cook until the tomatoes have reduced to make a good sauce. Add plenty of chopped marjoram. Mix with the hot pasta and serve grated pecorino/romano separately.

SPAGHETTI WITH GARLIC AND BACON

1 lb. spaghetti
½ lb. pancetta or
unsmoked streaky bacon
3 oz. grated pecorino/romano

3 cloves garlic
salt and pepper
4 tablespoons olive oil

Heat the oil and lightly brown the finely sliced garlic, then the diced bacon. Mix with the hot pasta and serve with freshly ground black pepper and grated pecorino/romano.

MINESTRONE WITH BACON

¾ lb. short pasta
1 lb. vegetables: lettuce,
cabbage, 3 tomatoes, 2 sticks celery,
1 carrot, escarole
3 oz. grated parmesan

4 oz. pancetta or
unsmoked streaky bacon
4 tablespoons olive oil
salt and pepper

Boil about 30 ounces of water in a deep pan and add all the chopped vegetables at once, then the finely chopped bacon. Season with salt and pepper and cook until soft, then add the pasta. When this is al dente pour in the olive oil. Serve grated parmesan separately.

Variation Brown the bacon in a little oil before adding.

1 lb. macaroni	2 large tomatoes
6 oz. olive oil	2 aubergines/ eggplant
2 oz. pancetta or	3 oz. sliced caciocavallo cheese
unsmoked streaky bacon	2 medium onions
salt and pepper	

Peel, finely slice the aubergines/eggplant, sprinkle with coarse salt and leave for one hour under a lightly weighted plate. Fry in the oil with a little salt. Lightly brown the chopped onion in two tablespoons oil, add the diced bacon and peeled, seeded, chopped tomatoes. Season with salt and pepper and cook until the tomatoes have reduced and thickened. Cook the macaroni, drain well and mix with part of the sauce. Put in layers in a greased ovenproof dish with the remaining sauce, fried aubergines/eggplant and finely sliced caciocavallo. Pour over a little oil and brown in a hot oven.

RICOTTA GNOCCHI WITH BACON **553**

10 oz. ricotta	3½ oz. flour
3 eggs	6 oz. butter
3 oz. pancetta or	salt and pepper
unsmoked streaky bacon	6 oz. grated parmesan

Lightly brown the diced bacon in a little oil. Work the ricotta until creamy and soft, then add the beaten eggs, half the grated cheese and the bacon, salt and pepper and enough flour to make a smooth, firm paste. Form into little balls, flour lightly and fry in a little butter. Serve with the remaining melted butter and grated parmesan.

1 lb. perciatelli
2 lb. aubergines/eggplant
¼ lb. lean veal
1 egg
3 oz. grated parmesan
3 oz. or 2 slices stale white bread
½ lb. shelled peas
2 oz. pancetta or
unsmoked streaky bacon
salt and pepper

2 lb. tomatoes
4 oz. sugna
2 oz. breadcrumbs
6 tablespoons white wine
½ oz. butter
parsley
basil
olive oil
2 oz. chicken livers
10 oz. sliced mozzarella

Another dish that is so rich in flavour and originality that it is well worth the extra effort in preparing it. Peel, cut the aubergines/eggplant in thin slices, sprinkle with coarse salt and leave for about an hour under a lightly weighted plate. Fry in plenty of hot oil and sprinkle with salt. Heat two tablespoons oil with two ounces sugna and make a tomato sauce in the usual way (see recipe 15) with the pureed tomatoes, salt and pepper and basil. Chop the cleaned chicken livers and fry very quickly in two tablespoons butter. Make a firm paste with the finely minced veal, beaten egg, stale bread soaked in a little water and squeezed dry, a little parmesan and chopped parsley, and a pinch of salt. Form into little balls and fry in plenty of hot oil. Lightly brown the diced bacon in one tablespoon oil and one ounce sugna, then add the peas and cook until tender. Mix the meat balls, livers and peas with a few tablespoons of the tomato sauce. Slice the mozzarella. Grease an ovenproof dish and line with greaseproof/waxed paper sprinkled with breadcrumbs. It should be large enough to come up the sides of the dish. Cook the pasta and mix with half the tomato sauce and the grated parmesan. Put in layers in the dish with the meat ball sauce, livers, peas, sliced mozzarella, grated parmesan and more sauce. Finish with a layer of aubergines/eggplant, sprinkle with parmesan, cover with another sheet of greased paper and bake for at least 15 minutes in a hot oven. Turn out if desired onto a large plate.

1 lb. trenette
4 tablespoons olive oil
1 onion
2 oz. pancetta or
unsmoked streaky bacon

2 oz. gruyere
2 oz. lean cooked veal
6 oz. thick cream
2 teaspoons curry powder
salt

Heat the oil and lightly brown the chopped onion, the diced bacon and veal. Add the cream and curry powder. Stir well to blend, then add the diced cheese. When it starts to melt add the hot pasta, mix well and serve.

PAPPARDELLE WITH BACON AND ANCHOVIES **556**

1 lb. pappardelle
2 oz. butter
2 oz. pancetta or
unsmoked streaky bacon
2 oz. lean beef
2 salt-cured anchovy fillets
¾ lb. tomatoes

1 onion
1 carrot
1 stick celery
6 oz. white wine
3 oz. grated parmesan
salt
(meat stock)

Use commercial pappardelle, or make them with the usual pasta dough (see recipe 181) cut into ⅝ inch strips with a fluted pasta wheel. Make the sauce: heat the butter and lightly brown the chopped onion, carrot and celery, then the chopped bacon and beef. Moisten with the wine, let it reduce, and add the washed, chopped anchovy fillets and the pureed tomatoes. Stir well with a few tablespoons warm water and cook until the tomatoes have reduced and the sauce is well blended. Mix with the hot pasta and serve grated parmesan separately.

1 lb. macaroni
1 lb. lean stewing beef (more
or less as desired)
3 oz. pancetta or
unsmoked streaky bacon
1 oz. strutto or lard
1 oz. raisins
1 oz. pine nuts

2 lb. tomatoes
½ onion
1 clove garlic
6 oz. red wine
olive oil
3 oz. grated parmesan
salt and pepper

A slight variation on other stracotto or braised beef recipes as the meat should be larded with strips of pancetta and stuck with pine nuts and raisins, then tied up well and browned in the lard, together with the finely chopped garlic and onion, the remaining chopped pancetta or bacon and a little oil. Add the wine, let it reduce, then add the peeled, seeded, chopped tomatoes. Season with salt and pepper, stir gently, cover with boiling water and cook over low heat for at least three hours (see recipe 483). Serve the gravy with the hot pasta, and serve grated parmesan separately. Serve the meat as another course.

SPAGHETTI WITH BACON AND GORGONZOLA **558**

1 lb. spaghetti
5 tablespoons olive oil
7 oz. pancetta or
unsmoked streaky bacon
½ lb. gorgonzola

12 oz. thick cream
1 piece hot chili pepper
3 oz. grated parmesan
salt
(garlic)

Heat the oil and brown the chopped pepper and the bacon cut in very fine strips. Cook until the fat melts, then add the diced gorgonzola. Stir so the cheese melts, then add the cream and serve with the hot pasta. Serve grated parmesan separately.

Variation Use one or two crushed cloves garlic instead of the chili pepper and discard before mixing with the pasta.

1 lb. flour	½ lb. tomatoes
6 eggs	1 lb. scamorza or mozzarella cheese
3 hard-boiled eggs	6 oz. white wine
¾ lb. lean minced/chopped veal	4 oz. grated pecorino/romano
½ lb. lean minced/chopped beef	salt and pepper
3 oz. butter	(meat stock, grated parmesan)
¼ lb. prosciutto fat	

This recipe from the Abruzzi makes use of prosciutto fat and this gives the ragu a quite different flavour. Make pasta in the usual way with the flour, four eggs, a pinch of salt and a few tablespoons warm water as necessary (see recipe 181). Make the sauce: lightly brown the chopped prosciutto fat and add the beef. Brown all over and add white wine and the pureed tomatoes. Season with salt and pepper and continue cooking for about ¾ hour with a few tablespoons warm water if it seems too dry. Make meat balls with the finely minced veal, three tablespoons grated pecorino/romano, two beaten eggs, salt and pepper, and fry them in a little butter. When they are brown add the meat sauce. Cook the lasagne, drain well and dry on a cloth. Grease an ovenproof dish and put in alternate layers of lasagne, ragu, sliced scamorza, sliced hard-boiled eggs and grated cheese. Put a little ragu over the final layer, dot with butter and brown in a hot oven.

Variations 1. Use parmesan instead of pecorino/romano or a mixture of both.
2. Use stock instead of water to dilute the sauce.

PASTA AND PEAS WITH PROSCIUTTO **560**

1 lb. short pasta	1 onion
3 tablespoons olive oil	1 stick celery
2 oz. pancetta or unsmoked	parsley
streaky bacon	salt and pepper
2 oz. prosciutto	(meat stock)
½ lb. shelled peas	

Heat the oil and lightly brown the chopped celery and onion, then the diced pancetta. Add the peas (use only small tender ones), stir a little, then add the prosciutto cut in narrow strips. Just heat it through as it needs less cooking than the pancetta. Season with salt and pepper, add a handful of chopped parsley and a few tablespoons warm water if it seems too dry. Serve with the hot pasta.

Variation Use stock instead of water.

PASTA WITH BROAD
BEANS AND PROSCIUTTO

561

1 lb. short pasta
2 oz. pancetta or unsmoked
streaky bacon
2 oz. prosciutto
½ lb. shelled broad beans
or lima beans

3 tablespoons olive oil
1 onion
1 stick celery
6 tablespoons vinegar
½ teaspoon sugar
salt

Cook the beans in boiling water until just tender. Lightly brown the chopped onion and celery in the oil, then the diced pancetta. Add the beans and then the prosciutto cut in thin strips. When the beans are soft enough to disintegrate when pressed with a spoon, add the vinegar and sugar for an old-fashioned sweet/sour flavour. Mix with the hot pasta.

Variation The vinegar and sugar can be omitted, but the flavour is less interesting.

TUBETTINI WITH
BEANS AND PROSCIUTTO

562

1 lb. tubettini
1 lb. fresh or tinned/canned
baby lima beans
3 large tomatoes
5 tablespoons olive oil
2 oz. prosciutto
1 onion

1 carrot
1 stick celery
basil
bay leaf
rosemary
3 oz. grated parmesan
salt and pepper

Heat four tablespoons oil and lightly brown the chopped onion, carrot and celery, then add a little rosemary and a bay leaf. Add the beans (if using fresh ones), cover with water and cook over low heat until soft. Tinned/canned beans will just need heating in their own water in the pan. Heat the remaining oil in another pan and brown the finely sliced prosciutto, the pureed tomatoes, a few basil leaves and a little pepper. Drain the beans and add to the sauce with the prosciutto and tomatoes, stir well and add the hot pasta. Serve grated parmesan separately.

SPAGHETTI WITH BREAD AND PROSCIUTTO 563

1 lb. spaghetti	2 oz. prosciutto
3 oz. butter	2 oz. stale bread
2 oz. lardo or fat salt pork	salt and pepper

A very simple but appetizing dish. Heat the butter and lightly brown the diced lardo, the thinly sliced prosciutto and the diced stale bread. Add plenty of freshly ground black pepper and cook until the bread is browned. Serve with the hot pasta.

BUCATINI WITH PROSCIUTTO AND MUSHROOMS 564

1 lb. bucatini	parsley
3 oz. butter	3 oz. grated parmesan
3 oz. mushrooms	salt and pepper
3 oz. prosciutto	(tomatoes, tomato puree, peas)
1 onion	

Heat half the butter and lightly brown the chopped onions. Add the sliced mushrooms, a pinch of salt and pepper and a little chopped parsley. Cook for a few minutes then add the finely chopped prosciutto. Add warm water if the sauce seems too dry and serve with the hot pasta.

Variations 1. Add pureed tomatoes or tomato puree to the sauce.
2. Add about four ounces shelled peas to the mushroom mixture before adding the prosciutto.

PENNE WITH BLACK OLIVES AND PROSCIUTTO 565

1 lb. penne	1 large tomato
4 tablespoons olive oil	8 oz. thick cream
1 tablespoon butter	basil
1 onion	3 oz. grated parmesan
2 oz. prosciutto	(white wine)
2 oz. small seeded black olives	

Lightly brown the chopped onion in the oil and butter, then the diced prosciutto, chopped olives, pureed tomatoes and the cream. Stir well to bind, then add the hot pasta, a little basil and the grated parmesan.

Variation Add four tablespoons white wine to the prosciutto, let it reduce then add the cream. Omit the pureed tomatoes.

MACARONI WITH CREAM AND PROSCIUTTO **566**

1 lb. macaroni	1½ oz. butter
3 oz. lardo or fat salt pork	6 oz. thick cream
3 oz. prosciutto	salt and pepper

Chop the lardo or fat salt pork and the prosciutto very finely and mix with the softened butter in a hot serving dish. Cook the pasta, drain very well and pour into the serving dish, where its heat will mix the ingredients nicely. Pour over the warm cream and serve with freshly ground black pepper.

BUCATINI WITH YOGURT, PROSCIUTTO AND HERBS **567**

1 lb. bucatini	parsley
2 oz. butter	bay leaf
3 oz. prosciutto	12 oz. yogurt
1 onion	2 oz. grated parmesan
thyme	salt and pepper
marjoram	(spring onions/scallions)

Brown the chopped onion in the butter and add a pinch each of chopped marjoram, parsley, thyme and bay leaf. Stir in the diced prosciutto. Add the yogurt, season with salt and pepper and cook until reduced a little. Add the grated parmesan and serve immediately.

Variation Use spring onions/scallions and leave them whole.

LINGUINE WITH PEAS, SWEET PEPPER AND PROSCIUTTO **568**

1 lb. linguine	1 onion
1 sweet pepper (about 4 oz.)	3 oz. butter
¼ lb. shelled peas	3 oz. grated parmesan
3 oz. prosciutto	salt and pepper
½ lb. tomatoes	(black truffle)

Roast the pepper over an open flame to remove the skin (peel it off with moistened fingertips), and cut in strips. Heat two ounces butter and lightly brown the chopped onion, add the pureed tomatoes, season with salt and pepper and let the sauce cook until thick. Add the peas and the sweet pepper. Stir well, then add the diced prosciutto, cook for a few more minutes and mix with the hot pasta and the remaining butter. Serve grated parmesan separately.

Variation Add a little crumbled truffle to the sauce when it is almost ready.

PASTICCIO OF CAPELLINI WITH PROSCIUTTO 569

1 lb. capellini	3 oz. butter
10 oz. mozzarella	3 oz. grated parmesan
3 eggs	2 tablespoons breadcrumbs
4 oz. prosciutto	salt and pepper

Cook the capellini, drain well and mix with most of the butter and the parmesan. Put half of this mixture in a greased ovenproof dish and sprinkle with the breadcrumbs. Cover with slices of mozzarella and the thinly sliced prosciutto mixed together. Pour over the beaten eggs with two tablespoons parmesan and a pinch each of salt and pepper. Cover with the remaining pasta and breadcrumbs, dot with butter and brown in a hot oven.

SPAGHETTINI CROQUETTES WITH PROSCIUTTO AND MOZZARELLA 570

1 lb. spaghettini	salt and pepper
5 oz. prosciutto	breadcrumbs
½ lb. mozzarella	strutto or lard
4 eggs	(gruyere)

Cook the pasta in lightly salted boiling water. Drain and cool. Mix with the diced prosciutto and mozzarella, three beaten eggs and a pinch each of salt and pepper. Make into small croquettes, dip them in beaten egg and breadcrumbs and fry in plenty of very hot strutto or lard. Serve very hot.

Variation Use grated gruyere instead of mozzarella.

FETTUCCINE WITH PROSCIUTTO AND MASCARPONE 571

1 lb. flour	3 oz. prosciutto
5 eggs	hot chili pepper
1 egg yolk	3 oz. grated parmesan
3 oz. mascarpone cheese	salt

Make a paste with the mascarpone, the prosciutto cut in strips, one beaten egg, one egg yolk, two tablespoons grated parmesan, a pinch of chili pepper and as much boiling water (taken from the pan where the pasta is cooking) as necessary to make a thin sauce. Make the fettuccine in the usual way with the flour, four eggs, a pinch of salt and a little warm water (see recipe 181). Mix with the hot pasta and serve grated parmesan separately.

SOUFFLE OF ZITONI WITH PROSCIUTTO 572

1 lb. zitoni	18 oz. milk
6 oz. butter	6 eggs
4 oz. grated parmesan	3 oz. grated gruyere
6 oz. mozzarella	parsley
¼ lb. prosciutto	salt and pepper
2 oz. flour	

Another elaborate and delectable Neapolitan recipe. Use a round ovenproof dish with sides at least four inches high. Cook the zitoni whole, drain well and reserve the water, then carefully cut the zitoni with a three inch slit down one side. Heat again by returning for an instant to the cooking water. Drain again and toss with two ounces butter and two tablespoons grated parmesan. Grease the ovenproof dish and line the sides with zitoni standing upright like a crown, then put alternate layers of zitoni and thin strips of mozzarella and prosciutto in the middle. Make a firm bechamel with two ounces butter and two ounces flour, the milk and seasoning. Cool. Away from the heat stir in the egg yolks one at a time, then three ounces grated parmesan and three ounces grated gruyere, mixed with salt and pepper and plenty of chopped parsley. Fold in the stiffly beaten egg whites and pour this mixture over the zitoni, using a spoon to push it into the holes. Pour what remains in the central cavity and bake in a moderate oven for about one hour or until the mixture is set.

1 lb. linguine	1 lb. peeled tomatoes
2 oz. butter	6 tablespoons white wine
½ onion	6 tablespoons thick cream
¼ lb. prosciutto	salt and pepper
¼ lb. smoked salmon	(cognac)

Heat the butter and cook the onion over low heat until it softens completely. Add the prosciutto cut in strips and cook again for a few minutes, stirring, then pour over the wine. Add the tomatoes and crush them with a fork. Cook for about ten minutes until you have a thick sauce, then add the chopped salmon, a little pepper and the cream. Stir in the hot pasta and serve immediately.

Variation Use cognac instead of wine.

1 lb. macaroni	4 oz. chicken livers
2½-3 lb. chicken	3 oz. prosciutto
4 tablespoons olive oil	3 oz. mushrooms
1½ oz. prosciutto fat	¾ lb. flour
3 oz. butter	4 egg yolks
½ onion	4 oz. strutto or lard
1 small carrot	18 oz. milk
1 stick celery	salt and pepper
6 tablespoons white wine	

Make the pastry in the usual way: put one ounce flour in a mound on a pastry board and mix in three egg yolks, the strutto or lard and a pinch of salt (see recipe 181). Try not to use any water for a smooth, firm dough, as for tagliatelle and other pasta. Form into a ball and leave to stand under a cloth. Roll out and make into one large and one small sheet for the top and bottom crust of your pie. Grease a pie dish and line with the large sheet of pastry. Put a circle of greaseproof/waxed paper on the bottom and cover with dried peas or rice. Brush with beaten egg and bake in the oven about ten minutes or until firm and golden with the top crust on another greased baking sheet. Remove the peas and the paper and prepare the filling: cut the chicken into serving pieces, sprinkle with salt and pepper, then brown on all sides in the oil with a little chopped onion, carrot, celery and prosciutto fat. Cover with the wine and cook until tender in a moderate oven. Add boiling water if it seems too dry. Clean and chop the livers and the mushrooms. Fry the mushrooms gently in two tablespoons butter, add the livers, season with salt and pepper and cook for a few minutes until lightly brown on the outside. Make a bechamel with two ounces butter, two ounces flour and the milk. Remove all the flesh from the chicken and cut in strips. Sieve the sauce and return the chicken to it with the livers, mushrooms and their juice and the prosciutto cut in strips. Mix all this gently with the hot macaroni, the parmesan and the bechamel sauce. Put in the pastry case, cover with the top crust, and heat in a moderate oven for about ten minutes.

TAGLIATELLE WITH PROSCIUTTO AND BRAIN 575

1 lb. flour	½ onion
4 eggs	1 clove garlic
4 oz. lamb's brain	cloves
4 oz. chicken giblets	3 oz. grated parmesan
2 oz. prosciutto	grated lemon peel
2 tablespoons olive oil	sage
2 oz. butter	salt and pepper
6 tablespoons white wine	(cinnamon)

A very old recipe: make the tagliatelle in the usual way with the flour, eggs, a pinch of salt and warm water as necessary (see recipe 181). Lightly brown the chopped onion and garlic (or crushed cloves of garlic to be discarded when brown) and a little sage in the olive oil. Add the chopped chicken giblets (excluding the livers) and the prosciutto cut in strips. Brown gently, then add two or three cloves, ½ teaspoon grated lemon peel, and the cleaned chopped chicken livers. Season with salt and pepper and add the brain, cleaned, blanched and roughly chopped. Simmer for about 20 minutes, put through a food mill or blender and return to the heat. Add the butter and stir to make a smooth, thick sauce. Mix with the hot pasta and serve grated parmesan separately.

Variation Add a little cinnamon to the sauce when you return it to the pan.

1 lb. flour
4 eggs
3 oz. prosciutto
¼ lb. sweetbreads
3 oz. butter
6 oz. thick cream

3 oz. grated parmesan
flour
thyme
marjoram
nutmeg
salt and pepper

Make the tagliolini in the usual way (see recipe 181). Heat two ounces butter with a little thyme and marjoram. Add one tablespoon flour and then the diced prosciutto. Brown a little and stir in the cream with a pinch of nutmeg. Cook for a few minutes and put through a food mill or blender. Plunge the sweetbreads in boiling water, remove the membrane and chop finely. Cook for about 20 minutes in two tablespoons butter with some salt and pepper. Add the pureed prosciutto and stir well, then mix with the hot pasta. Serve grated parmesan separately.

MACARONI WITH COLD ROAST MEAT AND PROSCIUTTO 577

1 lb. macaroni
½ lb. cold roast or braised meat
¼ lb. prosciutto
2 oz. grated parmesan
3 egg yolks

2 oz. butter
1 lb. tomatoes
5 tablespoons olive oil
salt and pepper

An excellent way of using leftover meat. Finely chop the meat and the prosciutto. Mix in a bowl with the grated cheese and beaten egg yolks to bind. Cook the macaroni and toss with this mixture. Transfer to a greased ovenproof dish and bake in a moderate oven for ½ hour in a bain-marie (set the dish in a pan of warm water). Put into a serving bowl and pour over a tomato sauce made in the usual way with the tomatoes and oil (see recipe 15).

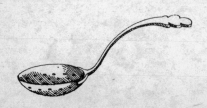

1 lb. maccheroncini	3 oz. grated parmesan
3 oz. prosciutto	salt
3 oz. cooked tongue	black truffle
2 oz. butter	(flour, meat stock, cream)

Heat the butter and lightly brown the diced prosciutto and tongue, then add about one tablespoon crumbled truffle. Mix with the hot pasta and serve grated parmesan separately.

Variations 1. Use a little less butter and add one tablespoon flour and a few tablespoons stock to the meat in the pan.
2. For a smoother sauce add three ounces cream.

1 lb. flour	3 oz. grated parmesan
12 eggs	½ lb. diced mozzarella
¼ lb. prosciutto	breadcrumbs
6 oz. meat gravy	salt
6 oz. butter	

Make the lasagne in the usual way with the flour, four eggs, a pinch of salt and a little water as necessary (see recipe 181). Cook them in plenty of boiling salted water. Cut the prosciutto into very fine, long strips. Grease an oven-proof dish and line with the meat brushed with some beaten egg. Put in half the lasagne mixed with the meat gravy, butter and parmesan. Cover with a layer of meat and diced mozzarella mixed with the remaining beaten eggs. Put a final layer of lasagne, sprinkle with grated parmesan, dot with butter and brown in a hot oven.

1 lb. flour	2 oz. butter
4 eggs	3 oz. grated parmesan
4 oz. prosciutto	½ onion
6 oz. meat gravy	salt and pepper
½ lb. shelled peas	

Heat the butter, cook the chopped onion until it disintegrates, then add the peas. Cook over low heat with salt and pepper. Add the diced prosciutto and brown a little, then stir in the meat gravy (see recipe 483) and cook for a few more minutes. Make the fettuccine in the usual way with flour, eggs, a pinch of salt and a little warm water as necessary (see recipe 181) but do not cut them too finely. Cook in boiling, salted water, drain well and serve with the sauce and grated parmesan.

PASTICCIO OF PASPADELLE

581

1 lb. flour	¾ lb. tomatoes
3 eggs	1 onion
6 oz. butter	1 carrot
¾ lb. spinach	1 stick celery
½ lb. lean minced/ground beef	18 oz. milk
¼ lb. chicken giblets	6 tablespoons thick cream
2 oz. minced/ground veal	3 oz. grated parmesan
2 oz. prosciutto	salt

Make the paspadelle with the flour, eggs, one tablespoon softened butter, the cooked, well drained and finely chopped spinach and a pinch of salt (see recipe 191). Roll out thinly and cut into irregular lozenge-shaped paspadelle. Make the sauce: lightly brown the chopped onion, carrot and celery in two ounces butter. Add the diced prosciutto, chopped beef, chicken giblets and veal. Let them brown slightly, then cover with the cream. When the sauce has thickened add the pureed tomatoes and bring to a boil. Make a bechamel with two ounces butter, two ounces flour and the milk. Cook the paspadelle in plenty of boiling salted water and drain well. Put in layers in a greased, ovenproof dish with the meat, bechamel and grated parmesan, finishing with a layer of bechamel. Cook in a moderate oven for 30 minutes.

LINGUINE WITH COOKED HAM **582**

1 lb. linguine
8 oz. cooked ham
2 oz. butter

1 stick celery
3 oz. grated parmesan
salt and pepper

Heat the butter in a large pan and brown the chopped celery, then the diced ham. Season with salt and pepper and add a few tablespoons hot water if it seems too dry. Cook for a few minutes to bind the sauce. Add the hot pasta, mix well and serve grated parmesan separately.

LINGUINE WITH COOKED HAM AND MUSHROOMS **583**

1 lb. linguine
2 oz. butter
5 oz. cooked ham
3 oz. mushrooms
1 onion

3 oz. grated parmesan
1 tablespoon marsala
nutmeg
salt and pepper
(tomatoes, garlic)

Heat the butter and brown the chopped onion and the sliced mushrooms. Add the diced ham, let it brown a little, then moisten with marsala and a pinch of nutmeg. Season with salt and pepper and let the wine reduce. Cook slowly, adding a little warm water if it seems too dry. Serve with the hot pasta and serve grated parmesan separately.

Variations 1. Add a few tablespoons pureed tomatoes after adding the ham and marsala.
2. Use garlic instead of onion, or both together.

MACCHERONCINI WITH COOKED HAM, WALNUTS AND CREAM **584**

1 lb. maccheroncini
2 oz. butter
7 oz. walnut kernels
2 oz. cooked ham

6 oz. thick cream
3 oz. grated parmesan
basil
salt and pepper

Heat the butter with a little chopped basil, then add the chopped walnuts, diced ham, salt, pepper and cream. Mix with the hot pasta and grated parmesan.

MACARONI WITH COOKED HAM, BECHAMEL AND TOMATO SAUCE

1 lb. macaroni	½ onion
7 oz. cooked ham	olive oil
½ lb. butter	nutmeg
3 oz. flour	basil
18 oz. milk	salt and pepper
3 oz. grated parmesan	(thick cream)
1 lb. tomatoes	

Make a good quantity of bechamel: heat four ounces butter and stir in the flour, then the milk, salt and pepper and nutmeg. Make a tomato sauce with the pureed tomatoes, the onion, two ounces butter, one tablespoon oil, a little basil, salt and pepper. Cook the macaroni, toss with the remaining butter and the grated parmesan and then the bechamel. Mix well, add the diced ham and plenty of freshly ground black pepper. Cover with the tomato sauce and serve immediately.

Variations 1. Make slightly less bechamel and then make up the quantity with heavy cream.

              2. Put the pasta in layers with the bechamel, ham and tomato sauce in a greased overproof dish. Dot the final layer with butter, sprinkle with grated cheese and cook for about ten minutes in a moderate oven.

CONCHIGLIE WITH COOKED HAM AND MAYONNAISE

1 lb. conchiglie	18 oz. olive oil
½ lb. cooked ham	juice of ½ lemon
1½ oz. butter	salt and pepper
3 egg yolks	

Make a mayonnaise in the usual way with the egg yolks, oil, lemon juice and some salt and pepper. Cook the conchiglie, drain well and toss with the butter. Mix in a serving bowl with the diced ham, cool and pour over the mayonnaise before serving.

1 lb. maccheroncini
1 chicken (2½-3 lb.)
12 oz. light meat gravy
¼ lb. chicken giblets
¼ lb. cooked ham
6 oz. shelled peas
parsley
4 egg yolks
2 hard-boiled eggs

1 lb. flour
6 oz. butter
6 oz. sugar
olive oil
vanilla or cinnamon
truffle
3 oz. grated parmesan
salt

This is a more refined version of the famous Sicilian dish, still make in some of the great houses of Sicily. Make a sweet pastry with the flour, five ounces butter and five ounces sugar, a pinch of salt and a little vanilla (see recipe 499). Use meat gravy from a roast. Dice the ham or cut in fine strips. Boil the chicken and remove the flesh. Chop ½ pound of it and mix together with two tablespoons grated parmesan, one beaten egg and a little chopped parsley. Form into small balls and fry in the hot oil. Cut the remaining chicken into strips. Clean and chop the chicken giblets. Cook the peas. Heat the meat gravy and add all these ingredients, cook for a few minutes, add a little crumbled white truffle and the sauce is ready. Grease a deep pie dish, line with the larger sheet of pastry and put in the hot maccheroncini. Make a hollow in the middle and pour in the sauce so it covers the pasta. Add a little more meat gravy, the sliced hard-boiled eggs and a few tablespoons grated parmesan. Cover with the top crust, press the edges well together and cook for about 40 minutes in a hot oven.

BUCATINI WITH SALAMI **588**

1 lb. bucatini
5 oz. salami (a mild-flavoured variety)
4 tablespoons olive oil
1 onion

6 tablespoons white wine
salt and pepper
1 lb. tomatoes
3 oz. diced caciocavallo cheese

Heat the oil and lightly brown the chopped onion. Add the diced salami and the wine. Cook until it reduces, sprinkle with pepper, stir well and add the pureed tomatoes. Let this reduce to make a good sauce, then add a few tablespoons of hot water if it seems too dry. Cook the bucatini in lightly salted boiling water, drain well and mix with the sauce and diced cheese.

BUCATINI WITH SALAMI AND RICOTTA 589

1 lb. bucatini
3 oz. lardo or fat salt pork
4 oz. salami
½ lb. tomatoes
½ lb. ricotta
1 onion
basil
salt and pepper

Chop the bacon and brown lightly with the chopped onion. Add the diced salami and stir gently, then add the pureed tomatoes and a little basil. Cook until the sauce is thick and well flavoured and serve with the hot pasta, some crumbled ricotta and plenty of freshly ground black pepper.

PASTICCIO OF MACARONI WITH VEAL, CHICKEN AND SALAMI 590

1 lb. macaroni
2 oz. lean veal
1¼ lb. tomatoes
2 oz. chicken livers
2 oz. salami
2 oz. mozzarella
2 aubergines/eggplant
2 oz. peas
2 hard-boiled eggs
1 clove garlic
olive oil
grated pecorino/romano
basil
salt and pepper

Peel, slice the aubergines/eggplant, sprinkle with coarse salt and leave to drain under a lightly weighted plate for at least one hour. Fry in plenty of hot oil, drain on absorbent paper and keep warm. In another pan lightly brown the chopped garlic in four tablespoons oil with the finely chopped veal. Add the pureed tomatoes and season with salt and pepper. Cook for a few minutes then add the cleaned, chopped chicken livers and the peas and continue cooking over low heat for about ½ hour. Dice the mozzarella and salami and slice the hard-boiled eggs. Cook the pasta, drain well and mix with some of the sauce, the mozzarella and salami. Make layers in a greased ovenproof dish with the sauce, fried aubergines/eggplant, sliced eggs and finely chopped basil, and a little oil to moisten the top. Sprinkle with grated pecorino/romano and brown for ten minutes in a hot oven.

MACARONI WITH PORK SAUSAGE

1 lb. macaroni
3 oz. lardo or fat salt pork
2 medium onions
2 oz. fresh pork sausage

1 lb. tomatoes
3 oz. grated parmesan
salt
(ricotta)

Chop the lardo or fat salt pork and fry over low heat with the chopped onion. When the onion starts to disintegrate add the sausage cut in slices. Cook for a few minutes together, then add the pureed tomatoes and cook until thick. Serve with the hot pasta and grated parmesan.

Variation When you have mixed the pasta with the sauce stir in crumbled ricotta, and omit the parmesan.

SPAGHETTI WITH FRANKFURTERS

1 lb. spaghetti
½ lb. frankfurters
¼ lb. butter
1 onion

3 oz. grated parmesan or gruyere
paprika
parsley
salt

Cut the frankfurters into thick slices. Heat two ounces butter and lightly brown the chopped onion. Add the frankfurters, stir well, add some chopped parsley, a pinch of paprika and very little salt. Cook for about ten minutes, add the hot spaghetti tossed with the remaining butter and grated cheese.

PASTICCIO OF LASAGNE WITH FRANKFURTERS

1 lb. flour
4 eggs
½ lb. frankfurters
6 oz. butter
½ onion
1 lb. tomatoes
6 tablespoons meat gravy

2 oz. flour
18 oz. milk
nutmeg
salt
paprika
2 oz. grated parmesan

Cut the frankfurters into thick slices. Heat two ounces butter and lightly brown the chopped onion. Add the frankfurters, stir well, add some chopped parsley, a pinch of paprika and very little salt. Cook for about ten minutes, add the meat gravy (see recipe 483) and cook until well blended and thickened. Make a bechamel in the usual way with two ounces butter, the flour, milk, nutmeg and some salt and pepper. Use commercial lasagne, or make them in the usual way with the flour, eggs, a pinch of salt and some warm water (see recipe 181). Put in layers in a greased ovenproof dish with the sauce, a little bechamel and some grated parmesan. Finish with a layer of pasta and sprinkle with parmesan, dot with butter and brown in a hot oven.

LINGUINE WITH RAGU AND MORTADELLA/BOLOGNA **594**

1 lb. linguine	1 lb. tomatoes
¼ lb. butter	6 tablespoons white wine
½ lb. lean beef	3 oz. grated parmesan
¼ lb. mortadella/bologna	nutmeg
1 onion	salt and pepper
1 carrot	(salami)
1 stick celery	

Make the beef ragu: lightly brown the chopped onion, celery and carrot, then add the coarsely chopped beef and diced mortadella/bologna. Brown for a few minutes, then moisten with white wine and let it reduce. Add the pureed tomatoes, a pinch of nutmeg and some salt and pepper. If it seems too dry add a few tablespoons hot water. Cook the pasta, drain well, toss with the remaining butter, the parmesan and the ragu.

Variation Add a little diced salami as well as the mortadella/bologna.

PASTA AND CAULIFLOWER WITH PORK RIND **595**

¾ lb. pasta (e.g. penne or maccheroncini)	2 cloves garlic
	olive oil
1 large cauliflower	3 oz. grated pecorino/romano
¼ lb. fresh pork rind	salt and pepper
2 oz. cooked ham	(tomatoes, tomato puree)
½ onion	

Prepare the pork rind: blanch in boiling water for about ten minutes, drain, rinse in cold water. Scrape away any hair or fat from the inside and singe for a minute over an open flame to remove any final hairs. Chop into ½ inch squares. Remove the florets from the cauliflower and cook in lightly salted water until just tender. Heat two tablespoons oil in an earthenware pan and add the chopped onion and garlic. Brown lightly and add the diced ham. Stir well, season with salt and pepper and add one or two tablespoons warm water if it seems too dry. Add the pork rinds. Let the liquid reduce and add the water in which you blanched the rinds. Bring to a boil, add the pasta and cook for about three minutes. Add the cauliflower florets and cook until tender. Serve as a thick soup. Serve grated pecorino/romano separately.

Variation   Add a little pureed tomato or tomato puree before frying the pork rind.

PASTA AND BEANS WITH PORK RIND   596

¾ lb. flour	1 stick celery
3 eggs	1 carrot
¾ lb. dried white beans	olive oil
4 oz. fresh pork rind	salt and pepper
1 onion	(parmesan, garlic, parsley)

Soak the beans for at least 12 hours. Blanch and clean the pork rind as in the previous recipe. Put the beans in a large pot and cover with water. Bring to a boil, add the whole piece of blanched pork rind, the chopped onion, carrot and celery. Remove the fat as it rises to the surface. When the beans are soft remove half from the pan and put through a food mill or blender and return to the pan to thicken the soup. Make the tagliatelle in the usual way with the flour, eggs, a pinch of salt and warm water as necessary (see recipe 181). Add the tagliatelle to the soup and serve all together when they are al dente, with a little fresh oil and some freshly ground pepper.

Variations 1. It is not usual to serve cheese with this soup but you can serve grated parmesan separately if desired.
2. Add a chopped clove of garlic and some chopped parsley with the other chopped vegetables.

RIGATONI WITH PORK SAUSAGE—I   597

1 lb. rigatoni	salt
¾ lb. fresh pork sausage	2 oz. butter
1 onion	4 oz. grated parmesan
6 oz. dry white wine	(olive oil, sugna, strutto,
1 tablespoon tomato puree	tomatoes, carrot, celery)

Melt the butter and cook the chopped onion until transparent, then add the skinned, crumbled sausage meat. Stir well, add the wine and cook until it reduces over low heat. Add the tomato puree diluted in a little hot water and continue cooking until well blended and until the sausage meat is cooked, adding more hot water if it seems too dry. Cook the pasta, drain well and mix with this sauce. Serve grated parmesan separately.

Variations 1. Fry chopped celery and carrot with the onion.
2. Use olive oil instead of butter, or a mixture of other fats such as strutto, sugna etc.
3. Use fresh pureed tomatoes instead of concentrated tomato puree, or a little of both.

RIGATONI WITH PORK SAUSAGE—II   598

1 lb. rigatoni
¼ lb. fresh pork sausage
3 oz. shelled peas
1 lb. tomatoes
3 tablespoons olive oil
3 oz. butter
1 onion

1 carrot
1 clove garlic
6 tablespoons white wine
2 oz. grated parmesan
2 oz. grated pecorino/romano
salt

Heat the oil with two ounces butter and lightly brown the chopped onion and carrot and the crushed garlic (to be discarded). Moisten with wine, cook until it evaporates and add the pureed tomatoes. Season with salt and add the peas. Cook for a minute then add the skinned, sliced sausage meat and cook until done. Mix the hot pasta with part of this sauce and the two grated cheeses. Put in a greased ovenproof dish, cover with the remaining sauce and two tablespoons oil, dot with butter and brown in a hot oven.

PASTA AND BEANS WITH PORK SAUSAGE   599

¾ lb. short pasta
½ lb. dried white beans
¼ lb. fresh pork sausage
2 oz. lard

parsley
salt and pepper
(ham bone)

Soak the beans for at least 12 hours, then drain and cook in a pan covered with plenty of water. When they are soft add the whole sausages, the chopped lard, a handful of chopped parsley and some freshly ground pepper. When the sausage is cooked, bring to a boil, add the pasta and remove the sausage. Skin and slice the sausage and return to the pan. Mix well, then leave to stand for a few minutes before serving.

Variation Cook a ham bone with the beans and remove the little bits of meat on it when cooked to mix with the pasta and beans.

MACARONI WITH MASCARPONE
AND PORK SAUSAGE

1 lb. macaroni	3 tablespoons olive oil
6 oz. fresh pork sausage	salt and pepper
10 oz. mascarpone cheese	2 oz. grated parmesan

Heat the oil and add the skinned, crumbled sausage, then one or two table-spoons hot water so the sausage cooks without burning. When the meat is cooked remove from the heat and work in the mascarpone. Cook the pasta and when draining leave a little water on it to help dissolve the cheese. Mix with the sausage and cheese mixture and serve with freshly ground pepper and grated parmesan.

MACARONI WITH PORK
SAUSAGE AU GRATIN

1 lb. macaroni	4 oz. fresh pork sausage
1¾ lb. tomatoes	2 oz. grated pecorino/romano
3-4 tablespoons olive oil	basil
½ onion	sugar
6 oz. mozzarella	salt and pepper

Make a tomato sauce in the usual way with the oil, onion and pureed tomatoes (see recipe 15). Cook the pasta, drain well and mix with part of the tomato sauce. Grease an ovenproof dish and sprinkle with breadcrumbs. Put in alternate layers of pasta, more tomato sauce, sliced mozzarella, a little basil, diced sausage and grated pecorino/romano. Sprinkle the final layer with bread-crumbs, the remaining sauce and mozzarella and a little oil. Brown for about ten minutes in a hot oven.

MACARONI WITH PORK SAUSAGE AND EGGS

1 lb. macaroni	5 eggs
6 oz. fresh pork sausage	3 oz. grated parmesan
2 tablespoons olive oil	salt and pepper
1½ oz. butter	

Heat the oil and butter and add the skinned, diced sausage. Cook over low heat with two tablespoons warm water. Crush the sausage with a fork and mix with the hot pasta. Pour over the eggs beaten lightly with a pinch each of salt and pepper. Remove from the heat, leave to stand for a minute, then serve with grated parmesan.

½ lb. flour
1½ lb. potatoes
1 egg
½ lb. pork sausage (small thin variety)

1 oz. margarine
6 tablespoons white wine
3 oz. grated parmesan
salt

Brown the sausage in one tablespoon margarine and add a little white wine. Remove from the heat when nearly cooked, drain off the fat and cool. Cut into one inch thick slices. Cook the potatoes, peel and mash. Work together with the flour, one egg and a pinch of salt to make the gnocchi mixture (add more flour if it is not firm enough). Take large pieces of this mixture to wrap round the slices of sausage and make into small balls. Press round lightly and cook in plenty of boiling salted water so they do not stick together. Drain after four or five minutes and serve very hot with grated parmesan.

TAGLIATELLE WITH PORK SAUSAGE AND AUBERGINES/EGGPLANT **604**

1 lb. flour
4 eggs
½ lb. fresh pork sausage
¼ lb. diced pancetta or
unsmoked streaky bacon

2 aubergines/eggplant
¾ lb. tomatoes
olive oil
salt
3 oz. grated parmesan

Skin the sausage and crumble the sausage meat. Peel, dice the aubergines/eggplant and leave to drain sprinkled with coarse salt under a lightly weighted plate. Fry in the oil over medium heat. Chop the pancetta and lightly brown, then add the pureed tomato and cook until the sauce has reduced and thickened. Make the tagliatelle in the usual way with the flour, eggs, a pinch of salt and warm water (see recipe 181). Cook in plenty of boiling water, drain well and mix with the sausage meat sauce and the grated cheese.

Variation Omit the pureed tomato and add warm water if the sauce seems too dry.

¾ lb. flour	2 oz. lard
8 eggs	3 oz. grated parmesan
6 oz. fresh pork sausage	nutmeg
10 oz. ricotta	salt and pepper
2 oz. butter	(strutto, mozzarella, roast meat gravy)

Make the lasagne in the usual way with the flour, four eggs, a pinch of salt and warm water as necessary (see recipe 181). Roll out and cut into broad strips. Skin the sausage and crumble the meat, or cut into thick slices if it is a compact type of sausage. Brown the sausage meat with the chopped lard. Remove as soon as it browns all over and keep warm. Sieve the ricotta and work with two tablespoons hot water (use the lasagne cooking water). Mix in four beaten eggs, salt, pepper and a pinch of nutmeg. Combine with the hot pasta, then put in layers in a greased ovenproof dish with a little sausage meat sauce and some grated parmesan between each layer. Dot the final layer with butter and brown in a hot oven.

Variations 1. Use strutto or butter to brown the sausage instead of ordinary lard.
2. Hard-boil four eggs, slice them and put between the layers of pasta. Omit the beaten egg with the ricotta.
3. Cover the lasagne with a meat gravy when it is ready to go in the oven.
4. Top the lasagne with diced or sliced mozzarella.

PASTICCIO OF LASAGNE WITH PORK SAUSAGE **606**

¾ lb. flour	8 oz. roast meat gravy
6 eggs	1 oz. butter
4 oz. fresh pork sausage	3 oz. grated parmesan
¾ lb. ricotta	salt and pepper
6 oz. mozzarella	

Brown the sausage lightly in one tablespoon butter, then remove the skin and cut into slices. Sieve the ricotta and work with two beaten eggs, two tablespoons grated parmesan and a pinch each of salt and pepper. Make the lasagne in the usual way with the flour, four eggs, a pinch of salt and warm water as necessary and cook in boiling salted water (see recipe 181). Drain well and arrange in layers in a greased ovenproof dish with a little ricotta, some meat gravy, sliced mozzarella, sliced sausage and grated parmesan. Top with sliced mozzarella and grated parmesan and brown in a hot oven.

¾ lb. flour
4 eggs
6 oz. chicken livers
½ oz. dried mushrooms
3 oz. butter

3 oz. lard or strutto
1 small onion
4 oz. grated parmesan
olive oil

15 oz. meat ragu made
with the following:
½ lb. lean beef
½ lb. knuckle of veal
1 small piece of fresh pork rind
1 small piece of salt-cured pork rind
½ small onion

1 small carrot
1 small piece of celery
bouquet garni (parsley,
bay leaf, thyme)
½ clove
½ clove garlic
1 teaspoon coarse salt

This classic Roman dish is given in all its detail, but you can obviously adapt the ingredients to your own requirements. Make the ragu: dice the meat, slice the carrot, onion and celery. Grease the bottom of a pan and add the pork rinds, bones, vegetables, chopped garlic and cloves. Add the diced meat and bouquet garni. Cook over medium heat so everything browns gently, then add a few tablespoons warm water, season with salt and cook for about two hours. Skim the fat from the surface and add more liquid as necessary. Remove the fat and strain the liquid, reserving the meat for a separate course. Make the fettuccine in the usual way with the flour, eggs, a pinch of salt and a little warm water (see recipe 181). Leave to rest for ½ hour, roll out not too thin and cut into fettuccine about ½ inch wide. Meanwhile clean and dice the giblets (excluding the livers). Soak the mushrooms in warm water, drain and slice or chop. Heat one ounce butter and the same amount of lard and brown the chopped onion. Add the giblets and mushrooms, mix well, season with salt and pepper. Add the chopped chicken livers and the strained ragu. Cook the fettuccine in lightly salted boiling water, drain well and toss with one tablespoon butter and some of the sauce. Put in layers in a hot serving bowl with the sauce and grated parmesan. Serve more grated parmesan separately.

1 lb. flour
2 eggs
10 oz. pork
1½ oz. lard or strutto

¾ lb. tomatoes
basil
salt and pepper
3 oz. grated pecorino/romano

Make a pasta dough with the flour, eggs and a little warm water (see recipe 181). Knead well, roll out and cut into small squares. Roll these round a knitting needle, remove the needle carefully then leave these home-made macaroni to dry for at least 12 hours. Make the sauce: heat the lard and add the chopped pork, brown lightly and add the pureed tomatoes, a little basil and some salt and pepper. Cook until the meat is tender, adding a little water if necessary, then serve with the hot pasta. Serve grated pecorino/ romano separately.

LASAGNE WITH RAGU OF PORK AND RICOTTA **609**

1 lb. flour
4 eggs
5 oz. ricotta
1¼ lb. lean pork
¼ lb. fresh pork sausage
1½ oz. lard or strutto
1 onion
1 carrot

1 stick celery
1 clove garlic
6 oz. white wine
1 lb. tomatoes
parsley
hot chili pepper
salt
3 oz. grated parmesan

Make the lasagne in the usual way with the flour, eggs, a pinch of salt and warm water as necessary (see recipe 181). Melt the lard and lightly brown the finely chopped carrot, onion, celery, garlic and parsley. Add the chili pepper broken in pieces and the pork. Lower the heat and brown the meat on all sides, then pour over the wine, let it evaporate and add the pureed tomatoes. Season with salt and pepper and continue cooking until the pork is done (about 1½-2 hours). Check from time to time to see if it is too dry; add warm water as necessary. When it is almost cooked add the skinned, crumbled sausage. Sieve the ricotta and work with a little of the lasagne cooking water. Cook the lasagne in plenty of boiling salted water, drain well and put in layers in a hot serving bowl with the meat sauce, ricotta and grated parmesan. Serve the pork as a separate dish.

LASAGNE WITH PORK CHOPS AND MEATBALLS

1 lb. flour	1 onion
¾ lb. loin pork chops	1 carrot
¼ lb. minced/ground pork	1 stick celery
1 egg	3 oz. grated pecorino/romano
3 hard-boiled eggs	olive oil
9 oz. shelled peas	nutmeg
6 oz. mushrooms	bay leaf
¼ lb. mozzarella	meat gravy
3 tender young artichokes	salt and pepper

This Neapolitan dish is usually make in the spring, and especially at Easter. Make the lasagne in the usual way without eggs, (or use commercial lasagne), with the flour, a pinch of salt and some warm water (see recipe 181). Roll out not too thin and cut into lasagne. Brown the pork chops in two tablespoons oil. Mix the minced/ground pork with two ounces grated parmesan, one beaten egg, nutmeg and salt and pepper. Form into little meatballs and fry these in plenty of hot oil. In another pan lightly brown the chopped onion, carrot and celery in two tablespoons oil, then add the cleaned, sliced mushrooms, the well trimmed atrichokes cut in wedges, the peas and bay leaf. Cut the hard-boiled eggs in quarters. Cook the lasagne and leave to dry under a cloth, then put in layers in a greased ovenproof dish with a few tablespoons meat gravy, meat balls, chops, hard-boiled eggs, sliced mozzarella and grated pecorino/romano. Finish with a layer of meat gravy and pecorino/romano and cook in a moderate oven for at least thirty minutes.

MACARONI WITH SPINACH, PORK AND VEAL 611

1 lb. macaroni	4 tablespoons olive oil
10 oz. lean veal	3 oz. butter
6 oz. lean pork (loin)	1 onion
1 lb. spinach	2 carrots
2 eggs	parsley
6 oz. grated parmesan	breadcrumbs
6 oz. mozzarella	salt and pepper
1 lb. tomatoes	

Use half the butter to fry the chopped onion, carrots and parsley. Add the veal and pork and brown on all sides, then add the pureed tomatoes. Season with salt and pepper and cook for 1½-2 hours until the meat is tender. Cook the spinach, drain very well and chop finely. When the meat is cooked, chop finely and mix with the spinach, beaten eggs, breadcrumbs, grated parmesan and make into two large rolls or loaves. Brown these in the remaining oil and butter, then add the juice from the pork and veal pan. Mash the meat rolls into this gravy with a fork and mix with the hot pasta, together with the diced mozzarella and more grated parmesan. Serve immediately, or put in a greased ovenproof dish and cook for a few minutes in a hot oven.

MACARONI WITH RAGU OF VEAL AND PORK **612**

1 lb. macaroni	1 stick celery
¼ lb. lean veal	parsley
¼ lb. lean pork	3 oz. butter
3 oz. fresh pork sausage	3 oz. white wine
2 oz. prosciutto	meat stock
3 lb. tomatoes	3 oz. grated parmesan
1 onion	salt and pepper
1 carrot	

Heat the butter and lightly brown the chopped onion, carrot, celery and parsley. Add the chopped pork and veal, the prosciutto cut in thin strips and the skinned, crumbled sausage. Pour over the wine and let it evaporate, then add the pureed tomatoes. Season with salt and pepper and cook until the meat is tender, adding more hot water if necessary. Mix with the hot pasta and serve grated parmesan separately.

LASAGNE VERDI WITH RAGU OF PORK AND VEAL **613**

1 lb. flour	1 carrot
1 lb. spinach	1 stick celery
4 eggs.	1 bay leaf
¼ lb. lean pork	parsley
¼ lb. lean veal	6 oz. white wine
3 oz. prosciutto	1 lb. tomatoes
2 oz. chicken livers	3 oz. grated parmesan
3 oz. butter	meat stock
1 onion	salt and pepper

Make the lasagne verdi in the usual way with the flour, eggs, cooked, drained and pureed spinach and a pinch of salt (see recipe 191). Roll out and cut into strips about ½ inch wide, then leave to dry. Heat three ounces butter and lightly brown the chopped onion, carrot, celery and parsley. Add the choppped pork and veal and the crumbled bay leaf. Let the meat brown on all sides and add the diced ham. Cook for a minute, then pour over the white wine and let it reduce. Add the pureed tomatoes and cook until thickened. Season with salt and pepper and dilute with a few tablespoons meat stock. Lightly brown the chopped chicken livers in two tablespoons butter and add to the other ingredients. Cook until the meat is ready, adding more stock if it seems too dry. Mix with the hot pasta and serve grated parmesan separately. Alternatively you can cook the lasagne, mix them with a little butter and put in layers in a greased ovenproof dish with the meat sauce and the parmesan. Dot the final layer with butter and cook for a few minutes in a hot oven.

MACARONI PIE WITH RAGU OF PORK, VEAL AND PIGEON 614

1 lb. macaroni
1¼ lb. loin of pork
6 oz. lean veal
1 egg
2 hard-boiled eggs
3 egg yolks
1 pigeon breast
6 oz. tomato puree
6 oz. mozzarella
½ lb. flour
6 oz. butter
¼ lb. sugar
3 oz. chicken livers

¼ lb. fresh pork sausage
6 oz. shelled peas
3 tablespoons olive oil
2 oz. lard or strutto
2 oz. proscuitto fat
2 oz. pancetta or streaky bacon
1 oz. dried mushrooms
1 medium onion
2 oz. stale bread
6 oz. white wine
parsley
salt and pepper
4 oz. grated parmesan

There are a number of steps in this recipe, but it is not as complicated as it may seem. Make a good Neapolitan ragu for the meat gravy: heat two tablespoons oil and two tablespoons lard or strutto and lightly brown the chopped onion with two ounces chopped prosciutto fat. Cook until the onion is soft, add the diced pancetta, let it brown and then brown the pork on all sides. Add the wine and let it reduce. Stir in the tomato puree diluted in a little warm water. Cook for a few minutes, season with salt and pepper, stir well and cook covered over low heat for at least three hours to get a rich gravy. Meanwhile heat two tablespoons olive oil and two tablespoons lard or strutto in another pan and brown a chopped onion. Add the sliced mushrooms (soaked in warm water) and the chopped chicken livers. Boil the peas for two minutes and add to the pan. Lightly brown the sausage in one tablespoon oil and one tablespoon lard or strutto. Moisten with white wine, let it reduce and remove from the heat. Remove the skin from the sausage and chop into thick slices. Mix seven ounces finely chopped or minced veal with the stale bread soaked in water, squeezed and crumbled, one tablespoon parmesan, one beaten egg and a little salt, pepper and parsley. Form into small meatballs and fry in the butter. Mix the meatballs, mushrooms, livers and peas with the juices from the pans and cook together for about ten minutes with one tablespoon meat gravy from the ragu. Lightly brown a little chopped onion in one tablespoon butter, then the pigeon breast. Moisten with a little white wine, season with salt and pepper and cook with a few tablespoons warm water until the pigeon is tender. Dice the cooked pigeon breast or cut into thin strips. Make the pastry in the usual way with the flour, four ounces butter, sugar, egg yolks and a pinch of salt (see recipe 499). You can omit the sugar, but the recipe is then less traditional. Leave the dough to rest for about one hour then roll out into one larger sheet and one smaller one. Cook the macaroni, drain well and mix with the ragu and parmesan. Grease an ovenproof dish and line it with the larger sheet of pastry. Put in the macaroni in alternate layers with the pork gravy, the meatball and sausage mixture, the pigeon, sliced mozzarella, the sliced hard-boiled eggs and grated parmesan. Finish with a layer of mozzarella and parmesan, cover with the top crust, press the edges well together and cook in a hot oven about 45 minutes or until the pastry is firm and golden.

MACARONI WITH RAGU OF PORK   **615**

1 lb. macaroni	6 tablespoons red wine
6 oz. loin of pork	1 lb. tomatoes
6 oz. lean beef	3 oz. grated pecorino/romano
6 oz. lamb	parsley
2 oz. pancetta or	salt
unsmoked streaky bacon	hot chili pepper
3 tablespoons olive oil	meat stock
2 cloves garlic	

Heat the oil and brown the chopped pancetta, the chopped garlic and parsley, and a few pieces of hot chili pepper. Add the meat in whole pieces, brown on all sides and add the wine. Let it evaporate and add the pureed tomatoes. Mix well, season with salt and pepper and cook for two hours over low heat, adding more warm stock or water if it seems too dry. Remove the chili pepper and the meat (to be used for another dish) and mix the meat gravy with the hot macaroni. Serve grated pecorino/romano separately.

Variation Chop the meat before browning and serve in the sauce with the pasta. Use about half the quantity indicated.

1 lb. flour
5 eggs
1¼ lb. loin of pork
½ lb. lean veal
½ lb. fresh pork sausage
¼ lb. lard or strutto
1½ oz. prosciutto fat
6 tablespoons olive oil
2 onions
6 oz. red wine
6 tablespoons tomato puree

3 tablespoons tomato sauce
½ lb. ricotta
6 oz. mozzarella
1 egg
3 oz. or 2 slices stale white bread
6 oz. grated parmesan
parsley
salt and pepper
(pancetta, sugna, beef stock,
salami, scamorza cheese)

This is a traditional Neapolitan carnival dish. Make a ragu: heat two ounces lard or strutto and two tablespoons oil with the chopped prosciutto fat and lightly brown the chopped onions. Add the whole piece of pork, brown on all sides and moisten with the wine. Cook until it reduces, then add the tomato puree diluted with a little water and the tomato sauce. Season with salt and pepper and cook for at least three hours, covered, adding more water if it seems too dry. In Naples this ragu is made the day before carnival so the fat can be skimmed off the surface the next morning. The lasagne are also made the day before: they should be quite firm so use only three eggs to one pound flour, a pinch of salt and warm water as necessary (see recipe 181). Roll out the dough fairly thin and cut in broad strips about three inches wide and four inches long. Make little meat balls with the minced or chopped veal, the stale bread soaked in water, squeezed dry and crumbled, one beaten egg, one tablespoon grated parmesan, a little chopped parsley and a pinch each of salt and pepper. Fry the meat balls in plenty of hot oil. Fry the fresh pork sausage in one tablespoon lard or strutto, skin and cut into thick slices. Mix the meat balls with the sausage in a pan with a little of the meat gravy and cook for a few minutes. Sieve the ricotta and mix with a few tablespoons meat gravy to make a smooth, dark cream. Slice the mozzarella. Cook the lasagne very carefully and drain when just al dente. Spread out to dry on a cloth large enough so they are not overlapping. Lightly grease a large ovenproof dish with lard and put in a thin layer of meat gravy, then a layer of lasagne, then the ricotta mixture, grated parmesan, slices of mozzarella, meat balls and sausage, more meat gravy and so on. Cover the final layer with gravy, sprinkle with plenty of parmesan, then bake in a moderate oven for 30 minutes.

Variations 1. Chop the cooked pork and return to the gravy instead of serving it separately.
2. Cook the sausage, remove the skin and put it in the pork ragu with the meat balls.
3. Use sugna instead of strutto.

4. Use pancetta instead of prosciutto fat.
5. Use stock instead of water to dilute the ragu.
6. Use scamorza cheese instead of mozzarella.
7. Add diced salami when making layers of lasagne, etc.
8. Mix two beaten eggs with the ricotta and meat gravy mixture.

MACARONI WITH CHICKEN AND HAM AU GRATIN **617**

1 lb. macaroni	6 oz. cooked chicken breast
1¼ lb. loin of pork	4 oz. prosciutto
2 oz. lard or strutto	3 egg yolks
2 tablespoons olive oil	2 oz. butter
2 onions	6 tablespoons thick cream
1 carrot	72 oz. beef stock
1 stick celery	5 oz. grated parmesan
6 oz. white wine	salt and pepper

This glorious recipe may have had French beginnings, but the distinction is never very clear in Neapolitan cooking. Heat the oil and lightly brown the chopped onion, carrot and celery. Add the whole piece of pork, brown on all sides and add the wine. Let it reduce, season with salt and pepper and dilute with a few tablespoons stock. Cook for at least three hours until you have a rich gravy. Mix the gravy with the hot macaroni (serve the pork as a separate dish), then put in layers in a greased ovenproof dish with the chopped chicken and prosciutto and the grated parmesan. Beat the egg yolks with the melted butter, cream and enough parmesan so the sauce is smooth, but still thin, then pour over the macaroni. Brown in a hot oven.

TORTELLINI BOLOGNESE **618**

1¼ lb. flour	2 oz. beef marrow
8 eggs	2 oz. butter
10 oz. loin of pork	3 oz. grated parmesan
1 turkey breast	nutmeg
3 oz. prosciutto	salt and white pepper
3 oz. mortadella/bologna	72 oz. chicken stock

There is always much argument about the authentic filling for tortellini Bolognese: this version has been handed down in a Bolognese family where cooking traditions are fiercely guarded and maintained. Make the egg pasta dough in the usual way with the flour, eggs, a pinch of salt and warm water as necessary (see recipe 181). Knead the dough and try not to use any water, or at least as little as possible; you want a soft, smooth dough. Roll it out very thin and cut into circles ¾ inch in diameter. Make the filling: heat three ounces butter and brown the pork. Add a few tablespoons warm water and a pinch of salt. Cook over low heat for two or three hours until the meat is tender. Cook the turkey breast in the same way, but obviously it will not need quite as long. Chop or mince the pork and turkey together with the prosciutto and mortadella/bologna. Add two beaten eggs, the beef marrow and one ounce butter. Unless the mixture is too firm you can also add four tablespoons grated parmesan. Mix well, check the seasoning, add a little freshly ground white pepper and some nutmeg. Put ½ teaspoon of the mixture on each circle of pasta, fold over and press the edges together (a soft dough sticks together best). Set the tortellini aside up to 12 hours to dry the pasta to perfection. If they are quite fresh cook in boiling stock for 10-12 minutes, but if made in advance they need about 20 minutes. The stock should not be too heavy as this might detract from the delicate flavour of the tortellini. Serve with melted butter.

TORTELLINI WITH CREAM **619**

1 lb. flour	2 oz. beef marrow
7 eggs	¼ lb. butter
½ lb. loin of pork	6 oz. grated parmesan
1 turkey breast	6 tablespoons thick cream
3 oz. prosciutto	nutmeg
3 oz. mortadella	white pepper

Make the tortellini as in the previous recipe. Cook them in stock or water, drain well and put in a pan with a little butter and cream. Sprinkle with white pepper and nutmeg. Gradually add all the cream and grated parmesan, stirring very gently over low heat. Serve with more grated parmesan. It is claimed that this is a very unorthodox way of serving tortellini, inherited from the French in the 18th century. Nevertheless, it is a perfectly delicious dish, as long as it is made with real cream and not bechamel.

1¼ lb. flour
7 eggs
½ lb. loin of pork
1 turkey breast
3 oz. prosciutto
3 oz. mortadella/bologna
2 oz. beef marrow

4 oz. butter
6 oz. grated parmesan
nutmeg
salt and white pepper
6 oz. thick cream
18 oz. milk

Make the tortellini in the usual way (see recipe 618) with the same ingredients. Make a bechamel sauce with two ounces butter, two ounces flour and the milk. Season with salt and pepper. Cook the tortellini in stock or water, drain and put in a greased ovenproof dish in layers with the cream and grated parmesan. Top the final layer with all the hot bechamel, sprinkle with parmesan, dot with butter and brown in a hot oven.

1 lb. flour
5 eggs
1 large chicken breast
2 oz. loin of pork
2 oz. lean veal
1 lamb's brain
2 oz. mortadella/bologna

2 oz. prosciutto
2 egg yolks
2 oz. butter
salt and pepper
nutmeg
3 oz. grated parmesan
72 oz. chicken stock.

Make the tortellini as in recipe 618, but the filling is slightly different: brown the pork, veal and chicken in the butter. Add the brain (cleaned, blanched in boiling water and the membrane removed, then chopped). Cook very gently with salt and pepper until all the meat is tender. Chop very fine together with the prosciutto and mortadella. Mix in the beaten egg yolks and bind with parmesan. Season with salt, pepper and nutmeg. Put about ½ teaspoon of this filling on each circle of pasta, fold over and cook in the stock. Serve as soup with grated parmesan, or drain and serve with melted butter.

1 lb. flour
5 eggs
3 egg yolks
10 oz. braised beef
¼ lb. fresh pork sausage
3 oz. pancetta

3 oz. chicken livers
2 oz. grated parmesan
2 oz. butter
72 oz. chicken stock
salt and pepper

Make the tortellini as in recipe 618 and make the filling in the following way: lightly brown the chopped livers in butter. Mix with the chopped beef from a really good stracotto (see recipe 483). Add the chopped pancetta and skinned sausage, then three beaten egg yolks, the grated parmesan and salt and pepper. Put ½ teaspoon of this filling on each circle of pasta, fold over to make tortellini and cook in the stock. Serve as soup or drain and serve with melted butter.

TORTELLINI PIE **623**

¾ lb. tortellini
12 oz. ragu Bolognese
½ lb. flour
6 oz. butter
4 oz. sugar

72 oz. beef stock
3 oz. grated parmesan
breadcrumbs
salt
(truffle)

Use tortellini made as in recipe 618. Make the ragu Bolognese as in recipe 504. Make a pastry with the flour, four ounces butter and the sugar as in recipe 499 for a smooth, not too elastic dough. Make into a ball, leave to rest for one hour under a cloth, then roll out into two sheets, one larger to line the greased pie dish, and one smaller for the top crust. Cook the tortellini in the stock. Sprinkle the greased pie dish with breadcrumbs and line with the pastry, then put in layers of tortellini and ragu, small pieces of butter and grated parmesan. Cover with the top crust, press the edges together, glaze with a little beaten egg if desired and cook in a hot oven for about 45 minutes or until the pastry is firm and golden.

Variation Put a little crumbled truffle between the layers of pasta.

1 lb. flour	72 oz. chicken stock
7 eggs	rosemary
1 chicken breast	lemon
3 oz. loin of pork	nutmeg
2 oz. ricotta	sage
2 oz. grated mozzarella	salt and pepper
1 tablespoon grated parmesan	ragu
½ oz. butter	

Make the pasta dough in the usual way with the flour and five eggs (see recipe 181) and roll out into a thin sheet. Cut into small circles or squares, about two inches in diameter. Lightly brown the chicken breast and pork in a little butter with some sage, rosemary and a pinch each of salt and pepper. Chop the meat, mix with the grated parmesan, crumbled ricotta and grated mozzarella, two beaten eggs and a pinch of nutmeg, a little grated lemon peel and salt and pepper. Put ½ teaspoon of this filling on the pasta circles, fold them over and press the edges together, then draw the oppposite ends together to form a crescent- shaped cappelletto. Cook in the stock and serve as a soup, or cook in water, drain well and serve with a ragu (see recipe 504).

CAPPELLETTI WITH PORK,
CHICKEN AND BRAIN FILLING

625

10 oz. flour	2 oz. lamb's brain
4 eggs	6 oz. grated parmesan
3 oz. cooked loin of pork	3 tablespoons marsala
1½ oz. mortadella/bologna	nutmeg
1½ oz. prosciutto	72 oz. stock
3 oz. cooked chicken breast	salt and pepper

Make the pasta dough with the flour, three eggs, a pinch of salt and a little water as necessary (see recipe 181). Finely chop the pork, mortadella, prosciutto, and chicken. Clean, blanch and remove the outer membrane from the lamb's brain. Chop fine and add to the other meat with two tablespoons grated parmesan, the marsala, and a pinch each of salt, pepper and nutmeg. Set aside for about ½ hour. Roll the pasta dough out thin and cut into circles about two inches in diameter. Put ½ teaspoon filling on each circle. Fold them over, press the edges together and make into cappelletti. Cook in the stock and serve as soup with grated parmesan, or drain and serve with melted butter and parmesan.

---

1 lb. 2 oz. flour	16 oz. stock
5 eggs	4 oz. olive oil
1 egg yolk	¾ lb. butter
6 oz. lean veal	6 tablespoons white wine
6 oz. lean pork	6 oz. red wine
3 oz. prosciutto	nutmeg
2 oz. mortadella/bologna	cloves
½ lb. grated parmesan	rosemary
9 oz. thick cream	sage
2 oz. breadcrumbs	parsley
1½ lb. chicken gizzards	bay leaf
3 oz. onion, carrot, celery	salt and pepper
1 medium tomato	

This is such a beautiful and tasty dish that it is worth the effort to prepare it for special occasions. Melt four ounces butter and two tablespoons olive oil with a little rosemary, sage and chopped parsley. Brown the veal and pork and season with salt. Add the white wine, let it reduce, cover the pan and cook, adding up to four ounces stock as the sauce dries out. Remove the meat when tender and chop with the prosciutto and mortadella/bologna. Mix with one beaten egg, five ounces grated parmesan and two tablespoons breadcrumbs. Make the pasta dough in the usual way with one pound flour, four eggs, a pinch of salt and warm water as necessary (see recipe 181) and knead thoroughly for a smooth, soft dough. Roll out and cut into two-inch squares. Put about ½ teaspoon filling on each square, fold over the pasta and make into cappelletti (see recipe 624). Make a ragu: lightly brown some chopped onion, celery and carrot in five ounces butter and three tablespoons olive oil. Add a pinch of nutmeg and a clove, then the well-cleaned, chopped gizzards. Add the red wine, let it reduce and add the pureed tomato. Cook for a few minutes, stir in 12 ounces stock and cook, covered, over low heat for at least three hours for a thick ragu. Cook the cappelletti in plenty of boiling, salted water, drain well and mix with the ragu, four ounces grated parmesan and the warmed cream. Make a pastry case with six ounces butter and six ounces flour, a pinch of salt and six ounces warm water (see recipe 499). Fold the pastry over several times and leave to rest in the refrigerator, then roll into one larger sheet for the bottom crust and one smaller one for the top crust. Grease a pie dish and line with the larger sheet. Put in the cappelletti mixture, cover with the top crust, press the edges well together and cook for about one hour in a moderate oven until the pastry is firm and golden.

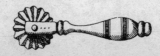

1 lb. flour	2 cloves garlic
5 eggs	rosemary
10 oz. lean beef	nutmeg
4 oz. fresh pork sausage	6 oz. grated parmesan
2 oz. pancetta	salt and pepper
6 oz. butter	1 onion
2 tablespoons olive oil	(ragu)
6 oz. white wine	

Make incisions in the beef and add pieces of garlic and some rosemary. Lightly brown the chopped onion in 1½ ounces butter and four tablespoons olive oil. Add the meat and brown all over. Season with salt and pepper and pour over the wine. Let it reduce and cook, covered, over low heat for at least three hours, adding a few tablespoons warm water if it seems too dry. Lightly brown the chopped pancetta and sausage in another 1½ ounces butter. When the beef is cooked chop it fine and mix with the skinned, crumbled sausage and the pan juices, the pancetta, one beaten egg, a pinch of nutmeg, three ounces grated parmesan, or as much as you need to make a soft mixture for the agnolini filling. Make a pasta dough in the usual way with the flour, four eggs, a pinch of salt and warm water as necessary (see recipe 181). Set aside to rest, then roll out and cut into 1¼ inch squares. Put ½ teaspoon filling on each square and fold the pasta over to make a triangle. Press the edges together carefully then draw the opposite points of the triangle together to make cappelletti, or angolini, as they are called in Mantua. Cook in plenty of salted water, drain well and serve with melted butter and grated parmesan.

Variation Serve with a ragu (see recipe 504).

AGNOLOTTI WITH TRUFFLE **628**

1 lb. flour	¼ lb. butter
3 eggs	3 oz. grated parmesan
6 oz. loin of pork	3 oz. white wine
6 oz. lean veal	1 small truffle (about ½ oz.)
3 oz. prosciutto	salt and pepper

The truffle goes into the filling for these agnolotti. Lightly brown the veal and pork in about two tablespoons butter, then add a little wine and let it reduce. Cook until the meat is tender, adding warm water as necessary. Finely chop together with the prosciutto. Mix with the chopped truffle (use more or less to taste), one beaten egg and two tablespoons grated parmesan to bind. Make the pasta dough in the usual way with the flour, a pinch of salt, two eggs and a little water as necessary (see recipe 181) and roll out into two sheets as for ravioli. Put mounds of the filling on the first sheet (see recipe 251) and make into ravioli with the other sheet. Set aside to dry for a few hours, then cook in stock or water. Drain well and put in layers in a hot serving bowl with a little melted butter, grated parmesan and more crumbled truffle.

AGNOLOTTI WITH VEAL AND MORTADELLA/BOLOGNA FILLING   **629**

1 lb. flour	1 oz. butter
3 eggs	72 oz. beef stock
6 oz. lean veal	4 oz. grated parmesan
¼ lb. calf's brain	nutmeg
3 oz. mortadella/bologna	milk
2 oz or 1 slice	salt and pepper
stale bread	(ragu)

Lightly brown the veal in one tablespoon butter, then add a few tablespoons stock and cook slowly for about one hour until tender. Chop the veal fine. Blanch the brain, remove the outer membrane, chop fine and mix with the veal together with the chopped mortadella/bologna. Soak the stale bread in stock, squeeze dry and crumble. Mix with the meat, one beaten egg, a pinch of nutmeg, salt and pepper and half the grated parmesan. Mix together well and set aside. Make the pasta dough in the usual way with the flour, two eggs, a pinch of salt and a little milk (see recipe 181). Roll out fairly thin into two sheets and put mounds of filling on one sheet as for ravioli (see recipe 251). Set aside to dry for at least one hour and cook in stock or water. Serve as soup, or drain and serve with melted butter and grated parmesan, or with a good ragu (see recipe 504).

RAVIOLI WITH FONTINA AND CREAM   **630**

10 oz. flour	6 oz. fontina
4 eggs	6 oz. thick cream
3 oz. mortadella/bologna	1 oz. butter
2 oz. beef marrow	salt and pepper
½ lb. braised beef	(white truffle)
3 oz. grated parmesan	

Make the pasta dough in the usual way with the flour, three eggs, a pinch of salt and warm water as necessary (see recipe 181). Finely chop the braised beef (see recipe 483) and mortadella. Mix with the beef marrow, one beaten egg, two ounces grated parmesan, salt and pepper to make the filling. Roll out the dough and make ravioli with the filling (see recipe 251). Cook them in stock or water. Grease an ovenproof dish and put in the diced fontina mixed with the cream. Leave in a hot oven for a few minutes, or cook gently over medium heat, and when the cheese has started to melt add the ravioli and mix well. Sprinkle with parmesan and brown for a few more minutes in a hot oven.

Variation Grate a little white truffle over the dish.

RAVIOLI WITH BEEF AND VEGETABLE FILLING 631

1 lb. flour	2 oz. lamb's brain
4 eggs	2 oz. fresh pork sausage
1 lb. shin of beef	6 oz. heavy cream
4 tablespoons olive oil	6 tablespoons white wine
½ oz. fat from the kidney,	1 onion
or beef suet	1 clove garlic
2 lb. tomatoes	rosemary
10 oz. borage	6 oz. grated parmesan
10 oz. Swiss chard	salt and pepper
10 oz. spinach	

Heat four tablespoons oil with the kidney fat and lightly brown ½ chopped onion and the chopped garlic. Brown the beef with a little rosemary and a pinch each of salt and pepper. Add the wine, let it reduce, and add the pureed tomatoes. Cook over low heat for at least three hours for a good thick sauce. Strain the gravy and chop half the meat (the rest can be used for another dish). Boil the borage, Swiss chard and spinach until just tender, drain, squeeze out all the moisture and chop fine. Lightly brown another ½ onion in two tablespoons oil, add the skinned, crumbled sausage and the brain (cleaned, blanched to remove the outer membrane and chopped), and cook for a few minutes. Add the vegetables and chopped meat. Stir well and mix in two beaten eggs, the grated parmesan and the cream. Season with salt and pepper and set aside. Make the pasta dough in the usual way with the flour, two eggs, a pinch of salt and a little oil. Roll out into two sheets to make the ravioli with the filling (see recipe 251). Dry, cook in boiling water, drain and serve with the beef gravy and more grated parmesan.

SMALL RAVIOLI IN SOUP

1 lb. flour
4 eggs
6 oz. roast chicken
3 oz. fresh pork sausage
3 oz. salami
2 oz. butter

2 onions
breadcrumbs
parsley
72 oz. stock
salt and pepper

Heat two ounces butter and lightly brown the finely sliced onion. Add plenty of chopped parsley, then the chopped chicken and salami, the skinned, crumbled sausage and one tablespoon grated parmesan. Cook for a few minutes, remove from the heat and pound in a mortar with two beaten eggs and a pinch each of salt and pepper. Make the pasta dough in the usual way with the flour, two eggs, a little salt and some water as necessary (see recipe 181). Roll out and put mounds of the filling quite close together and make small ravioli (see recipe 251). Cook them in the stock and serve as soup. Serve grated parmesan separately, or strain the ravioli and serve with melted butter.

RAVIOLI WITH RICOTTA AND VEAL FILLING ABRUZZI

1 lb. flour
1¼ lb. ricotta
6 eggs
1¼ lb. lean veal
2 oz. lardo or
fat salt pork
1 onion
6 tablespoons white wine

1 tablespoon sugar
cinnamon
3 oz. grated pecorino/romano
cloves
garlic
salt and pepper
1 tablespoon tomato puree
(olive oil)

One of the few recipes to have a sweet and savoury flavour. Make a ragu in the Abruzzi way: make incisions in the veal and put in tiny pieces of lardo or fat salt pork and garlic, then brown the meat with the remaining chopped lardo and the onion stuck with cloves. Season with salt and pepper, moisten with wine, let it reduce, and add the tomato puree, diluted with warm water. Cook over low heat until the meat is tender—at least three hours. Make the pasta dough in the usual way with the flour, four eggs, a pinch of salt and warm water as necessary (see recipe 181) and roll out very thin. Make the filling: mix the ricotta with two beaten eggs, the sugar and a pinch of cinnamon. Put mounds of this filling on one sheet of dough and make very small ravioli (see recipe 251). Cook in plenty of boiling, salted water. Drain and arrange in a hot serving dish in layers with a little gravy from the veal ragu on each layer (use the meat for another course). Sprinkle with grated parmesan and serve immediately.

Variation   Increase the amount of sugar in the filling and fry the ravioli in hot oil. Serve sprinkled with vanilla sugar, for a pasta dish with a different taste.

NEAPOLITAN RAVIOLI   **634**

1 lb. flour
3 eggs
10 oz. scamorza cheese
3 oz. ricotta
3 oz. prosciutto
6 oz. grated parmesan

2 lb. tomatoes
4 tablespoons olive oil
parsley
basil
salt and pepper

Make a pasta dough in the usual way with the flour, two eggs, a pinch of salt and a little warm water (see recipe 181). Make the filling: mix the ricotta with one beaten egg, two tablespoons grated parmesan, the prosciutto and scamorza diced very fine, some chopped parsley and pepper. Put mounds of this filling on the dough (rolled out fairly thin into two sheets). Cut in circles and fold into crescent shapes as they do in Naples. Cook in boiling, salted water drain well and mix with a tomato sauce made in the usual way with the olive oil, pureed tomatoes and some basil (see recipe 15). Serve grated parmesan separately.

1 lb. flour	6 tablespoons soy sauce
4 eggs	vinegar
1 lb. lean pork	hot chili pepper
6 water chestnuts	salt and pepper
3 spring onions	(stock, chicken, shrimp, cabbage)

Chinese cooking includes an enormous variety of stuffed pastas: this one is best known in the west. Make the pasta dough in the usual way with the flour, two eggs, a pinch of salt and warm water as necessary (see recipe 181). Knead until smooth and elastic and set aside for about one hour under a cloth. Roll out and cut into 2½ inch squares. Make the filling: mix the finely chopped raw pork with two eggs, the finely chopped water chestnuts and spring onions, two tablespoons soy sauce and a pinch each of salt and pepper. Put mounds of this filling on the pasta squares, then fold them into triangles and press the edges well together. Cook in plenty of boiling, salted water and toss in a cold sauce made with more soy sauce, two tablespoons vinegar and a pinch of hot chili pepper.

Variations
1. Cook and serve the ravioli in beef stock.
2. Use a chicken breast instead of pork.
3. Add a few cooked shrimps to the filling.
4. Add a little chopped cabbage instead of water chestnuts.

FRIED RAVIOLI WITH SHRIMP AND PORK FILLING **636**

1 lb. flour	1 oz. soy sauce
2 eggs	ginger
1 lb. lean pork	sugar
½ lb. shelled shrimps	salt
1 large onion	soybean or peanut oil

Make the pasta dough in the usual way with 11 ounces flour, two eggs, a pinch of salt and warm water as necessary (see recipe 181). Make the filling: lightly brown the chopped onion in three tablespoons oil. Add a little chopped ginger and the chopped pork, then the minced or pureed shrimps, the soy sauce, ½ teaspoon sugar and a pinch of salt. Roll out the dough and cut into one-inch squares, put ½ teaspoon filling on each square. Fold over to make a triangle, press the edges together well and fry in plenty of oil. Drain on absorbent paper and serve immediately.

1 lb. flour	36 oz. milk
4 eggs	½ onion
10 oz. ricotta	nutmeg
6 oz. mozzarella	parsley
3 oz. prosciutto	salt and pepper
6 oz. grated parmesan	(ragu)
6 oz. butter	

Make the pasta dough in the usual way with 11 ounces flour, two eggs, a pinch of salt and warm water as necessary (see recipe 181). Roll it out and cut into five-inch squares. Make the filling: mix the ricotta with two beaten eggs, four ounces grated parmesan, salt and pepper, a little nutmeg, some finely chopped parsley and the finely diced mozzarella and prosciutto. Cook the pasta squares for just 20 seconds (if they are freshly made) or 50 seconds if they are a little dry. Drain well and dry on a cloth. Put the filling on the pasta squares and roll them up to make cannelloni. Make a bechamel with four ounces butter and three ounces flour, the milk, the juice of ½ onion and some salt and pepper. Put two or three tablespoons bechamel on the bottom of a greased ovenproof dish, arrange the cannelloni in a single layer so they do not overlap and cover with the remaining bechamel. Sprinkle with grated parmesan and brown for a few minutes in a hot oven.

Variation Use a good ragu instead of bechamel.

CANNELLONI WITH CHEESE AND TOMATOES **638**

10 oz. flour	3 tablespoons olive oil
4 eggs	2 oz. lard or strutto
10 oz. ricotta	basil
6 oz. mozzarella	4 oz. grated parmesan
3 oz. prosciutto	salt and pepper
1¼ lb. tomatoes	(cooked ham)

Make the pasta dough in the usual way with the flour, two eggs, a pinch of salt and a little water if necessary (see recipe 181). Roll out and cut into five-inch squares. Make the filling: mix the ricotta with two beaten eggs, add the diced mozzarella and prosciutto, three tablespoons grated parmesan and some salt and pepper. Cook the pasta quickly in boiling, salted water (see recipe 637). Put a little filling on each square, roll up and make cannelloni. Make a tomato sauce in the usual way with the oil, one tablespoon strutto or lard, salt, pepper and basil (see recipe 15). Grease an ovenproof dish, put in a little sauce, then cannelloni, cover with the remaining sauce, sprinkle with grated parmesan, dot with butter and brown in a hot oven.

CANNELLONI WITH PORK AND SPINACH FILLING **639**

10 oz. flour	4 oz. grated parmesan
4 eggs	3 oz. butter
16 oz. pork gravy	nutmeg
6 oz. lean pork from a ragu	salt and pepper
1½ lb. spinach	(prosciutto)

Make a good ragu with the lean pork (see recipe 614). You can use a larger quantity of pork and serve that as a separate course. Make the filling: cook the spinach, drain well, chop fine and cook for a minute in two tablespoons butter. Mix with one beaten egg, three tablespoons grated parmesan, nutmeg, salt and pepper, and a few tablespoons gravy (use more or less according to the consistency of the filling). Make a pasta dough in the usual way with the flour, three eggs, a pinch of salt and warm water as necessary (see recipe 181). Roll out and cut into five-inch squares, cook them in boiling water for 20 seconds, drain well and dry on a cloth. Divide the filling between them, roll up and make cannelloni. Grease an ovenproof dish and put in the cannelloni not too close together. Pour over the remaining ragu, sprinkle with grated cheese, dot with butter and brown in a hot oven.

Variations 1. Add a little diced prosciutto to the filling.
             2. Put a little chopped pork in the gravy that you pour over the cannelloni.

1 lb. flour
3 eggs
1¼ lb. spinach
1 lb. lean beef
4 oz. butter
4 tablespoons olive oil
18 oz. milk
white wine
4 oz. prosciutto

6 oz. thick cream
2 oz. grated gruyere
2 oz. grated parmesan
1 onion
1 carrot
1 stick celery
salt and pepper
(truffle)

This Bolognese speciality is the ultimate of all stuffed pastas. Make a pasta dough in the usual way with ½ pound flour, two eggs, a pinch of salt and a little warm water (see recipe 181). Make a green pasta dough with the remaining ½ pound flour, one egg, and the cooked, well drained and chopped spinach (see recipe 191). Heat two ounces butter with four tablespoons olive oil and lightly brown the chopped onion, carrot and celery. Add the chopped beef, with some salt and pepper and some white wine. Let it reduce, then cook slowly for at least one hour, adding more warm water as necessary. Dice the prosciutto and gruyere. Roll out the plain egg pasta dough and cut into five-inch squares. Roll out the green pasta dough and cut into very thin strips or taglierini (¹⁄₁₆ inch wide). Make a bechamel with two ounces butter, two ounces flour and the milk. Season with salt. Cook the pasta squares for about 50 seconds in boiling water, drain and dry on a cloth. Cook the taglierini very quickly also, drain and mix with the beef ragu together with the diced prosciutto and cream. Use individual, preferably earthenware, soup pots or gratin dishes and line them with a pasta square (the size of the square may have to vary depending on the size of your pots). Fill with a little of the taglierini mixture, some diced gruyere and grated parmesan. Cover with some bechamel and draw the edges together in folds to make a little purse. Heat in a hot oven for 10-15 minutes until the folds of pasta are slightly brown.

Variation Put a little crumbled white truffle in each pasta case.

VIII
PASTA WITH GAME

BIGOLI WITH DUCK

1 lb. maize or yellow
cornflour/cornmeal or
commercial bigoli
2 eggs
1 duck
2 oz. butter
2 tablespoons olive oil
2 tablespoons pomegranate juice

1 onion
1 carrot
1 stick celery
2 sage leaves
2 bay leaves
3 oz. grated parmesan
salt and pepper

You can use wild or domestic duck for cooking; originally wild duck was used but gradually the domestic variety gained favour. Wild duck must be cooked young or they have too strong a flavour. Bigoli are a homemade pasta from the Veneto without a hole. Make the dough with the flour, eggs, a pinch of salt and a little water if necessary and knead well until smooth and elastic. Feed into a special pasta press a little at a time to make bigoli or cut long spaghetti-like strands of pasta. The duck should be well cleaned and singed; remove the giblets and boil the duck in plenty of salted water with the chopped carrot, onion and celery. When the duck is tender remove from the stock and serve as a separate dish. Heat two sage leaves and two bay leaves in the butter and brown the cleaned and chopped duck liver and gizzards. When almost done add the pomegranate juice—an old Venetian tradition—and season with salt and pepper. Cook the bigoli in the duck stock with plenty of salt and serve with the giblet sauce. Serve grated parmesan separately.

FETTUCCINE WITH WILD DUCK

1 lb. flour
4 eggs
2 tablespoons olive oil
one young duck
2 oz. butter
2 medium slices fat bacon
2 onions
1 clove garlic

a few cloves
¾ lb. tomatoes
1 stick celery
1 carrot
6 oz. white wine
beef stock
3 oz. grated parmesan
salt and pepper

Clean the duck and remove the liver and giblets. Put an onion stuck with cloves inside the duck to remove any remaining gamey flavour during the cooking. Truss well, brown in butter and oil with the chopped garlic and bacon and a thinly sliced onion. Cook gently, adding stock when the pan seems too dry. Add the sieved tomatoes and diced celery and carrot. Season with salt and pepper and cook until tender, adding the wine as the liquid dries out in the pan. The duck is cooked when the legs can be easily detached from the body. Remove the duck from the pan, chop the meat and return to the pan, stirring well to make a good sauce. Make the fettuccine in the usual way with the flour, eggs, a pinch of salt and a little water if necessary (see recipe 181). Serve with the duck sauce and serve grated parmesan separately.

MACCHERONCINI WITH QUAILS **643**

1 lb. maccheroncini (penne)
10 oz. quail breasts
4 oz. chopped mushrooms
3 oz. butter
3 egg yolks

6 tablespoons red wine
beef stock
3 oz. grated parmesan
salt and pepper

Cook the quail breasts gently in the butter with a little salt and pepper, then put through a food mill or puree in the blender. Cook the mushrooms in the same pan, add the pureed quail, moisten with a little wine, let it evaporate and add a few tablespoons stock. Let this evaporate very little—the pan should still have plenty of liquid—and mix in the egg yolks. Stir rapidly and serve with the hot pasta. Serve grated parmesan separately.

PASTA WITH QUAILS **644**

1 lb. pasta
6 quails
10 oz. loin of pork
5 tablespoons olive oil

6 oz. red wine
sage
rosemary
salt and pepper

Clean the quails well and put in a large baking tin/pan with the pork, plenty of oil and the sage, rosemary and a little salt and pepper. Cook in a moderate oven for about 45 minutes or until tender, basting from time to time with the wine. Remove the quails and the pork; chop the pork and keep the quails hot. Sieve the juice in the pan and stir in the pork over moderate heat. Mix this sauce with the hot pasta and put in a serving dish crowned with the quails.

MACCHERONCINI WITH PHEASANT

1 lb. maccheroncini (penne)
1 pheasant
1½ medium slices bacon
2 tablespoons butter
1 onion
1 stick celery

3 egg yolks
6 oz. red wine
nutmeg
3 oz. grated parmesan
salt and pepper

Make sure the pheasant has hung for at least four or five days. Clean well and roast on a spit or in the oven for about 45 minutes. Remove the best flesh from the pheasant and chop. Put the rest to cook in plenty of lightly salted water. Lightly brown the chopped bacon, onion and celery, then add the chopped pheasant meat, stir well and add a little salt, pepper and nutmeg. Moisten with wine and let it evaporate, then cook gently adding some of the pheasant stock. Stir in the egg yolks to thicken and mix well, then serve with the hot pasta. Serve grated parmesan separately.

LASAGNE WITH TEAL DUCK

1 lb. flour
4 eggs
3 teal ducks
6 oz. butter
2 onions
12 oz. cream
18 oz. milk

2 tablespoons marsala
nutmeg
stock
3 oz. grated parmesan
salt
(truffle)

Heat two ounces butter in a pan and cook the finely sliced onion until transparent, but do not let it brown. Add the cleaned teal, brown on all sides and moisten with a little of the cream. Let them absorb the cream, then add the rest to make a gravy; season with salt and pepper. Cook until the cream reduces and add the marsala. Let this reduce also, then cook until the teal are tender, adding stock if it seems too dry. Meanwhile make the lasagne with 14 ounces flour, four eggs, a pinch of salt and a little water if necessary (see recipe 181). Roll out and cut into broad strips. Make a bechamel with two ounces butter, two ounces flour, the milk, salt and a little nutmeg. Bone the teal and put the flesh through a food mill. Return to the sauce in the pan and stir in one tablespoon butter. Mix some of this sauce with the hot lasagne, then put layers of lasagne in a greased ovenproof dish and cover each layer with more sauce, a little bechamel and some grated parmesan, ending with just bechamel and parmesan. Bake in a moderate oven for 15 minutes.

Variation Sprinkle each layer with a little grated white truffle.

1 lb. macaroni	3 oz. tomato sauce
2 coot	beef stock
4 tablespoons olive oil	6 oz. red wine
1 onion	3 oz. grated parmesan
1 carrot	6 tablespoons vinegar
2 sticks celery	parsley
2 oz. prosciutto	bay leaf
salt and pepper	

Remove all the skin from the coot as well as the feathers and the fat under the skin as this has an unpleasant flavour. The flesh makes a delicious sauce. Cut off the head and legs and leave for six hours in a marinade made the following way: boil the vinegar with 16 ounces water, the chopped onion, two bay leaves, some parsley, salt and pepper. Remove from the heat and add the red wine, then pour over the coot. When ready to cook dry the coot and brown in the olive oil so they are crisp and golden. Add a chopped onion, carrot, celery and fat prosciutto. Brown the vegetables and add the tomato sauce diluted with a little stock. Mix well, season with salt and pepper and continue cooking, adding more stock as necessary. Remove the coot and mix the sauce with the hot pasta. Serve grated parmesan separately.

PAPPARDELLE WITH HARE **648**

1 lb. flour	parsley
5 eggs	milk
1 hare	nutmeg
4 oz. olive oil	garlic
1 onion	rosemary
1 carrot	salt and pepper
1 stick celery	(parmesan, truffle)
6 oz. red wine	

Clean and skin the hare, reserving the blood and giblets. The head and shoulders are traditionally used for this dish in Tuscany as the hindquarters would get stringy in the sauce (they can be reserved for another dish). Heat five tablespoons oil in a casserole and lightly brown the chopped onion, carrot, celery and parsley, then the head and shoulders of the hare. Moisten with wine, let it evaporate, then add the blood diluted with a little hot water. When the blood thickens and reduces a little add several tablespoons of milk for a fairly liquid, but not thin sauce. Season with salt and pepper and a pinch of nutmeg and cook until the hare is tender, about one hour. Remove the flesh from the bones and chop fine. Heat two tablespoons oil and brown one clove garlic with a sprig of rosemary. Brown the chopped heart, liver and lungs of the hare. Stir in the meat from the hare with the juice from the pan and cook for a few minutes until thick. Meanwhile make the pappardelle with the flour, eggs, a pinch of salt and water as necessary (see recipe 181) and cut the dough in broad strips. Cook in plenty of boiling, salted water, drain well and mix with the hare sauce.

Variations 1. Eliminate the blood but the dish loses much of its characteristic flavour. Substitute some wine or hot water in the pan.
  2. When frying the heart etc. add a puree made by breaking the hare bones and putting them through a food mill.
  3. Grated parmesan is not generally served with this dish, but it can be served separately.
  4. Freshly grated truffle gives a delicious flavour to each serving if added at the last moment.

PAPPARDELLE WITH HARE SAUCE   **649**

1 lb. flour	1 onion
4 eggs	1 stick celery
2½ lb. hare	thyme
12 oz. red wine	bay leaf
4 tablespoons olive oil	beef stock
2 oz. pancetta or bacon	salt and pepper
1½ oz. butter	(parmesan)
nutmeg	

This sauce is quite different from the previous recipe. Clean and skin the hare, then cut into small pieces. Leave to stand in a marinade made with the red wine, the chopped onion and celery, a few peppercorns and a little crumbled thyme and bay leaf for 12 hours. Make the pappardelle with the flour, eggs, a pinch of salt and a little warm water (see recipe 181). Roll the dough out thin and cut into broad strips. Heat the oil, brown the chopped pancetta and add the drained hare. Brown on all sides, season with salt and little nutmeg and cook for about one hour over low heat, adding some of the marinade and some stock as the liquid dries out. Remove the pieces of hare and strain the sauce. Mix with the hot pappardelle and some melted butter.

Variations Serve grated parmesan separately.

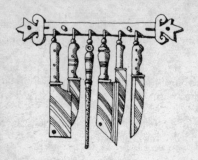

MOCK PAPPARDELLE 650

1 lb. flour	parsley
3 eggs	nutmeg
1 leg of hare	sage
½ lb. lean veal	rosemary
6 tablespoons olive oil	1 tablespoon tomato puree
1 onion	6 oz. brandy
1 carrot	6 oz. red wine
1 stick celery	beef stock
1 clove garlic	salt and pepper
2 cloves	(parmesan)

They are mock pappardelle because the sauce is not a true hare sauce as it contains veal. Heat the oil and brown the chopped onion, carrot, celery, parsley and garlic. Add the chopped veal and the chopped meat from the hare and brown on all sides. Season with cloves, a little nutmeg and some salt and pepper. When the sauce is thick add a sprig of rosemary and a few sage leaves: this is the best moment to get their full flavour. Cook for a few more minutes, add the brandy and let it evaporate. Stir in the tomato puree diluted with very little brandy and add the wine. Continue cooking until the meat is tender, adding stock if it seems too dry. Make the pappardelle with the flour, eggs, a pinch of salt and a little warm water (see recipe 181). Roll the dough out thin and cut into broad strips. Cook in plenty of boiling salted water and serve with the hare sauce.

Variation Serve grated parmesan separately.

BUCATINI WITH HARE SARDINIAN STYLE **651**

1 lb. bucatini
1 large hare
6 tablespoons olive oil
2 medium slices of bacon
1 onion
1 clove garlic
18 oz. red wine

rosemary
flour
cloves
cinnamon
salt and pepper
3 oz. grated pecorino/romano

Clean and skin the hare and reserve the blood. Wash the meat well and cut in serving pieces. Dry and roll in flour. Heat the oil with the chopped bacon. Brown the hare pieces and add the chopped onion and garlic. When the vegetables are brown and the liquid has thickened, add enough wine to cover the hare (increase the quantity if necessary). Let it cook for a few minutes then add a few cloves and a little cinnamon, salt and pepper. Stir well, add a sprig of rosemary (remove it before serving) and cook over low heat for two hours. Stir in the blood and cook until it is well mixed with the sauce. Mix with the hot pasta and serve with pieces of hare on each plate (or serve them as a separate dish). Serve grated pecorino/romano separately.

SPAGHETTI WITH HUNTER'S SAUCE OF WILD BOAR (VENISON OR ROE-BUCK) **652**

1 lb. spaghetti
1 lb. boar, venison or roe-buck
6 tablespoons olive oil
2 cloves garlic
rosemary

4 tablespoons tomato sauce
1 oz. dried mushrooms
6 oz. red wine
flour
salt and pepper

Heat the oil and brown the chopped or crushed garlic, which can then be discarded. Dice the meat, roll in flour and fry in the oil with a sprig of rosemary, salt and pepper, adding some wine if necessary. Add the mushrooms which have been soaked in water and coarsely chopped, and cook for a few minutes. Moisten with the wine, let it evaporate, then add the tomato sauce (see recipe 15) diluted with a little warm water. Cook for about 2 hours or until the meat is tender, adding more warm water as necessary, then mix with the hot pasta.

1 lb. maccheroncini (penne)	thyme
10 oz. roast game (boar,	marjoram
venison, roe-buck)	2 tablespoons brandy
4 oz. butter	2 tablespoons tomato sauce
2 medium slices bacon	salt and pepper
juniper berries	(mushrooms)

Heat two tablespoons butter and cook the chopped bacon, pounded juniper berries and a pinch each of thyme and marjoram. Add the finely chopped meat and stir well with some salt and pepper. Pour over the brandy, let it evaporate, and add the tomato sauce (see recipe 15) diluted with warm water. Cook until the sauce is thick and well blended. Mix with the hot pasta, together with the remaining butter.

Variation   Add some dried mushrooms, previously soaked in warm water and coarsely chopped, after adding the meat.

METRIC CONVERSION TABLE

DRY MEASURE

1	ounce	=	2.8	grams
4	ounces	=	114	grams
1	pound	=	454	grams
2.2	pounds	=	1000	grams/1 kilogram

LIQUID MEASURE

1	ounce	=	2.8	centilitres
3½	ounces	=	10	centilitres
9	ounces	=	25	centilitres/¼ litre
17.5	ounces	=	50	centilitres/½ litre
35	ounces	=	100	centilitres/1 litre

INDEX OF RECIPES

Recipes are indexed according to types of pasta and types of dishes. Within these categories, the principal ingredients used in the various recipes are listed. Numbers shown are not page numbers but recipe numbers.

THAI COOKING

Jennifer Brennan

Thai cooking blends Chinese, Indian and Arabic influences into a unique cuisine. This is the first comprehensive and authentic book on Thai (Siamese) cooking and it brings the delicious secrets of Thai cuisine within the grasp of every cook.

A typical Thai dinner consists of an assortment of curry dishes, soups, salads, vegetables and sauces served simultaneously around a central bowl of plain boiled rice. Recipes range from *Quail Egg Flowers, Prawns caught In a Net* and *Bamboo Shoot and Pork Soup* to *Sweet and Sour Beef* and *Whole Fried Fish with Ginger Sauce*. The final chapters are dedicated to desserts and sweets — everything from *Thai Fried Bananas* to *Mangoes and Sticky Rice*.

'Sublimely varied, exciting, colourful and intensely delicious'

The Sunday Times

Futura Publications
Non-Fiction/Cookery
0 7088 2555 9

POT LUCK
Scrumptious Stews and Cheerful Casseroles

Sonia Allison

From the delicate flavour of Grape Chicken with
Almonds to the cheerful Drunken Duck with
Chestnuts, from the delicious Brandied Beef in a
Garden to the wholesome and comforting Lamb
Cobbler, Sonia Allison, cookery editor of *Ideal Home*
brings you

POT LUCK

A feast of tasty and tempting stews and casseroles
which can be cooked either in the oven or on the
hob. Including some old favourites as well as original
recipes of her own, there are meals for every occasion
from a light and simple snack to a complete family
meal or a dish to entertain with. Especially enticing
for those who don't want to spend too much time in
the kitchen, there are chapters on beef, lamb, pork
and bacon, offal, poultry and game, eggs and cheese
as well as vegetarian recipes.

'Exciting and imaginative' *Express*

Futura Publications
Non-Fiction/Cookery
0 7088 2643 1

GLYNN CHRISTIAN'S

Radio and TV Cookbook

Mouthwatering recipes from BBC TV Breakfast Time's Cook

Glynn Christian has become famous as an original and creative cook. His radio broadcasts and television appearances attract a wide and increasing audience.

Collected here are the *crème de la crème* of his most delicious recipes, presented with wit and clarity. Pink Cloud Pâté, Saffron Seafood Millefeuille, Passion Fruit Paradise Pancakes . . . a host of dishes to catch the imagination, please the eye and tempt the palate.

Futura Publications
Non-Fiction/Cookery
0 7088 2438 2

THE BOOK OF SANDWICHES

Gwen Robyns

When Lord Sandwich first wrapped a chunk of beef in two slabs of bread, little did he know that he had achieved immortality. More than two hundred years later the sandwich is one of the basics of the western diet, whether it be a mouth-watering American club sandwich, a ratatouille-filled pouch of pitta bread or a good old English ham sandwich.

Gwen Robyns believes there is an art to making a good sandwich — and the soggy plastic sandwiches we've all encountered suggest she's right. THE BOOK OF SANDWICHES shows you how to produce sandwiches fit for a gourmet. Once you've mastered the traditional English sandwiches you can move on to delicious new spreads like curry butter or avocado and lemon and surprising fillings like chicken with capers and sour cream or ham and currant jelly with cayenne. There are sandwiches for vegetarians, sandwiches for children, sandwiches for the sweet tooth — in fact, sandwiches for every taste.

THE BOOK OF SANDWICHES tells you how to make the world's most appetising sandwiches — for every occasion.

Futura Publications
Non-Fiction/Cookery
0 7088 2476 5

THE MIRACLE COOKBOOK

Rosemary Stark

THE SHOPS ARE CLOSED. THE DOORBELL RINGS.
SUDDENLY YOU'VE GOT FIVE STARVING FRIENDS
TO ENTERTAIN. YOU NEED

THE MIRACLE COOKBOOK.

For everyone who has been stunned into
embarrassed silence and desperate rummaging
through the fridge and bread bin, Rosemary Sark,
cookery editor of OPTIONS magazine, has the
answer. Adding an extra course, expanding what's
to hand with goodies from your cupboard or
producing a whole new meal from your hoard of
canned and frozen food: with these solutions that
sinking feeling will never hit you again.

Beginning with a practical chapter on stocking up,
THE MIRACLE COOKBOOK ensures you can conjure
up steaming bowls of soup, comforting spicy pasta
dishes and tempting tarts at a moment's notice.
And the ingenious index will tell you at a glance
just what you can do with what you've got.

An essential book for every home — whether it's a
mansion or a bedsit.

Futura Publications
Non-Fiction/Cookery
0 7088 2460 9

THE COMPLETE BOOK OF BARBECUES

Mary Norwak

Outdoor parties in the long summer evenings; the smell of wood smoke and charcoal fires; the fragrance of herbs and spit-roast lamb — all these and more make up the charm of the barbecue.

Whether you're planning a barbecue party, a family feast or a quiet meal for two, Mary Norwak's THE COMPLETE BOOK OF BARBECUES is the perfect guide.

Mary Norwak provides all the practical information you need — types of barbecue, fire building, basic cooking rules and equipment — and a host of delicious recipes for main courses, sauces, marinades and dressings, from the simple but delicous hamburger to such gourmet delights as veal chops with kirsch, spiced orange glazed spare ribs, mussels and bacon and spit-roasted duck.

Futura Publications
Non-Fiction/Cookery
0 8600 7209 6

All Futura Books are available at your bookshop or newsagent, or can be ordered from the following address:
Futura Books, Cash Sales Department,
P.O. Box 11, Falmouth, Cornwall.

Please send cheque or postal order (no currency), and allow 55p for postage and packing for the first book plus 22p for the second book and 14p for each additional book ordered up to a maximum charge of £1.75 in U.K.

Customers in Eire and B.F.P.O. please allow 55p for the first book, 22p for the second book plus 14p per copy for the next 7 books, thereafter 8p per book.

Overseas customers please allow £1 for postage and packing for the first book and 25p per copy for each additional book.